Basic Counseling Techniques:
A Beginning Therapist's Toolkit

C. Wayne Perry, D.Min., LMFT

ISBN: 1-4033-8326-X (e-book)
ISBN: 1-4033-8327-8 (Paperback)

This book is printed on acid free paper.

1stBooks – rev. 11/15/02

This text is dedicated to my wonderful wife, Donna. She loved me enough to encourage me in my clinical work, and she loved me enough to force me to practice in my personal life what I teach in my professional life. She has been and continues to be a real blessing of God.

Acknowledgments

I wish to sincerely thank the students in my Basic Counseling Techniques classes at Southern Christian University during 2002. They critiqued this text in its draft form and helped me make needed improvements. To the extent that I achieve my goal of providing a text that the beginning counselor or therapist will find truly useful, these students deserve a big "Thank you."

I also want to thank my wife for her careful proof-reading of this text. Her careful attention to even the most minute details was invaluable in producing the final edition.

Finally, I want to thank God for giving me the high privilege of being a therapist. As a Christian saint from the Middle Ages, Anthony of Padua, once said, "I bandaged his wounds. God healed him." For more than 30 years I have read the research and taken courses in an attempt to learn how to bandage emotional wounds more skillfully, more appropriately, more effectively. My clients deserve nothing less than my very best, and that definitely includes my best efforts to stay current on the trends of my chosen profession. Even so, I am keenly aware that every healing I get to witness in the therapy room is the result of God's work, not my skill. As the kids say today, "It's a God thing." When lay people ask me how I listen to my client's troubles for hour after hour, day after day, I tell them this is how: I get to watch a miracle unfold before my eyes. I can ask for no greater privilege than this.
- Wayne Perry

Table of Contents

Foreword

I did not set out to write a textbook of counseling and therapy techniques. My original purpose was to find a textbook I could use for a class I would be teaching beginning master's level students. What I found, to my surprise, is that I could find no suitable book. There are many books of theories, and many books which address important issues that this one does not. This text aims to fill in the gaps left by those other texts, to supplement them and not to replace them. Specifically, the purpose of this text is to give the beginning therapy or counseling student the nuts-and-bolts of how to actually apply some of the major theories. I assume that in other courses the student will study theories of therapy in depth to gain a more complete understanding, and I assume the student will take a practicum or internship to learn how to actually do therapy. No book, including this one, can teach someone how to counsel. You learn therapy by doing therapy under the careful guidance of a skilled supervisor.

I do want to express my gratitude to my clients over the last twenty-five years. They have taught me so much. All of the case material in this text is drawn from my clinical experience with these wonderful people. Their actions do not necessarily reflect this author's position on moral issues, but they do reflect the reality of therapy as I have experienced it. Some of the "clients" in this text are actual people. Others are composites of several real people. In all cases, enough of the facts are altered so that the client's confidentiality is protected. If you, the reader, think you recognize one of these clients, chalk that up to the universality of human experience and know that you cannot possibly identify who these real people are. Please do read these cases carefully to get a "feel" of the client and the client's situation. Use your imagination to put yourself in the client's shoes. This is a skill which will not only help you get the most out of this text, it will also serve you well in your future profession.

I also want to express a word of caution to those beginning counselors and therapists who read this text. All of the case material in this text comes out well. The client gets better. That is not always the case in real life therapy. Most of us know that, but no one ever tells you that even the best therapy properly performed will not be 100-percent successful. Do work hard to improve your skills and remember that, sadly, some people are more dedicated to staying in their illness than they are to improving. If we therapists could fully understand the client's world from the client's point of view, we could understand why that makes sense to them and perhaps help them move toward health. However, as Salvador Minuchin reminds us, "Life is more complex than that." You will always lose some.

There is one more word of caution. This text presents a variety of techniques because no one style of therapy has yet been proven superior to all other styles in all cases. Likely, you will gravitate toward one or two styles of therapy because they "fit" your personality, and that is usually a good thing. The therapist's primary tool is his or her personality, so finding a style of therapy which allows the therapist to make the most of that tool is a great goal. When that usual style does not work, however, be ready to change your way of working. If you do not see behavior change in the client by the second session, whatever your style of therapy, your client is non-verbally telling you that there is a disconnect between your preferred style and this particular client's needs. Do something different. As I often remind my supervisees, "Insanity can best be defined as doing the same thing over and over expecting different results every time." That applies to us as well as to our clients.

I wish you the best as you learn how to help people. Therapy is an honorable profession with many frustrations and many joys. May your joys outweigh your frustrations.

Wayne Perry
November 2001

Introduction

When there is a disagreement between the book and the bird, always believe the bird. - James Audubon

I will never forget that September afternoon when, for the first time in my life, I set foot on a locked ward in a mental hospital. This was the second week of internship during my master's degree work, and I was frightened out of my wits. A thousand questions zipped through my mind. "What will I say? What will I do? Will I hurt someone? Will they hurt me?" My supervisors had done their best to prepare me, and certainly I knew the theories that were supposed to be helpful. Still, walking toward that first encounter with the unknown, I felt a lump in my throat the size of Alaska.

Like most interns I have known, I eventually had a good learning experience. By the time the year was over, I was relaxed and enjoying my work. I had become comfortable in what had previously been a frightening, unknown setting. At the time I was too happy to have survived and to have actually learned a few things to think very deeply during the experience of those first, very uncomfortable weeks. Now, however, I think about those weeks a lot. I see my experience repeated again and again in the lives of the interns I now supervise. With years of experience behind me, I have come to believe there has to be a better way to train budding professionals than simply giving them theories about swimming for two years, then taking them to the deep end of the pool and throwing them in, without ever giving any specific, practical tips on how one swims. This book is specifically written as an attempt to discover that "better way." Students, after reading this book and doing the practice units, should start to feel like they have "been there, done that."

There is a second major purpose for this book which is closely related to the first. Virtually every handbook of therapy is intellectual or academic and lists a variety of schools of therapy, each with its own history and "star" figures. Broderick and Schrader (1991, p. 34.) quote Carlos Sluzki as calling the rise of so many competing schools of therapy a "Balkanization of the field into sectors based on political rather than scientific boundaries. . . . The consequence of all this has been the development of more and more 'brand-name' models and increased bickering about whose technique washes whiter." Yet Broderick and Schrader go on to say that they believe that the future of therapy belongs not to any one of these many schools of therapy, but rather to some form of integrated therapy. Indeed, it seems that ever year that passes, the differences that separate practicing clinicians become less distinct. Clinicians still praise their favorite "stars" of the therapy world, but practice from a patchwork of theoretical models.

The problem for the beginning student is that there are so few guidelines for actually doing this work of integration. My experience as a supervisor of therapy teaches me that what usually happens is that students "fly by the seat of their pants," grabbing a little bit of technique from this school, that technique from another school, without ever thinking about how any of this fits together. The net result of this un-examined patchwork is that therapy feels and looks patched together. Clients and therapists alike come away wondering what happened. Should the work actually be successful, the therapist likely will be unable to repeat the success since she or he will have no clear idea just what they did or why. They lack a good model for integrating techniques.

Therefore, the second major purpose of this book is to provide a model for integrating techniques from a variety of schools and perspectives. Naturally, given the first purpose of providing a practical "how-to" guide for the beginning professional counseling/therapy student, this book will be limited to the basics. Subtle nuances and advanced developments will have to wait for another volume.

[1]The Metasystems Model

The model for integrating these basic skills followed throughout this book is the Metasystems Model. The name is quite descriptive. "Systems" refers to the multiple layers of connections of which we are all a part. "Meta" is a Greek word which means "with" or "along side of." So "meta-systems" is an integrated model of therapy which places the individual "with" or "along side of" the multiple systems of which the individual is an integral part. It is a practical application of what Nichols (1987) called "the Self in the system."

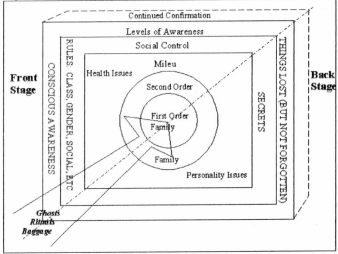

From the moment of our conception we are part of multiple systems. The first system is, of course, the womb, and it is primarily (if not exclusively - I won't enter into that debate) a biological system. After birth we are part of a system called a family. As we grow older, our system expands to the neighborhood, and then to the community, and later to the nation (perhaps even the world). Throughout our development we are still the same individual, and yet we change as we interact with our various systems. Of course, our interactions influence the systems of which we are a part, just as we are influenced by them. The fundamental premise of the Metasystems Model, then, is in order to understand behavior, one must understand both the individual and the system. A very closely related corollary is that all change takes place within the individual. The individual

---

[1]The basis for the model was first developed by John H. Curtis, Ph.D. I am grateful for his seminal work which laid the foundations on which I have built.

makes changes and thus changes the systems of which she or he is a part (Nichols, 1987).

Not all of this is available to our conscious awareness, of course. Erving Goffman (1956) provided a helpful concept by describing human social behavior in terms of a theater metaphor. Metasystems builds on that metaphor. All human life takes place either on "Front Stage" or "Back Stage."

Near the city where I live is the Alabama Shakespear Festival - rated as one of the top five Shakespear theaters in the world, according to their publicity. Anyone who pays the admission price can enter the theater and watch the play being presented. The action that the audience sees takes place on "front stage." It is the public part of the theater. However, as anyone who has worked around theater knows, there is a great deal of action taking place "back stage," where it is hidden from the view of the audience. In fact, there is some action taking place back stage that is hidden even from the actors. Still, all of this back stage action combines to make possible the action the audience sees on the front stage.

The same is true of human behavior. Part of our lives are lived on the front stage. This is the public part of us, the part of which we are consciously aware, and the part of which others could become aware if they were to "pay the admission price" - i.e., take the time to get to know us. However, there are parts of our lives which are certainly hidden from others, and some parts which are hidden even from our own conscious awareness. This is the back stage. Obviously, the "back stage" includes the areas that traditional psychodynamic psychology labeled as the "unconscious," but it is a much broader concept than that.

The distinction between front stage and back stage is more substantive than just being descriptive of awareness. It also defines how change takes place. Because front stage is open to conscious awareness, change can take place through education, psychoeducation, relabeling or reframing, or similar techniques that address the neocortex of the brain. To change the back stage requires the application of techniques which can tap into more developmentally primitive parts of the brain (e.g., the amygdala and other parts of the "limbic system") - techniques such as dream interpretation, lifestyle analysis, or revising schemas or private fictions[2].

Even the most neophyte counseling/therapy student has heard that the presenting problem isn't necessarily the real problem. The Metasystems

---

[2]For the most current information about the role of the brain in mental disorders, the reader can consult the National Institute of Mental Health web site: http://www.nimh.nih.gov .

Model helps the beginner determine which part of the life space - front stage or back stage - contains the real problem. Once that is accomplished, selecting the appropriate intervention comes easily. The main body of this book will develop a variety of therapeutic situations and demonstrate when an intervention might be appropriate and which tools the therapist/counselor might employ to produce the desired change.

What are the various systems of which one is a part? As already indicated, the family of origin ("first order family") is the first system. The Metasystems Model is grounded in Adlerian psychology which understands that each person is unique (hence Adler's term "individual psychology" for his theory), and yet each person is influenced by the social system of the family. On the front stage, birth order becomes a major influence (Tomm, 1993). Just as obviously, gender is a front stage influence. Children learn very quickly, for example, "I am a girl and I am older than my brother." Not only do children learn these facts, but they also learn the family's emotional meaning of those facts. Perhaps in this family girls are more highly favored than boys, or perhaps the younger child, being a boy, receives more privileges than his older sister because he is a boy. Parents communicate these values, whatever they may be, both verbally and non-verbally through their interactions with their children. Depending on the family constellation, the extended family (e.g., grandparents, aunts, uncles, etc.) may be just as significant influences as the birth parents - perhaps even more so. So the child's basic identity and sense of personal competence are forged first of all in the first order family.

Very quickly another significant influence comes on the scene. This is the second order family. Second order family includes all of those people who are not biologically related to the child but who are nevertheless uniquely important to the child. Some examples of second order family might include scout leaders, church or synagogue teachers, school teachers, or even a neighbor down the street. Street gangs are, unfortunately, also a form of second order family, which illustrates the reality that second order family, while potentially even more influential on the child than first order family, is no more likely to be truly functional than first order family. For better or worse, the value of the second order family is that it provides additional opportunities for the child to learn "appropriate" social behavior by observing others. In turn, this helps confirm the self-concept the child had already developed in those early interactions in the first order family. For the 27 percent of U.S. children who live in single parent families, second order family can supply some of the relationship pieces missing in first order family. For the 54 percent of U.S. children from birth through the third grade who regularly receive child care from someone other than a biological relative, learning from second order family becomes inevitable

(America's Children 2000, 2000). However, even children in intact traditional families can benefit from the enrichment of second order family relationships.

Also on the front stage for both first and second order family is health issues. As any parent knows, children are acutely aware of any difference from "normal" (i.e., "like me"). Children with physical characteristics desirable to their peers will be more popular, and thus will move more easily toward the healthy goal of personal superiority. On the other hand, children who have some physical inferiority (e.g., vision defects, over weight, poor coordination, etc.) will have to compensate in some way (Lundin, 1989). Whether these compensatory mechanisms are healthy (i.e., promoting the child's ultimate welfare and growth) or not will depend on a host of other factors.

One powerful example of the influence the family has on the health issues of the individual is a study which showed that in families where parents and grandparents were clinically depressed, a discomforting 49 percent of the grandchildren showed signs of psychopathology, with a very high risk of anxiety disorders (Warner, Weissman, Mufson, and Wickramaratne, 1999). Whether this is genetically determined to some degree or is purely the result of social learning can be debated. The clear fact is that health patterns do tend to repeat in families across generations. Children cannot help but learn the emotional meaning of these patterns.

On the back stage for both first and second order family is personality issues. The more we learn about child development, the more clear it becomes that basic temperament is genetically influenced. As any parent knows, some children are born very active and happy, while other children come into the world cranky and fearful. There is evidence that these observations are biologically based. Some studies have shown, for example, that fearful children have a higher heart rate in the womb than the average child, and their amygdalas (which controls learned fear) may be more excitable than normal ("Personality Disorders", 2000). Bandura's concepts of "reciprocal determinism" and "self-system" (1978) help make sense of the complexity of real human life. Human behavior is determined by genetic and environmental factors, but humans in turn select, through a variety of cognitive (though unconscious) processes, to which stimuli they will respond and how they will respond. All of this is happening back stage, beyond the individual's consciousness, guiding the front stage interactions with family, friends, and community.

Social Control

As humans develop, the number of systems with which they interact expands. On the front stage, humans learn a variety of gender, ethnic, sociocultural, and subcultural rules. Through observation and sometimes through direct teaching, children learn "boys do this, girls do that." Take a very common example: at a holiday gathering, the male child, hungry for attention, wanders into the adult gathering and performs some feat. If the adults respond, "Oh, isn't he smart! Look what he can do!", the boy will quickly learn that boys in this culture are rewarded for doing. However, if a female child, just as hungry for attention, wanders into that same gathering and receives a response from the adults like, "Oh, isn't she sweet! Look how cute she is!", she will quickly learn that girls in this culture are rewarded for being. Euro-Americans follow rules which stress individualism, while Asian-Americans tend to follow rules which stress family and group loyalty.

The function of these rules is, of course, to teach the "right" perceptions. This behavior conforms to the rules and therefore is "right." That behavior does not follow the rules and therefore is "wrong." At least to this degree, perception, and therefore behavior, is socially constructed. While few people consciously think about these many layers of rules, they remain front stage because anyone can, with sufficient effort, list them. In keeping with Adler's concept of "fictionalism," it really does not matter whether these rules are true. We follow them "as if" they were true (Lundin, 1989). Many older African-Americans, for example, can testify how the rules of American society prior to the 1960s tightly restrained where they could eat, where they could sleep, or even in what part of the bus they could sit. These "Jim Crow laws," as they were known, were enforced "as if" society depended on it, and everyone knew that this was the way things were done in America.

The back stage of awareness contains secrets. However, not all secrets are created equal. Evan Imber-Black (1998) makes some useful distinctions. There are "sweet secrets." These are time-limited and made for the purpose of fun. Some common examples of "sweet secrets" would include surprise parties, gifts, or unexpected visits. Since "sweet secrets" are by definition time-limited, they do not linger on the back stage.

Then there are "essential secrets." These are secrets which appropriately protect boundaries. For example, one essential secret between couples would be their sexual intimacy. This secret contains activity that only they share and thus draws them closer together. It truly is no business at all of others. Incidentally, violations of these "essential secrets" such as adultery are so deeply hurtful precisely for this reason - the offended party rightfully feels that their partner has stolen something essential from the relationship.

There are also "toxic secrets." Toxic secrets poison relationships and haunt the back stage of life for long periods of time. The 1999 film *American Beauty* bitingly portrays the effect of toxic secrets on a relationship. The film is, in fact, full of toxic secrets, all of which combine to literally prove fatal by the end of the film. Toxic secrets usually build up like arsenic, until their cumulative effect is fatal to the relationship if not to human life.

Finally, there are "dangerous secrets." In contrast to toxic secrets, which usually build over long periods of time before they cause serious harm, dangerous secrets can explode suddenly, inflicting great harm. A common example is domestic violence. The dangerous secret of domestic violence allows one-third of all female homicide victims and four percent of all male homicide victims to be murdered by a spouse, ex-spouse, or boy/girl friend (U.S. Department of Justice, 2000).

For better or worse, secrets control us. Take the example of a college-age male who has come to believe he is homosexual, who also believes that his parents will never accept his sexual identity. He decides to keep the secret from his family, but this decision starts in motion a dance of distance in the family. He pulls away from his parents because he feels he is living a lie, and the parents awkwardly respond with puzzlement. The real reason for his pulling-away behavior remains a secret which affects everyone in the family. It is hard to fight an enemy you cannot see.

When the beginning counselor/therapist notices sudden silences or quick side-ways glances, there is a good chance that the conversation just accidentally tripped over a secret. Similarly, if the individual or family appears to be stuck at a particular developmental level, the odds are high that there is some secret lurking on the back stage, tying the family to the past and restricting future growth. Secrets keep us stuck (Imber-Black, 1998).

Levels of Perception

The front stage of perception deals with conscious awareness. Psychologists who have studied perception have noted that there are far more events happening in the environment than we ever consciously perceive. One of the reasons for that reality is "preparatory set," that is, we see (or hear, or smell, etc.) what we expect to see. Artists and movie makers make use of this principle to trick us into believing we are seeing something that is not really there. Another common example of preparatory set from everyday life concerns looking for a set of lost keys. We can look right at them and never see them if we don't expect them to be where they are.

There is another brain-mediated principle of perception, and that is "pay value." We see only what has "pay value" for us. All of us develop what Adler called a "style of life" which basically remains unchanged over time (Lundin, 1989). Part of this style of life will be the goals for which we are striving. Obviously, whatever helps us reach our goals will have pay value for us, and therefore we will lock onto that. Whatever conflicts with our previously held beliefs will not have pay value, and therefore will either not be perceived at all or will be dismissed as irrelevant. This is true whether the person is striving toward healthy goals ("superiority" in Adler's language) or unhealthy ("neurotic") goals.

This bit of front stage knowledge can help the beginning counselor/therapist. If a client appears to be totally unaware of the effect of her/his behavior on others, it may not be denial. The person may indeed be unaware. Or perhaps the client may claim to be unaware of how self-defeating the client's behavior is, despite the counselor's attempts to point it out. In either case, the counselor/therapist knows to start looking at the client's goals, because perception is ruled to a large degree by "pay value" - by the goals we are striving for. That is why Harry Stack Sullivan said, "All behavior makes sense when you see it from the right perspective" (Levenson, 2000). That perspective is always the client's perspective.

Back stage of perception are those things which the Metasystems Model labels "Things forgotten but not lost." Much of what we know about this area of human life comes from the study of trauma, though traumatic events are certainly not the only things which can be forgotten but not lost.

For example, adult survivors of childhood sexual abuse frequently report sexual problems with their spouse, including sexual disinterest, aversion, dissatisfaction, and performance problems. This is true even when the abuse is not consciously remembered. One very common survival tool people employ during the trauma is dissociation - the splitting off of that part of life from the rest of life. In reality, these "walled-off" memories are really behind a very leaky dam. Almost anything can trigger a re-experiencing. Women who have been raped report that even with their partner, who they love and trust, the smell of semen can trigger painful memories. Males who were orally raped as boys may find that an oral swabbing at the dentist's office drives them to a near panic. This is because the walled-off material is highly emotional and relatively non-verbal. The memories trigger the amygdala, which in turn floods the body with stress/fear hormones, long before the thoughts have a chance to hit the cortex of the brain (Schiraldi, 2000). The same "leaky dam" applies to other, non-sexual, traumatic memories as well.

9

Schiraldi (2000) also cites a study which indicated that 80 percent of prostitutes come from abusive or alcoholic homes.   The same study supported the idea that people with sexual addictions come from similar backgrounds. In abusive or alcoholic homes, children quickly learn that sex is separate from love and is useful for purposes other than love. This is true even when the child is only an observer of the abuse. The facts of the home life may be open to conscious awareness, but the real emotional message will lurk on the back stage.   Thus, the adult tries, through repetition compulsion or addiction, to gain a sense of control over events of the past which still haunt the present, all without ever being aware of the connection.

How will the beginning counselor know that some things forgotten but not lost are at work? Obviously, if the client exhibits any of the symptoms of post-traumatic stress disorder, that would be a major clue.   Bodily complaints for which there is no medical explanation is another.   For example, if a client complains about chronic back pain but MRIs and mylograms find no somatic abnormalities, it would well be that someone is still "on this client's back," and the body is responding appropriately. Other common pointers include self-mutilation, death anxiety, or alexithymia (the shutting down of emotions, becoming an emotional robot).

Rituals, Ghosts, and Baggage

In the Metasystems Model, rituals, ghosts, and baggage are drawn as an arrow cutting across all levels of the paradigm and going right to the heart of the model - the family of origin. The arrow is part on the front stage and part on the back stage. This illustrates the self-evident truth: some of this material we are consciously aware of, and some we are not.

Rituals are set, customary, usually formal, ways of ordering behavior. Normally, when one thinks of organized religion she or he thinks of rituals, and certainly religious rituals do help order life. All organized religion contains rituals for the momentous transitions of life, including birth, marriage, and death, as well as rituals for worship. For those who have an active religious faith, these religious rituals can be a powerful source of help and comfort, especially during and following traumatic or highly emotional life events (Schiraldi, 2000).

Families have their own rituals, too.   These usually focus on the family's involvement in various holiday celebrations, including both civic and religious holidays, as well as birthdays, anniversaries, and other special occasions. Since rituals, by their very nature, tap into all spheres of life, they are very useful for the beginning counselor/therapist to inquire about and use. A client of mine was unable to face the death of his wife. As we talked, I discovered that other members of his family normally made regular visits to the grave of a loved one, yet he had not visited his wife's grave even once in the two years. By not participating in this family ritual, he had cut himself off even more completely from his family's support network than the death itself had, and thus he had unwittingly deepened his depression. I contracted with him to meet him on a given day and drive him to the cemetery. He canceled twice before he finally rode with me to the place where his wife's body was buried. I stood behind him, close enough to be supportive but enough out of his field of vision to let him focus on the visible evidence of his pain and loss, while he did what he had to do. When he was finished, he thanked me and said, "Thanks. I can make it now." And he did.

Ghosts are not apparitions or spirits or anything metaphysical. Ghosts are those people who, although not physically present, continue to influence our behavior as though they were present. The "ghost" in this sense may be a living person, or the person may be dead, or the person may be totally fictitious (Sullivan, 1964). Ghosts are an important concept because, as Sullivan noted, all behavior is relational. However, the relationship may be with a ghost, rather than with people who are physically present. In my clinical practice with teens, I have learned that one clue to their real, core relationships comes from the posters they have on their walls. In that vein, I had a troubled teenaged boy, a typical "bad-ass adolescent," in my office. I found that his hero was Freddie Krugger - the "hero" of the "Nightmare on Elm Street" series of films. He admired the way Freddie had overcome abuse, and he was constantly playing to "Freddie." Not all ghosts are so malicious. Many Christian teens wear a bracelet with the initials "W.W.J.D." - "What Would Jesus Do?" By reminding themselves of their relationship with Jesus, these teens give themselves permission to act in ways of which Jesus would approve.

Baggage refers to the beliefs one brings to the present moment. For example, one piece of my baggage is my belief that I am a good therapist. Another piece of my baggage contains my belief about myself as a husband. Note that these beliefs do not have the formal character of rituals or the "universal" character of rules. They do, however, equip the person for the journey of life. Obviously, the term "baggage" does draw on a travel metaphor, and just as obviously, no one would want to take a long trip without some baggage. Just as obviously, one would not want to take excess baggage on the trip. If, for example, I were going to the beach in the summer, I would be very unlikely to need my snow skiing outfit.

The task of the beginning counselor/therapist is to determine which baggage, which beliefs, truly help the person move toward "superiority" and which are excess or outdated for the trip. Often the easiest way to accomplish this is to use Adler's "fictionalism" - to encourage the person to act "as if" what they believe is true and note carefully what actually happens. If at all possible, because, as we have already noted, perceptions can be distorted, the person should also contract with another person to help observe. The flip side is just as effective. The therapist may suggest that the person discard an old belief and act "as if" it were excess baggage and not what happens. Feelings are not the issue. Observable results are.

The Metasystems Model is a dynamic model. Since it is grounded in Adlerian psychology, the model presupposes human creativity and activity. Humans shape their world as much as they are shaped by it, and ideally this process continues at least to the point of death. It is when that is not true that psychopathology becomes an issue. Applying this model in practical, "nuts-and-bolts" ways to various manifestations of psychopathology will be the focus of the rest of this book.

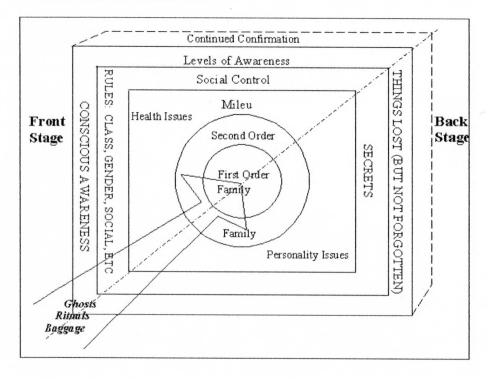

THE FUNDAMENTALS

Chapter 1 - The First Interview

Everyone is kneaded out of the same dough but not baked in the same oven. -
Yiddish Proverb

The first interview is a bit like going on a blind date. Each party to the relationship knows a little about the other, but not enough to feel comfortable. The therapist's or counselor's (the two terms will be used interchangeably, since this text addresses both) primary task during the first interview is to help everyone feel comfortable enough to want to continue the relationship.

The importance of accomplishing the task of forming a comfortable working relationship cannot be overstated. Research into what makes psychotherapy effective has consistently shown two facts. First, about 75% of the people who received psychotherapy were better off than non-treated people who had similar disorders. Second, the type of therapy did not seem to be as significant as the relationship between the therapist and the client (APA, 1994).

Because of the power inherent in the counselor's position, all of the major mental health organizations' codes of ethics recognize that the therapist bears primary responsibility for the relationship. For example, the American Psychological Association (APA)'s code of ethics states, in part, "Psychologists are sensitive to real and ascribed differences in power between themselves and others, and they do not exploit or mislead other people during or after professional relationships" (APA, 1992). The American Association for Marriage and Family Therapy's (AAMFT, 2001) Code of Ethics expresses a similar principle: "Marriage and family therapists advance the welfare of families and individuals. They respect the rights of those persons seeking their assistance, and make reasonable efforts to ensure that their services are used appropriately."

This chapter will provide the beginning counselor or therapist something few of us ever had on our blind dates - a step-by-step process for beginning the special relationship known as counseling or therapy. Of course, there will be variations on the themes listed here due to different agencies' standards of care and the counselor's personal preferences. Still, these themes should guide the beginner until they become as natural as breathing.

Setting Up the Room

Almost all, if not all, beginning counselors will work in an agency setting, and therefore will have little choice about the physical layout of the consultation room. However, they should take charge of the options they do have. If at all possible, use a table lamp rather than a bright overhead light in the room. It creates a more comfortable, "homey" atmosphere and seems less "clinical" and therefore less anxiety-provoking to most clients. Chairs should be positioned so that there is no furniture between the client and the therapist, with the possible exception of a low coffee table. Anything that creates a physical barrier also creates an emotional barrier.

Timing the session is always an issue. This author prefers to use a countdown timer on his watch that emits a loud, 20-second series of beeps. The author sets the timer for 40 minutes (10 minutes before the end of the session) and informs clients during the intake interview that the beep signals ten minutes remaining in the session. Other counselors prefer to position a clock behind the client, where the counselor can glance at it and keep track of time without being too obvious about it. However one does it, keeping track of time is a necessary task.

Most beginning therapists will also have to record their work for supervision purposes, either for their practicum during their degree program or for post-degree experience toward licensure. Either way, the client must consent, in writing, prior to actually beginning the recording. Since most schools and agencies have their own consent forms, this text will not provide a sample. Should the therapist need an example, most professional associations have sample forms they can provide their members. If the therapist is audio recording, the recorder should be somewhat out of sight but within easy reach of the therapist, so it can be started or stopped without disrupting the session. The microphone should be an area-type microphone instead of the usual directional microphone, and should be located away from the recorder but close to the client. The microphone wires should be carefully placed so that there is no danger of anyone tripping over them.

If the therapist is video taping the sessions and the agency is not equipped for video recording, the therapist can station the video camera on a tripod behind the clients. Since the intern is presenting the tape to her or his supervisor, the camera should be pointed at the therapist so that the therapist, not the client, has to look at the camera. Again, an external microphone works best, and it should be set up as for audio recording. Ideally, the therapist should use a remote control which allows starting and stopping the video recorder without having to disrupt the session by physically walking over to the camera.

If at all possible, the ringer on the telephone in the consultation room should be turned off. Murphy's Law ("If anything can go wrong, it will") dictates that a telephone will ring at precisely the wrong moment for the client. Even if the agency's secretary quickly answers the ring, the mood can be broken and the whole session's emotional work set back. Needless to say, the same applies to the therapist's cell phone and beeper.

Naturally, the therapist should have the room set up with materials the therapist can reasonably expect to need. Some like to have a note pad to make process notes during the session. Others like to have a pad and colored pencils to draw a genogram (see Chapter 11). Still others will want to have therapy games to help children and adults talk about emotional issues. Part of the set-up will depend on the specific needs of the client learned from the contact which established the appointment, and part will depend on the therapist's personal preferences. One thing is sure: nothing looks as unprofessional as having to repeatedly run out of the room to retrieve therapeutic aids.

The First Few Seconds

Some parts of therapy cannot be learned. The first few seconds of therapy definitely come under that heading. In those first few seconds when the client (or potential client) first lays eyes on the professional, much will transpire and most of it will be nonverbal. This is where the professional will need to draw upon her or his own interpersonal skills learned and practiced in countless "normal" interactions with others. The key is for the professional to communicate a genuine warmth and hospitality. As the Metasystems Model makes clear, the cultural rules of what constitute "warmth and hospitality" will definitely affect the specific behaviors exhibited by the professional. For example, in the deep South, where the author lives, greeting a stranger as though they were a long lost friend is still considered the norm. In other parts of the country, the greeting might be more restrained and formal, and yet, within that culture, still communicate hospitality. Observing these well-known, but often unspoken, rules helps set the client at ease, because these behaviors introduce a bit of the familiar into what is usually, for the client, a very strange and anxiety-provoking experience.

At the same time, the professional must act like a professional. Counseling is a very distinct type of relationship. It is a relationship undertaken by the client because the client hopes that it will result in the client "getting better" (whatever that may mean to the particular client). It is not a relationship for the mutual pleasure and benefit of both parties. The professional must maintain a certain emotional distance in order to be effective. To use the terms the Metasystems Model borrowed from Structural Theory, the therapist must join with the system without getting triangulated into the system (Figley and Nelson, 1989). Once again, the specific behaviors that constitute "professional" behavior will be dictated by the particular culture in which the professional operates.

Like the first few minutes of a blind date, the very brief time period between first eye contact with the client and the formal beginning of the interview are crucial. Those first minutes may not guarantee that the relationship will develop. There is still much work to do on both sides, even in the first interview. If the therapist is cold or officious or in any way offensive of the client's general expectations of professional hospitality, however, these few minutes can mean the death of the relationship before it ever really begins.

In this sense only, the author believes that therapists are born, not made. No one can teach that genuine warmth and caring. It has to come from within. However, if that warm caring is there, supervision and other training can shape and develop it.

The Formal Interview Begins

The formal part of the first interview begins the moment the client (which can mean one person, a couple or a whole family) and the therapist are comfortably seated in the consultation room. Every behavior, verbal and nonverbal, by the client becomes information from which the therapist can form the assessment which will guide the course of treatment. At the same time, the client is (usually unconsciously) assessing the therapist, looking for behaviors which will support the initial impression formed at the first meeting.

Even where the client sits can be part of the assessment. For example, in the author's counseling center, one of the consultation rooms has a love seat and two very comfortable chairs. The client is allowed to choose where to sit. If a couple chooses to sit together on the love seat, that communicates something about the emotional closeness they feel. If, on the other hand, one chooses to sit on the love seat and the other chooses to sit in a chair, that communicates a different, but equally valuable, message about the couple's level of closeness.

For couples, individuals, or families, body language is an important component of the assessment. However, generalizations about what constitutes "open" and "closed" body messages will likely lead the therapist to misunderstand what is actually going on. For example, instead of assuming that crossed arms automatically mean the person is closed, pay attention to how that cue fits with other cues. Interpret the body language cues in the light of what is the norm for the client's sociocultural group, rather than what some generalizations say these cues "ought" to mean.

Ideally, clients should be instructed to arrive early (15 to 30 minutes, depending on the amount of "paperwork" required by the agency) for their first interview to complete the required forms. If the therapist has not already done so, the therapist should take the completed forms from the client at this very early point and quickly glance at them. Then the therapist should put the forms away and focus on the client.

As soon as the therapist can conveniently transition from the casual conversation ("Is it cold enough for you?" "How about that baseball game?") which usually fills the walk down the hall to the consultation room, the therapist should begin to structure the counseling process. Remember, this is a blind date. Many clients only know about therapy what they have seen in the movies, and most of that is inaccurate. They need to know the rules of the relationship to feel comfortable, and it is up to the therapist to provide that necessary information.

Let us assume that beginning counselor Samuel Shmooze is meeting adult client Jane Bagodonuts for the first time. For this example, assuming that local cultural rules encourage the use of first names between adults, the opening conversation might go something like this:

> Jane, before I ask you to tell me anything about yourself, I want to tell you some things about me and about this counseling center. You have a right to know that I am a counseling intern at Southern Christian University. I have completed my work for my master's degree in counseling and I am being supervised in my internship by Dr. Wayne Perry, a licensed supervisor of marriage and family therapy. As you saw on the consent to tape form you signed, Dr. Perry will be reviewing the tapes of our sessions with me to ensure that you receive the best possible care. So in essence, you are getting two sets of eyes and ears instead of only one. I want to go over our center's Standard of Care, which you have in your hands, so you will know what to expect during our relationship.

> You need to know that we will meet for 50 minutes each time. I have just set a countdown timer on my desk behind me. It is set for 40 minutes, and it is rather loud and obnoxious when it goes off. I do that for two reasons. Because I have set the timer, I don't have to worry about the time. I can focus on you and your needs, and not worry about watching the clock. When the timer goes off, I will

know we have about ten minutes to go, and we can begin to wrap things up. However, just as importantly, you will probably hear the timer go off, and you, too, will know that we have about ten minutes to go. That frees you to make some decisions for yourself about what to do. You might say to yourself, "Hummm, only ten minutes to go. I really want to get this in so I better say it now." Or you might say, "Hummm, only ten minutes to go. I better hold this for next time." Either way, you stay in control, and that is important to me.

The orientation to the counseling should continue in the same vein. The agency's Standard of Care will dictate the specific areas covered. These are some common areas which will need to be addressed.

- Telephone contact. How are emergencies handled? Does the counselor or agency allow for telephone counseling? If so, what is the charge? What limits are there?
- Court appearances. Does the agency routinely allow counselors to testify in court? Obviously, courts can legally subpoena a counselor's appearance and records, and the counselor must always comply with the subpoena. Some agencies, however, try to discourage such appearances, so clients need to know in advance if the counselor is going to have the agency's support in trying to fight any subpoena which may be issued. Clients also need to know in advance what the charges for such court appearances will be. Ethics never allow exorbitant charges.
- Confidentiality. All major mental health associations have some statement about client confidentiality, and many, though not all, state laws grant privileged communication to therapists and counselors. Clients need to know in advance that their communications will be kept confidential to the maximum limits specified by state and federal law. They should be reassured that any information shared with the counselor's supervisor will be treated by the supervisor as confidential.
- "Duty to Warn." Most states have laws that compel therapists to comply with the "duty to warn" the identifiable potential victims of reasonably foreseeable violence. Clients need to know about these and any other statutory mandated reporting laws. For example, most states mandate reporting of suspected child abuse, but may or may not mandate reporting of spouse abuse.

- Financial policies. Clients have a right to know what the agency's financial policies are. If the agency has some sort of "sliding scale" of fees, that scale should be clearly explained, and the client directed to perform whatever actions may be necessary to apply for assistance. An agency that accepts insurance must inform the client which managed care companies they use, and what actions the therapist will take and what actions the client must take. If the agency bills the client for services, the client should know what the billing policies are, including the time for payment and penalties for nonpayment.
- The client's rights. Your agency should have these spelled out in their Consent for Treatment document. Some of the common ones include the right of the client to review your records on the client, and the requirements for doing so; the right to ask for a referral; and the right to terminate therapy and the process for doing so. Clients also have a right to know about the risks of therapy and to know that change in the desired direction is not guaranteed.

The Presenting Problem

Once the client verbally indicates an understanding of the agency's standard of care, the next question the therapist asks is usually one like this: "So, tell me, Jane, what brings you to see me today?" If the client is a couple or a family instead of an individual, the question may be phrased more generally to allow whoever wants to answer the question to speak up. This open-ended technique (referred to as "throwing up a jump ball") is often a very informative assessment tool. Watching the people in the room decide who will speak first often gives some clue to what is going on in the relationship. Who bows to whom? What sort of eye contact does the non-speaker maintain with the speaker? How freely does the non-speaker interrupt the speaker, and how does the speaker react to any interruptions?

Conventional wisdom in psychotherapy is that the presenting problem is seldom the real problem. There are at least three reasons why this may be true. First, clients may be applying a lot of effort at the wrong place. In other words, they may be actively trying to solve the wrong problem. For example, the client may believe the problem is their spouse's "unexplained" emotional distance, when the real problem is their own unacknowledged depression. Second, clients may be hesitant to reveal the real problem for fear the therapist will reject them in some manner. Never, in this author's experience, has an adult client come in with a presenting problem of having been sexually abused as a child. That real issue emerges only later, when trust is established. Third, the therapist may be so eager to "get to the root of the problem" that the therapist misses the main issue entirely. Abraham Maslow is quoted as saying, "To the man who only has a hammer in the toolkit, every problem looks like a nail." The therapist's own cultural and theoretical biases may cause the therapist to miss what the client is trying hard to say (Pipes and Davenport, 1999).

For all of these reasons, the therapist should "listen with the third ear" to the presenting problem. What emotions are being stirred in the therapist by the client's story? In the language of traditional psychotherapy, this is called paying attention to counter-transference. When did the client first notice what is being defined as the problem? What are the reported symptoms? When are these symptoms worse? When are they not as noticeable? What has been the course of the problem? Has it come and gone, or has it grown steadily more serious?

Depending on the situation, the counselor may simply allow the client to tell the story, or the counselor may need to actively guide the client via a diagnostic interview. Agencies that require a diagnosis under the *Diagnostic and Statistical Manual of Mental Disorders*, 4th Edition (usually referred to as DSM-IV) may also require a structured diagnostic interview for that purpose. Either way, the Metasystems Model suggests that the therapist make the appropriate diagnosis as a guide to accurate treatment planning and therapy (Figley and Nelson, 1989). Actually doing diagnosis is an advanced skill which is beyond the scope of this introductory text. Before seeing clients, the counselor should have taken course work in diagnosis and assessment which will fill this need.

If more than one person is in the room, the therapist will want to carefully invite comments about the problem from each person. This begins the process known as "joining." In joining, the therapist not only displays an active interest in and respect for each individual's point of view, the therapist also attempts to use the client's language and communication style (Griffin and Greene, 1999). Since therapy is primarily about relationship, to overlook any individual is to not only overlook a potentially valuable source of information about the problem, it is also a direct detriment to the effectiveness of therapy. In other words, joining is a critical therapy skill (Figley and Nelson, 1990).

A common question of beginning counselors and therapists is, what do I do if the client presents a problem I don't know how to treat? The professional associations' codes of ethics are clear that counselors and therapists should only treat problems within their scope of competence (e.g., AAMFT, 1998). Naturally, that scope will be very limited for the beginning professional, but that is not necessarily a problem. Before becoming licensed as an independent practitioner of a mental health profession, the beginning therapist must be under supervision. The supervisor's field of competence then becomes the limiting issue. As long as the beginning therapist keeps the supervisor informed about the progress of the counseling, and as long as the supervisor is comfortable with the professional's work, there is no need to seek a referral. More information about actually making referrals will come in Chapter 4 of this text.

Concluding the First Interview

In keeping with its Adlerian foundations, the Metasystems Model ends the first interview with a focus on goals. In the author's experience, few clients come to therapy simply to complain about their problems. They come expecting something to change for the better. While listening carefully to the client's problem definition is necessary to joining with the client, moving toward the client's goals is necessary to engendering a sense of hope - another critical therapy skill (Figley and Nelson, 1989).

Counselor Samuel Shmooze may want to transition to this phase of the first interview like this: "I really appreciate your sharing your story with me. I can see that you really are hurting, and I can appreciate how much you must want some help. So, let's suppose that our work together is wildly successful - that you get everything out of this counseling that you could want. Let's assume this counseling is so successful that even ten years from now you will look back on this experience and say, 'You know, that was the best investment of time and money I ever made.' Now, if all of that were true for you, what would be different?"

Frequently this question catches the client off guard. The client is probably more aware of what they do not want than they are what they want. That is one reason this question is so valuable. To answer the question, the client has to begin to envision a future which is different from the past. That new vision breaks what Milton Erikson would have termed a trance and introduces the possibility of change. (Chapter 5 includes much more about constructing goals.)

Ben Stein said, "The indispensable first step to getting the things you want out of life is this: decide what you want." Just as the counselor must listen carefully to each individual in the client system as each defines the problem (i.e., what they do not want), so the counselor must listen just as carefully as each begins to define, however hesitantly, what they do want. Having one or more persons who cannot define in even vague, general terms some desired outcome creates a very poor prognosis for the therapy. Likely the person is so discouraged that motivation to actually work to change anything will be very low. In this case, the counselor will need to work harder to really join with the discouraged person and engender a realistic

23

sense of hope before trying to rush off in the direction desired by the motivated person.

A special case arises when clients are mandated to treatment or otherwise feel compelled to come to counseling. For example, a young adult arrested for marijuana use may be ordered by the court to participate in drug rehabilitation, but the client may not see any problem with marijuana use. Or perhaps a husband comes to therapy only because his wife threatened to divorce him if he did not come. In these situations, the person who feels compelled may not see any need to change and therefore likely will not see any need to create personal goals for the therapy. Once again, the therapist carefully joins with the client. Counselor Shmooze may respond to the young adult, for example, this way: "I'm sorry you have to be here against your will, and I know it seems painful to you. But I have to tell the judge something. What kind of change do you think the judge is looking for? What would be different in your life if you actually did that?" To the resistant husband, Counselor Shmooze may say, "I know you think this is all your wife's fault, and I know you don't see any reason you should change. So what changes in her would you like to see? How will you have to change to help her do that?"

Once the client is able to articulate at least one concrete, specific behavioral goal, the counselor should conclude the first interview by assigning a task (known as "homework" or "a prescription" - see Chapter 2 for more on prescriptions in therapy) which will help the client begin to actually move in the desired direction. Confucius said, "The journey of 1000 miles begins with a single step." That is the basic principle for the conclusion of the first interview. The client needs to leave the consultation room with a realistic hope that things can be better. Having something to do between sessions which is logically connected both to the problem the client brought in and the goal the client took out is a powerful force for generating that hope (Figley and Nelson, 1990).

Last Issues

After the formal conclusion of the interview, there are still a few remaining issues which need to be taken care of. The next appointment will need to be scheduled. Payment will need to be arranged for the session just concluded. Just how these are taken care of will depend on the center. Sometimes the therapist takes care of these matters. In other agencies, the therapist takes the client to a receptionist who handles these matters. Whatever the agency's procedures, the way they are carried out will form the client's last impression of the agency and of the counseling - an impression which may make the client more or less likely to return for the second session. As at the beginning, so at the end a good balance of warmth and professionalism is the best bet for continuing the relationship which began as a "blind date" and hopefully will become increasingly therapeutic.

Living Into the Lesson

1.   List three people who have really made you feel welcomed in their home. What did they do? How did you respond? Which of these behaviors would be appropriate for you to use in greeting clients in a professional setting?

2.   Find a partner and role-play your greeting of a brand-new client. Escort your new client down the hall to your consultation room. When you reach the room, have your "client" give you feedback on what was and was not helpful. Then switch roles and repeat.

3.   Who in your family (first or second order) was the most empathetic person you knew? Who was the least? What did they do differently that you observed? From whom did you get your empathy skills?

4.   This text makes a point that the therapist or counselor should quickly glance at the intake forms and then put them away. Why? What's the point of glancing at the forms? Why not read them carefully at this point to get as much background as possible?

5.   The text emphasizes that the audio or video equipment should be "hidden in plain sight." What is the point of making the recorder as inconspicuous as possible? Since the client has to sign a release form to allow taping, doesn't the client know it is there?

6.   Obtain at least one sample of an agency's Standard of Care and Consent to Treatment statements (in some agencies, these may be combined into one document). Share these with your classmates. What similarities do you notice? What differences?

7.   Discuss client confidentiality. Who owns this confidentiality? What are the limits to confidentiality in your state? What types of behavior must be reported - and to whom?

8.   One client said to the author, "You're my best friend. I just have to pay you for your friendship." How do you feel about receiving money for being someone's "best friend?" How do you feel when you go to a professional (physician, tax preparer, lawyer, etc.) and have to pay for their services? Should mental health care be different? Why or why not?

9.   When you think of going "eyeball to eyeball" with a real client, what one presenting problem scares you more than any other? What presenting problem feels the most comfortable to you? What resources do you have for dealing with these problems?

10.   What are your professional goals right now? How do your goals actually affect your behavior? How do you tell the difference between wishes and goals? How can you apply your own experience to your work with your clients?

11.   Marriage and family therapy as a profession has historically resisted using mental health diagnoses because of concern about the medical model on which such diagnoses are based. Many mental health consumer groups (such as NAMI) have similar concerns for different reasons. So what do you think about the recommendation of making a diagnosis as appropriate for every client? Be ready to support your position pro or con.

12.   In the concluding section of this chapter the author gave two hypothetical examples of so-called resistant clients. Get with one other person and construct a behavior change assignment for each of these clients. Why did you choose the actions you did?

13.   Professionalism is a major theme in this chapter. What does that term mean to you? Who are the best models of professionalism that you personally know or have met? What qualities would you like to borrow from them?

Chapter 2 - Structuring Skills

It is not necessary to change. Survival is not mandatory. - W. Edwards Deming

Planning the Therapy Hour

In the college I attended, students often said that a certain professor in the education department did not have the twenty-two years' experience he claimed. He really had one year of experience repeated twenty-two times. That same trap can befall the beginning therapist. Once the counselor successfully completes the first interview, then what? Or, to use the phrase made famous by Eric Berne's 1973 book, "What do you say after you say hello?" To be successful, the counselor must plan each hour carefully, while remaining open to the unforeseeable "stuff" that is bound to happen in the course of any relationship.

The first session is, as Chapter One suggested, a "blind date." The primary goal of the first session is to begin to form the relationship, the therapeutic alliance, on which therapy will be based. A component of that goal is for the therapist to begin to assess what the major focus of therapy will be. The counselor goes into the first session with questions such as, "Who are these people? What brings them here? How do they define their problem? When did it first appear? What makes these symptoms worse? What makes these symptoms better?" Ideally, the first session ends with another component of that goal for the therapist: the client leaves the first session with a realistic hope that the problem will change.

To pull all of this off, the therapist has to balance two equally important yet very different skills. On the one hand, the therapist has to join with the client. This implies investing some very real emotional energy in the client. The therapist listens to the client so carefully that the therapist is able to begin to use the client's own language and symbols to talk about the issues. Each person in the therapy room receives focused attention from the therapist, and each has an opportunity to be heard. While not minimizing any of the reported pain, the therapist makes a point of highlighting individual and relational strengths revealed in these conversations. Joining, then, clearly implies that the therapist's assessment is jointly created, with each person in the room having a part in the assessment's creation.

On the other hand, the therapist has to remain detached from the client. One of the tenants that Metasystems borrows from Structural Theory is the belief that the client will try to triangulate the therapist into their problem (Nichols and Schwartz, 1998). One of the first skills the therapist must demonstrate (often long before actually talking about it) is the ability to maintain proper boundaries while also maintaining emotional contact. To say the same thing in other words, to remain effective, the therapist has to join with the client system without becoming enmeshed in that system. There is a second reason for maintaining this emotional detachment. The hard intellectual work of assessment requires it. The therapist has to be able to listen with the heart while thinking with the head.

As difficult as this balancing act is, most beginning therapists seem to get it fairly quickly. Although I have no research to back me up, I suspect this is because the structure of the first session is fairly clear-cut and somewhat standard. It is easily learned and practiced. For that reason, many beginning therapists seem to get stuck here. Like the education professor referenced at the beginning of this chapter, they do not grow or change. They simply repeat the same process over and over again.

All sessions after the first employ the same fundamental structural skills as the first: joining, maintaining boundaries, assessment, and ordinary human relational skills such as a sense of humor (Figley and Nelson, 1989). Yet there are major differences.

The counselor should walk into each subsequent session with some clearly defined, attainable "win/win" behavioral goals in mind (Figley and Nelson, 1989). These goals will build upon accomplishments in previous sessions, and should be both long term (i.e., the jointly created goals defining "success" in therapy) and short-term (i.e., immediate changes the therapist desires to effect in this specific session to help reach the long term goals). Subsequent chapters in this book will offer a variety of specific therapeutic techniques drawn from an assortment of theories to help learn ways to create these goals. They will also offer suggestions for dealing with the "stuff" that threatens to upset the goals of the therapy plan.

Prescriptions

Regardless of the counselor's orientation or therapy plan, these session goals should start with the homework (also called prescription) given to the client at the end of the previous session. Some authors make a distinction between homework assignments and prescriptions, but practically speaking, it is difficult, if not impossible, to distinguish the two (L'Abate, Ganahl, and Hansen, 1986). Therefore, in this text the two terms will be used synonymously.

This author often tells clients, "I have never seen anyone yet get well by sitting on some shrink's couch. However, I have seen lots of people get well by applying at home what they learned in my office." That is the principle behind using prescriptions. There are 168 hours in any week. Most clients spend only one hour in the therapist's office. If the only time they actually apply the new behaviors learned in therapy is during the office visit, the odds against the new behavior systematically becoming their routine are at least 167 to one.

Some counselors give homework assignments verbally. Others give them in writing. However one gives the task assignment, there are some general guidelines for creating the assignment. First, it must be logically related to the mutually agreed upon goals of therapy. However, "logically related" does not necessarily mean explicitly related. As with all other parts of therapy, prescriptions may operate on several levels at once. The client does not necessarily have to understand all of this complexity. All that is necessary is that the assignment makes enough sense that the client is willing to do it.

Let's assume, for example, Counselor Shmooze has a new client, Billy Bob Smith. Billy Bob and his wife, Anne May, have one child, a 10-year old son named Raymond. Billy Bob is very close to his son, and he is, in fact Raymond's primary caregiver when they are both at home. The presenting problem is that Raymond is frequently afraid to go to school, even though by everyone's assessment he is quite intelligent. There are no indications from teachers or anyone else that Raymond is the target of bullies, so there appears to be no logical reason for Raymond's frequent fear of school. Billy Bob is usually able to persuade Raymond to go to school, and usually when he goes he does stay all day, but these morning episodes often require Billy Bob to drive Raymond to school because Raymond has missed the bus, and they often make Billy Bob late to work. In listening to Billy Bob's story, Counselor Shmooze inquired if Billy Bob ever felt anything similar to what his son reported. Billy Bob replied that he did occasionally have "panic attacks" [the client's term], and that he had received some therapy for "panic attacks" from another therapist about two years before. Counselor Shmooze questioned what had helped him get over these "panic attacks." Billy Bob described a sequence of cognitive-behavioral interventions [see Chapter 6]. Counselor Shmooze then asked what were the triggers he had identified. After Billy Bob listed those, Counselor Shmooze instructed him to call a family conference and as a family construct a list of triggers for Raymond's fear of school.

Depending on the therapist's theoretical orientation, there are a number of possible explanations for the etiology of Raymond's behavior. The counselor should definitely have a working hypothesis of what that etiology might be, but the client does not need to be made aware of this to successfully complete the homework. Counselor Shmooze gave Billy Bob a homework assignment that made sense to him because it built on helpful skills that he had already used for himself. Specifically, this was an observational task which required no direct change in behavior. Yet implied in this task is the assumption that Raymond's triggers can be identified and changed, just as Billy Bob's had been.

The second requirement of prescriptions is that they be clearly stated. This is not always as simple as it first sounds. Because, by definition, a prescription requires a change in behavior (even if it is only observational change), and because change is always difficult, clients often forget or misunderstand precisely what the therapist asked them to do. This is one of the justifications for putting the prescription in writing (L'Abate, Ganahl, and Hansen, 1986). Even written assignments run the risk of misinterpretation, however. Whether the assignment is written or verbal, to the extent possible the task should be framed in the client's own language.

Suppose, for example, that Jane Bagodonuts is back for her third session with Counselor Shmooze. Her presenting problem is that she believes she is depressed, and Counselor Shmooze agrees with her self-assessment. Her stated goal for therapy is that she will feel happy and she will be able to laugh with her husband again. She has successfully completed the last two assignments, and she has reported feeling considerably less depressed. Counselor Shmooze might give her a prescription such as this: "Jane, this week I want you to pretend that your depression is gone. You and I both know that you are pretending, and that is okay. I want you to act like the depression is gone even though it isn't yet. Specifically, I want you to rent a funny video that you and your husband can watch together. All during this week, make a mental note of how differently your husband treats you from the way he has since you have been depressed. Don't tell him what is going on. What you are doing is just our secret. Let's see if it makes any difference to either of you, okay?" To be really safe, Counselor Shmooze might ask Jane to paraphrase the assignment back to him. This is a variation on the "do something different" homework theme.

Prescriptions serve several very valuable functions, in addition to extending the therapy into the client's home. They serve as a tool for continued assessment of the client. Whether the client completes the homework or not, the counselor learns more about the client's functioning. Indeed, the client's rationale for not doing the task can be as illuminating for the therapist as the client's success with it. Furthermore, failure to accomplish the task may help clarify the severity of the problem, since inability to follow directions is one possible indicator of high stress (L'Abate, Ganahl, and Hansen, 1986).

Prescriptions also serve to keep the counselor on track with the process of therapy. If the therapist gets too caught up in the client's emotions, the therapist will likely, at best, simply drift aimlessly from hot topic to hot topic, with no significant change ever being accomplished. In times of stress or conflict, family members often try to get other members to "chase rabbits" by changing the topic of conversation. The same dynamic often happens in therapy. The counselor who forgets the prescription and simply "chases the rabbits" with the client will find him or herself exhausted at the end of the session, while the client still has a seemingly endless supply of "rabbits" to chase. This ability to remain clear-headed while tracking behavior sequences even in highly emotional situations is a crucial therapy skill (Figley and Nelson, 1989).

The old joke asks, How do you eat an elephant? The answer is, of course, one bite at a time. That's the function of homework assignments for the client. They serve as evidence that the "elephant," the presenting problem, is indeed being eaten one bite at a time. This experiential evidence is a powerful means of engendering realistic hope in the client, and thus serves as a motivator for continued success in therapy.

Stopping Chaotic/Destructive Interactions

Once the counselor has "rejoined" the client and checked the homework from the previous session, the next structural step is to move the therapy forward toward the mutually agreed upon and contracted goals. Seldom is this an easy or smooth process. If change were easy, the client would already have done it without the counselor's help.

Human systems are unique among all other systems because humans, unlike, say, drops of water in a pond, are actively modified by their interactions (Chubb, 1990). The Roman philosopher, Seneca, observed that it was impossible to put one's foot twice into the same river, because by the time one put one's foot back in the river, it would have changed. The same changing milieu is true of individuals. As Metasystems holds, we are simultaneously the product of and creator of the events which shape us.

Sooner or later, whether one is dealing with an individual, a couple, or a family, the chaos the client feels is bound to be expressed in the counseling room. A common example happened to Counselor Samuel Shmooze. He was doing premarital counseling with a couple who were both over age 50 and whose children were all happily married and living away from home. The first several sessions had gone very well, and Counselor Shmooze had every reason to expect that session five would go just as well. The homework assignment was to create a joint budget; that was to be the basis for their discussions about the couple's financial goals and priorities. However, the instant the couple walked into the room, Counselor Shmooze could sense something was very different. Instead of the usual touching and other signs of affection, each partner sat stiffly in their respective chairs. The introductory jokes, which usually flowed easily, fell like ice to the floor. Already guessing the situation, Counselor Shmooze asked, "So, how did the homework assignment go?" "Terrible!" the woman exploded. Before anyone could say anything else, the man exploded in reply, and it was "off to the races."

In situations like this, when there is little time to understand what is going on before something else happens, it is helpful to remember that the therapist is affected by the chaos swirling all about just as the client is. It is also helpful to remember that therapists have influence but no real power (Chubb, 1990). The entire process of interaction is too complex and multiply determined for the counselor to be able to control anything, even if she or he wanted to. The best for which one can hope is to disrupt the interaction.

Counselor Shmooze chose to start his attempts to disrupt the action by silently holding his hands in the football "time out" signal. When that did not work, he swivelled his chair so that he was facing away from them and started reading a book on the credenza. This worked. The couple stopped their arguing and looked at Shmooze. As soon as he had a few seconds of silence, Shmooze swivelled his chair back around and very quietly said, "I see we need to use the Ten-Step Process [Olson, 1999] here. Now, this is the time and place, so that's step one. So, Janine, let's move to step two. What is the issue we need to discuss here?" Since the couple had successfully negotiated the Ten-Step Process twice in their earlier premarital counseling sessions, this return to earlier learning was both comfortable and yet different from the chaos they had allowed.

Counselor Shmooze's style of using gentle humor will not work for every situation or every therapist. Some therapists advocate the use of direct, authoritative instructions, with the consequence of not following the instructions being termination of therapy (e.g., Boszormenyi-Nagy, 1962). Others would advocate for directive interventions which provide structure without the authoritarian note. Minuchin (1996), for example, related a story of Murray Bowen's dealing with chaos by directing both the husband and wife to direct all of their comments only to him. " 'Don't tell me what you *feel*,' he said in his dry, unemotional way. 'I'm not interested in what you feel. Tell me what you think.' Throughout the session, Bowen inserted himself again and again, exerting cognitive control to monitor the intensity of the couple's exchanges" (p. 42). Other examples of providing structure without an authoritarian tone include Olson's Ten-Step Process and PREP, both of which will be discussed in more detail in Chapter Nine, along with some other psychoeducational methods. In session with individuals who are verbally escalating by feeding on their own inner chaos, this author has occasionally sat a trash can in front of the client and said in a soft, smiling, gentle voice, "Let me know when you're through throwing up."

There are probably many right ways to disrupt destructive or chaotic interchanges. Even so, there are two wrong ways to respond in these situations: a) do nothing and b) feed the system. Doing nothing gives tacit approval to the behavior and therefore makes it more likely to continue in the future. Even worse, one person may leave the interaction feeling attacked and betrayed both by the other person and by the therapist. After all, the therapist did nothing to stop what happened. The same applies to individual counseling. The individual may feel betrayed because the counselor "let" them get out of control. Either way, the therapeutic alliance may be seriously, if not irreparably, damaged.

The opposite extreme - feeding the system - is at least as bad. If the counselor attempts to shout down the combatants by raising his or her voice in response to the decibels of the voices in the room, the inevitable result is more chaos. The counselor may be successful in stopping the interaction temporarily. However, what the counselor's behavior really shows is that power counts. Sooner or later, the client is going to decide not to yield power. In the famous (author unknown) paraphrase of the Twenty-Third Psalm, "Yea, though I walk through the valley of the shadow of death, I will fear no evil...because I am the meanest son-of-a-gun in the valley." In short, the therapist's feeding the system will inevitably yield either counter-hostile behavior or regressive behavior or both on the part of the client (Paul and Grosser, 1964).

In their fall into chaos, the clients are teaching the counselor their normal rules for handling highly stressful situations (Minuchin, 1996). Perhaps the client only knows how to be intimate by fighting. Perhaps the client terribly fears conflict because of some past, very bad experiences with conflict, and therefore bottles it up until it explodes out of all proportion to the triggering event. Perhaps the client has learned through past experience that talking is a waste of time and that nothing ever gets solved. Whatever the client's core belief about the "rules" of conflict, the therapist's response has to displace these normal rules with new, more helpful rules that move the clients toward their goals.

Terminating Therapy

Next to the first session, the last is probably the most important in therapy. If the first session sets the expectations of the client for the course of therapy, the last will cement the impression the client carries away from therapy. The question is, which session will be the last?

Moshe Talmon published a book in 1990 called *Single Session Therapy* (Jossey-Bass, Publishers) which puts forth the extreme position that it is possible to effectively do single session therapy. In other words, the first session could literally be the last. The basic premise of solution-focused therapy is that each session should be treated as though it were the first, and each session should be treated as though it were the last (Walter and Peller, 1992). Regardless of one's theoretical orientation, there does seem to be wisdom in structuring each therapy session as though it were the last.

Clients may (and sometimes do) simply drop out of therapy for a variety of reasons. Spontaneous remission of symptoms does happen in physical distress as well as emotional distress. Clients may well decide they are no longer hurting and therefore do not need therapy. The counselor may have unwittingly violated one of the client's "Ten Commandments" (a Metasystems term for rules which the client treats as though they were of divine origin). Therapists may agree in principle with the title of theologian William Easum's 1995 book *Sacred cows make gourmet hamburgers* (Abingdon Press), but very few of us are so cavalier when it is our scared cows being ground up. Clients may also drop out because a more pressing problem (e.g., an unexpected business trip or an unforseen medical crisis) diverted the client's attention. Of course, these are only some of the possibilities.

One primary structuring skill the counselor can apply to meet this challenge is to review the learning of each session as a part of the homework assignment. Counselor Shmooze might say something like this to his client: "Daisy, I have been impressed with the way you have been willing to use the genogram to tell your story today. You made some connections between the way you feel now and the way your mother and her mother before her told you they felt. For some reason you all married emotionally abusive men. Now, I know your grandmother is dead, but your mother is still living, and even though you're not very close to her, here is what I want you to do before next session. I want you to ask her how she survived all those years in an emotionally abusive relationship. You can also ask your mother what she knows about what helped her mother survive. You may or may not be able to use their resources, but at least you'll know they have worked in your family in the past. Now, tell me in your own words what you're going to do this week."

Whether the client returns or not, reviewing what was learned in the session helps reinforce the learning for the client. Should the client not return for the next session, they will at least leave knowing that they made some progress. Clients who feel good about the progress they made may come back at some future time, or even refer friends to the therapist.

Most often, however, if the therapist establishes and maintains a therapeutic alliance with the client, the client will stay until the end. All of the professional codes of ethics specify that the counselor can keep the client only as long as it is reasonably clear that the client is benefitting (see, for example, AAMFT (1998)). So how does the counselor know when therapy "should" end? The answer is fairly obvious for those who have taken the time to establish clear, specific behavioral goals in the first session. Therapy ends when enough of the goals have been met that the client and the therapist jointly believe that the client can successfully complete the healing without the support of therapy.

If goals have been properly set and constantly reviewed, both the counselor and the client will usually be aware that the end of therapy is growing near. This author believes that it is normally best for the counselor to verbalize that awareness as soon as it becomes conscious. Verbalizing the possibility of termination gives the client "permission" to admit the client's own awareness, and it certainly gives a powerfully positive backstage message of confidence in the client's resources. One example of how to express this confidence comes from this author's own practice. Sally came in having been previously diagnosed with a bipolar disorder. Her previous therapist had prescribed appropriate medications, but Sally still felt out of control. She came to my practice because her behavior was causing problems with her husband and children. The following conversation took place at the end of tenth session.

T	Sally, I have been thinking. When you first came to see me, I asked you, on a one-to-ten scale, how bad you felt your problem was. Do you remember what you said? [In scaling, "one" is always low and "ten" is always best. See Chapter 5 for more on scaling.]
S	A three.
T	Right. And I agree that's where you were then. What about now? On that same one-to-ten scale, where do you think you are now?
S	I'm about a seven or an eight.
T	Right. I agree. So I have been thinking, when do you think we ought to consider ending our counseling relationship?
S	Ooo, I don't know. I hadn't thought about it. [Pause]. I'm doing so much better now, the thought of going it alone really scares me.
T	I'm certainly not going to push you out of the nest before you're ready. But this week, let's both think about your original goals and when the time will be right for you to start flying solo, okay?
S	Yeah. I need some time to think about this.

The next session began, as promised, with a review of Sally's goals. For each goal, I asked Sally to give several concrete examples of how she had met that goal. When she also gave some examples of setbacks, I asked her to describe how she had gotten back on track. Each time, with very little prompting from me, Sally was able to do so.

T   So, Sally, what does it look like to you? Are you ready to fly solo yet?

S   I don't know. I'm still scared.

T   Of course. However, it doesn't have to be an "all-or-none" decision. You have lots of options. You could decide you are ready to go it alone, and that will be fine with me. Or you could decide you want to build in a "safety net" and schedule another appointment four or five weeks down the road, just to be sure. Or you could decide you're not ready yet, and we'll keep on working on your goals until you are ready. Even if you decide that this is it, you can always call me anytime you need me, so it's not like you're burning any bridges or anything.

S   That helps. I guess I knew I could always call you, but it's nice to hear it from you. I guess I really am ready, but I would like to schedule an appointment four or five weeks from now. That would make me feel better.

T   Sure, no problem. If it turns out we still have work to do, fine. And if it turns out, as I suspect it will, that you are doing great, well, we'll just have time to sit and celebrate your victories.

S   I'd like that.

In the last few minutes of that eleventh session, we focused on dealing with relapses. This author usually teaches clients "Perry's Corollary to Murphy's Law": The probability that something will go wrong increases inversely with your desire that everything goes right. Since money was a very real concern for this client, we discussed the necessity of her staying on her medication and what she would do if that became a financial problem. We reviewed a second time how she had handled relapses during the course of therapy and projected those same skills into the future. Finally, we reviewed what specific behaviors she had created during the course of therapy which had moved her from a "three" to a "seven or eight."

Sally called the office three weeks later to cancel her next appointment. She was doing fine and felt confident she could make it on her own. When I called her for a routine six-month follow up, she reported that she was doing better than ever.

Not all cases will conclude as successfully as Sally's, of course. As Minuchin says, "Life is more complex than that" (AAMFT Conference presentation, 1998). Still, Sally's case does illustrate the structure for successfully terminating therapy. As the beginning counselor gains more experience, she or he will develop personal variations on these themes which make therapy truly theirs. Just as we can never use another person's finger prints, we can never totally use someone else's counseling techniques. Until the beginning professional develops a style as personal and as comfortable as her or his own fingerprints, these essential structural skills will provide a framework on which to build an effective counseling relationship.

Living Into the Lesson

1. This chapter introduces the concept of emotional triangles, a term used both by Bowen and Minuchin. Draw some of the emotional triangles which were present in your family of origin. What role(s) did you play in these triangles? What sort of situations would typically trigger these triangles?

2. To illustrate the process of goal setting in therapy: Plan a trip from your home to your state capitol. "Success" will be touring the state capitol building and taking memorable photographs of your trip. List in detail specific behaviors you will need to complete to achieve that goal (Hint: Don't forget to start out with getting dressed - unless you plan to visit your state capitol as a nudist).

3. The task given at the end of a session may be called a "prescription" or a "homework assignment." What images do those terms conjure in your mind? Which do you prefer? Since the language we use creates our reality, what sort of reality do you want to create in the minds of your clients when you assign the post-session task?

4. In this chapter, Counselor Samuel Shmooze has a client, Billy Bob Smith, who has a past history of "panic attacks" and whose son also appears to have "anxiety." What if there were no history of excessive anxiety in this family? Design a prescription for this worried father to use to help his 10-year old son.

5. Work with a partner. In the previous session, the client received the homework assignment of ignoring their six-year old child's temper tantrums [a "countersystemic prescription"], but the client reported this session failing to even attempt to change behavior. Role play the ways you would handle this "failed" assignment.

6. Work with a partner. You have a highly conflicted couple who have been unable to avoid fighting verbally with each other, despite their many protests that they both hate conflict. Prescribe the symptom (conflict) to your partner (the client) so that it appears logical to do more of it instead of trying to stop it. When you are finished, ask for feedback on whether the client would have tried to follow the homework. Then switch roles.

7. Working with a partner, role play the situation with Counselor Shmooze and the premarital couple escalating over financial issues. This time, however, assume neither you nor they have ever heard of the Ten-Step Model, so you will have to come up with an intervention to stop the chaos. Have one person play the escalating client and the other play the therapist. Then switch roles. Make sure each person comes up with a different intervention. Give each other feedback on how effective the intervention was.

8. Watch the classic movie "Who's Afraid of Virginia Wolfe?" or the more recent "War of the Roses." Notice how the male and female characters in these movies escalate each other's emotions. Plan how you would intervene if you were their counselor.

9. How were conflicts handled in your family of origin? Who held the power? Was it held actively or passively? Did anyone dare challenge the power person directly? In your current relationships, do you handle conflict differently? If so, how is your pattern of conflict different now?

10. Make a list of all of the structuring skills you found in this chapter. Compare your list with at least one other student. Which ones (if any) did you miss? Which ones do you find the most comfortable? Which ones appear the most uncomfortable to you?

11. Watch the movie "Good Will Hunting." What are the counselor's goals? Are these ever explicitly verbalized? Do these match the client's goals? Are the goals reached? How do you know?

12. Discuss with at least one other person: What constitutes a "failure" in therapy? Does a client dropping out indicate a failure? In Aesop's fable of the fox and the grapes, the fox who couldn't reach a bunch of grapes rationalized, "Those grapes were sour anyway." How do you know that you're not using a similar rationalization when you say, "Well, the client wasn't serious about therapy anyway"? How do you know you are correct?

13. When a client simply does not show up for the next scheduled session, do you call the client to find out what happened? Why or why not? What ethical principles are involved in your answer?

Chapter 3 - Process Skills

A loving person lives in a loving world. A hostile person lives in a hostile world.
Everyone you meet is your mirror. - Ken Keys

Psychiatrist Frank Pittman claims that therapy is what takes place in the head of the therapist (Master's Presentation, AAMFT Conference, 1991). That makes sense. The therapist's ability to conceptualize the case and track the interactions will directly affect the course of therapy for better or worse. Of course, even the most rudimentary experience with the world of counseling and therapy shows that the neophyte lags behind the master of therapy in these process skills. Hardly a supervisory session goes by without my commenting on some dynamic present in the case, and my supervisee crying out in frustration, "Oh, of course! Why didn't I see that for myself?" Well, there are very good reasons why.

The Developing Therapist.

S.A. Rigazio-DiGillio (2000) , building on the work of Ivey (1986), Piaget and others, articulated a holistic, recursive framework which can help the budding counselor or therapist understand their seeming blindness to the "obvious" insight that the supervisor points out. According to this framework, we enter the world of clinical training with a sensorimotor orientation. In terms of our professional development, we are similar to the young child in Piaget's theory. The neophyte is very focused on the here-and-now. Because of previous academic preparation, and perhaps personal predisposition, the counselor tends to focus on emotional issues. While this orientation does allow direct access to emotional material both in the client and in the therapist, it is not yet organized. The counselor knows very well what she feels, just not what to do with it. Similarly, the counselor can very accurately report what is going on in the therapy room without being able to make any predictions of what will happen next. This makes it difficult for the beginner to be able to effectively use the structuring skills essential for a therapeutic relationship. Furthermore, emotional chaos on the part of the client can trigger similar chaos in the counselor. With an underdeveloped ability to self-reflect or to predict the effect of interventions, the therapist can easily become overwhelmed by emotional issues. This therapy tends to be more a matter of "chasing rabbits" than actually making planned progress.

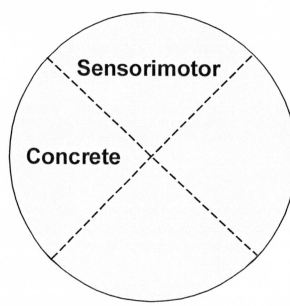

With experience, however, the counselor begins to add a concrete orientation. According to Rigazio-DiGillio, this orientation is analogous to Piaget's concrete-operational stage (age 7 to 12 years). The counselor with the concrete orientation is now able to rely on Front Stage facts to understand the clinical data. From the concrete orientation, the counselor is able to describe, in depth, actions and events and then describe, in linear, cause-effect, terms the relationship between the actions and the events. Ideally, the counselor retains all of the strengths of the sensorimotor orientation, and can access them as needed or desired for the progress of therapy. These new competencies, however, allow the counselor to feel more comfortable, more in control of the progress of therapy. The down side of this new-found sense of competence is that the counselor tends to rigidly adhere to one method, theory, or technique. After all, if it worked once, it must work the next time, too. That belief points to a second constraint of therapists with a concrete orientation, namely that the counselor relies on "truth" as he or she has already defined it from the facts. The concrete-oriented counselor will have difficulty applying circular reasoning or seeing the same situation from frames other than the one already constructed. Essential, non-confirming facts are easily missed or dismissed as "irrelevant." The limited foresight of which the person with a concrete orientation is capable makes fitting specific treatment interventions into a more comprehensive treatment plan difficult. Therapy for the therapist, then, becomes a bit like a game of billiards. I can predict that if I hit this ball this particular way, that will happen. However, that knowledge tells me nothing about what my next shot might be.

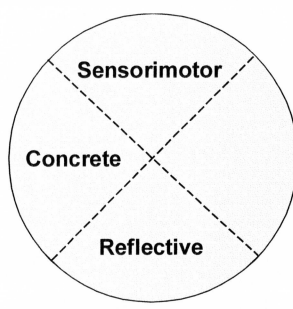

Gradually, experience grows and the therapist is able to add the reflective orientation to the previous two. The therapist is now able to synthesize ideas and strategies from multiple models of therapy, instead of rigidly adhering to only one or two. Both Front Stage and Back Stage data are beginning to make sense now. This greater ability to be reflective enables the therapist to modify treatment plans based on emerging data, and to see links between specific strategies and overall treatment plans. In other words, "truth" is no longer what the therapist decided it was at first. The greater comfort and self-confidence the therapist feels makes disconfirming data interesting and illuminating, rather than threatening. That same sense of comfort and self-confidence enables the therapist to examine their own patterns as these impact on the therapy and on the process of supervision. In other words, one of the hallmarks of the reflective orientation is the therapist's ability to use circular reasoning about his behavior and the client's behavior.

However, there are some constraints on the reflective orientation. If the therapist makes the mistake of leaving the previous strengths behind, all of the theorizing can really go off base. For example, if Counselor Shmooze is fixated in a reflective orientation, he will tend to minimize either affective (sensorimotor) or behavioral (concrete) data in favor of the more cognitive data. Samuel's big clue he has made this mistake comes when, after making an eloquent explanation of his client's situation, the client looks at him and says, "Huh?" The fascination with patterns of interaction can also lead the therapist to inaction ("paralysis by analysis"). As a supervisor, I frequently have to say to supervisees who are in a reflective orientation, "Yes, you are right, but what are you going to do about that?" Without the access to the here and now emotional data or behavioral sequence data from the previous orientations, the answer is not always clear.

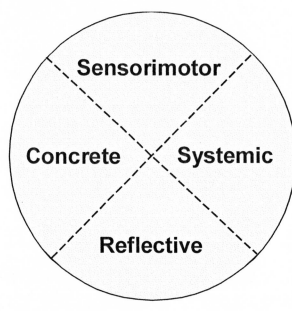

Still, if the counselor perseveres, professional development gradually enlarges to allow for the fourth orientation, the systemic orientation. Counselors who are fully able to use the systemic orientation realize the wider socio-cultural context of therapy. They can use the full complexity suggested by the Metasystems model to help the client question their own rules and assumptions which are sustaining the problematic behavior. They can also used that same complex analysis to help the client find and use resources from the larger social systems of which the client is a vital part. Counselors who operate from a systemic frame easily apply reframing to clients situations because they themselves are able to see any given situation from multiple frames of reference. They are as aware of the influence of context on their own assumptions as they are of the influence of context on the client.

However, the ability to accurately see multiple perspectives can be a curse as well as a blessing. Often supervisees operating from a systemic orientation can accurately articulate multiple possible paths to reach the client's goals, but are unable to choose any one. This is because they can accurately see the pros and the cons of each alternative path. Since to choose any one alternative is to automatically exclude the others, and since each alternative is limited in its benefits, the systems-oriented counselor can fall victim to "paralysis by context." The solution to the dilemma is to use the affective, behavioral, cognitive, and contextual data to select one alternative which best fits the client's goals, and trust the client's resources to take it from there.

This process of professional development has been symbolized in this text as a circle, with broken lines separating each of the orientations. That the process is a circle indicates that this is not a matter of hierarchal stages, with the more "mature" therapist leaving behind the earlier stage. On the contrary, the more mature in the profession the therapist is, the more easily the therapist will be able to use all of the orientations. That is why the boundaries between the orientations are drawn as broken lines. There can and should be flow in all directions within this open-ended system of professional development.

Effective Questioning

I often tell clients in my therapy practice that my expertise does not lie in my having a bag of answers. My expertise is in knowing which questions to ask in which situation. Certainly, being able to ask effective questions is a primary skill of therapists (Figley and Nelson, 1989).

One of the primary questioning skills is learning to ask direct questions rather than "shy" questions. "Shy" questions leave in doubt what the therapist really wants to know, which leaves open the possibility of misunderstanding. By contrast, a direct question is very clear and leaves minimum room for misunderstanding.

Counselor Shmooze is meeting with Mr. Joe Doakes, a 36 year old man. Mr. Doakes came to therapy to help him recover from his recent divorce from Lakesha, his wife of 13 years. Counselor Shmooze has begun to suspect that Mr. Doakes is slipping into a clinical depression, despite his verbal statements that he his dealing with the divorce "fine." If Counselor Shmooze were to ask about the depression in a "shy" way, the conversation might go something like this:

T	So, tell me, Joe, have you noticed any changes in your emotions lately?
D	Well, no. I'm feeling about like always.
T	Okay, well, any changes in your body?
D	No, I'm still as healthy as a horse.

This could go on for a while, with Counselor Shmooze no closer to confirming or denying his suspicions, and Mr. Doakes none the better.

If Counselor Shmooze were to use a more direct questioning style, the conversation might go something like this:

T	So, tell me, Joe, have there been any changes in your eating habits lately? More or less than usual?
D	Well, I really haven't been feeling like eating lately. No appetite. Guess that's good, though. I'll lose a few extra pounds, and I could use it.
T	How about changes in your sleeping habits? Sleeping more or less than usual?

45

D   I'm sleeping about three hours a night since the
         divorce. You know, that's really strange, because I
         used to sleep like a log. Now I just don't seem to
         be sleepy. So I read. I've read three books in the
         last week. Sure helps at work.

Despite Mr. Doakes' continued efforts to put a positive spin on his situation,
Counselor Shmooze has, because of his direct questioning, obtained data
which makes his suspicions of a major depression more reasonable.

Often it's personal discomfort, not lack of skill, that prompts the
therapist to resort to shy questions. Many therapists, including those who
have been in practice for years, avoid asking couples coming for marital
therapy about their sexual relationship. Even if they do ask, they ask "shy"
questions which do not tell much: "What's your sex life like?" "Fine."
More helpful would be direct questions:

T   How often do you have sex?
H   About once a week. (Wife nods in agreement).
T   And who decides when that once is?
H   (pause, looking at wife). I guess I do. (Wife looks
         away, looking toward the ceiling.)
T   I'm amazed. How do you always guess right?
H   (becoming irritated). I don't. Lots of times I try to
         kiss her or get her interested, but she just turns a
         cold shoulder.

By using direct questioning, the counselor (T) learns a great deal about the
couple's actual couple functioning. The counselor learns that rule of this
relationship is that he is the initiator in both sex and in the conversation, but
that the wife really controls what actually happens. Note that she did not
talk at all during the interchange, but her looking toward the ceiling when he
started talking about initiating sex communicated volumes.

Direct questions can also be used to "lend" feelings to a client where the
emotions seem to be either absent or unduly constrained (Minuchin and
Fishman, 1981). This author was working with a woman who had been in
an emotionally abusive marriage for 23 years. She had been referred to
therapy by a friend at church, who was worried about Sally's increasing
depression. In this particular session, Sally's affect had been unusually flat,
even for her.

T   So Scott [her son] just burst into your bedroom and
         started screaming at you for nothing?

S It wasn't so bad.

T And Harry [her husband] did nothing at all to help you?

S He never does, unless it affects him.

T Sally, I don't know how you are even sitting here. If my child had spoken to me like that, and my wife had just sat in the living room watching TV the whole time, I'd be mad, damn mad.

Sally looked up for a minute, and then gradually, like a locomotive gathering speed, began to let her hurt and anger pour out. By the end of the hour, she was animated and was able to articulate a plan to get herself out of this abusive relationship.

Two other styles of questioning were mentioned earlier in this chapter. Linear questions follow an "A causes B" format. Linear questions are very appropriate for clients whose primary orientation is concrete, or for clients who are educationally challenged. Of course, therapists operating from a concrete orientation will also find linear questions comfortable. The conversation segment between this author and Sally provides another example of linear questioning. This segment focused on what happened in a linear, time sequenced fashion.

From these examples, the reader should clearly understand that linear questioning is a perfectly valid style. The trick is to use it when it is appropriate, and to use circular questioning, the other style, when that is appropriate. Linear questions are appropriate when the counselor is concerned only with Front Stage issues, that is, when the counselor is trying to establish facts and track if-then sequences across time, regardless of other considerations. Circular questions, on the other hand, are appropriate when the counselor is trying to investigate the Back Stage.

One of the fundamental assumptions of family therapy is that human behavior, in contrast to inanimate objects, is usually made up of repetitive patterns. Going back to an analogy used earlier in this chapter, billiard balls on a table will move only if struck by some other ball (or the cue stick), and only in the direction of and in proportion to the energy transferred by that strike. Humans are not like that at all. Let's assume Jane Bagodonuts has had a fight with her son over the messiness of his room. Likely, she will say she yelled at him "because" the room was messy. Roger, her son, will likely defend himself by saying he yelled at her "because" she yelled at him. These linear explanations overlook the reality that they both participated in the fight; it could not have happened without both parties' active participation. Roger keeps his room messy, despite very good knowledge that Jane does not like it, because the messiness serves some function for him. Similarly, Jane argues with Roger, despite very good knowledge that he likes the room messy, because the messiness communicates something to her that feels like a threat in some sense. Trying to determine "who started it" would be a useless waste of time, very analogous to the old "chicken or the egg" argument.

This would be a perfect situation in which to apply circular questioning. Let's assume that Jane brought this incident to Counselor Shmooze, along with Roger, at their next scheduled counseling session. Counselor Shmooze, using circular questioning, might direct the conversation something like this:

T	Okay, Jane, tell me how you came to notice that Roger's room was messy.
J	How could I not notice! I walked by his room on the way to the den, and there it was (She went on to describe in detail the condition of the room. Meanwhile, Roger was looking out the window of the counseling room and appeared very bored).
T	And when you started yelling at Roger, how did he respond?
J	At first he just ignored me. So I told him again he needed to clean up that mess now! But he just kept on playing his video game.
T	Roger, when your mother first spoke to you and you kept on playing your video game, how did she respond?
R	(silent for approximately 45 seconds, then...) She started yelling louder. I mean, crap, I heard her the first time.
T	How were you hoping she would respond?
R	Huh?
T	Surely this isn't the first time something like this has happened. How did you think she was going to respond to your choosing to keep on playing your game?
R	I guess I thought she'd get mad.
T	Seems like you guessed right. Jane, how about you? How did you think Roger was going to respond when you told him again to clean up the room immediately?
J	I wanted him to get up and clean up his room. It was terrible!

T   I understand that's what you wanted, but is that what you expected him to do?

J   I guess not. He never does clean up the room unless I get real mad and just make him.

By using circular questions, Counselor Shmooze helped Jane and Roger move from a linear, "She/He did this to me,"position to understanding how their behavior contributed to getting the vicious cycle spinning again. From this point he would be in position to help each of them clarify what they really want to happen, and then construct alternative behavior sequences to help them actually achieve those goals.

The reader should note that Counselor Shmooze's circular questioning helps Jane and Roger deal with Back Stage issues without ever directly addressing those issues. Suppose Roger keeps his room messy as a way of exerting power in his relationship with his mother (certainly possible, since "I belong only when I have power" is one of the common mistaken beliefs which lead to misbehavior (Sweeney, 1989)). His secret [Back Stage] need for personal power never has to become a topic of conversation, or even speculation. That need can still be addressed by helping Roger claim what he needs from Jane to feel more in control.

Relabeling

Relabeling (also known as "reframing") is probably the most frequently employed technique in modern psychotherapy. In essence, relabeling gives a new frame of reference for the client, a new "label" for the client's experience (L'Abate, 1986). Which ever word one uses for the process, the action is the same. Reframing changes the Front Stage perceptions of an event or situation by changing the client's internal construction of reality. This new frame of reference (in therapy jargon usually simply referred to as a "frame") in turn affects the client's Back Stage by changing the emotional connotations ("pictures") which flash when an old frame is used. For example, if an alcohol abuser sees herself as "sinful," her Back Stage will likely be filled with pictures of one who is under condemnation for being self-indulgent, vile, and just plain no good. However, if that same alcohol abuser sees herself as medically ill, her Back Stage will likely be filled with pictures of one who needs to take positive steps to gain (or regain) health, and of one who can be helped.

This is really nothing new. According to history books, when Christopher Columbus sailed out of sight of land using his secret new charts, he was operating from a totally new frame of reference which said the world was round. Columbus' crew, however, was stuck with the old frames, which said the world was flat and if one sailed out too far, the ship and everyone in her would simply fall off the end of the world into destruction. No wonder, then, Columbus' crew was on the verge of mutiny when land was finally sighted. They were operating on the basis of their old frames, and consequently their Back Stage was filled with terror about their "certain" doom. Sighting land where land "should not be" gave them a whole new construct about the way the world was made, and made sailing out of sight of land "possible" for the first time in human history.

Columbus did not wisely apply his reframe to his crew. In the same way, many therapist do not successfully apply the seemingly easy task of reframing or relabeling to their client (L'Abate, 1986). L'Abate (1986) lists six steps to creating effective reframes.

The first step is to identify the client's frames of reference and world view. This is part of the fundamental skill of joining. The counselor listens to what the clients say and then uses the clients' own words. However, a key assumption here is "that the meaning of the communication in the family is the effect it has, regardless of one's own association to its meaning" (L'Abate, 1986, p. 65). In other words, identifying the client's world view is not simply a matter of copying word patterns. It also involves carefully noting client reactions when those word patterns are used, including any differences in reaction when different people use the same words. Of course, since communication is non-verbal as well as verbal, the counselor needs to pay attention to client non-verbals. What they do not say, and how they do not say it, is at least as significant as what they do say.

The second step in relabeling is to select specific behaviors or sequences of behavior to target for reframing. I often say that in my early days of therapy I felt like a mosquito in a nudist camp. I knew what to do, but not where to start. Knowing where to start is at least half the battle. Some of that knowledge will come from the counselor's clinical intuition, and some will come from experience. The beginning therapist can certainly begin to look for some predictable problem areas. Clients who are stuck in black or white thinking, or who can only frame things in terms of linear causality and blame (e.g., "he made me do it"), need a reframe. So do clients who only see things negatively. One of the differences between normal and dysfunctional families, according to many family therapy theories, is the inability of dysfunctional families to pay attention to the good that actually does occur. Indeed, any behavior which the therapist notes which the client appears to ignore may be a prime candidate for a reframe.

The third step is to collect details which will help the therapist fit the new frames with the client's reality. Closely related to this is the fourth step - creating a context for acceptance. If Columbus had used these two steps effectively, he might have had some conversations with his crew like this,

"Say, guys, have you noticed we haven't seen any of the sea monsters that are supposed to be out here? How do you think we managed to miss them if they're supposed to be everywhere? Oh, you think we're just lucky. Maybe you're right, and that luck will just keep on working for us. How about the noise of the waterfall? If water were falling off the end of the earth, we ought to hear that a long way off. Heard a waterfall? No, well, we must be a long way from the edge, huh?" And so on.

In step four, the therapist presents new ideas and listens for any signs of resistance on the part of the client. If the resistance comes, as it did in my illustration, the therapist simply reinterprets that to fit with the new frame. Often therapists can use a technique which comes out of sales called creating a "yes set." Sales people often ask clients a series of seemingly obvious questions, with the expected answer being "yes" in every case. What may not be so obvious at first, however, is that saying "yes" to these harmless questions makes saying "yes" to the "Do you want to buy...?" question more likely. Counselors can use their knowledge of the client's frame to do the same thing to get the client to say "yes" to the reframe.

That brings up the fifth step, which is actually introducing the reframe. In introducing the reframe, the counselor will carefully use client language and goals to extend the client's present reality into the desired direction. The author had an adult female client who had been verbally and emotionally abused as a child. She came to therapy complaining of "depression" (her term) and loss of interest in her marriage. Her husband played the care-taker role in this marriage, but that only increased her feelings of guilt ("He shouldn't have to take care of me. I should be taking care of him"). The author simply relabeled her role in the marriage from "bad" (her frame) to crucial ("If you weren't making such a self-sacrifice, your husband would have no way to get his need to take care of you met. He'd be pretty miserable"). Since she had stated often enough that he said he enjoyed taking care of her, she could not argue with this positive connotation of her current symptoms.

A different tactic came from another clinical experience. A husband and wife were in therapy to seek help dealing with their 19 year old son. He had been arrested several months previously on several felony charges. In addition, he had lost several jobs due to his coming up positive for marijuana on drug tests at work. In this particular family, the wife was and always had been the disciplinarian, while the husband had always taken the son's side. The author used negative connotations to grab the husband's attention. "Bill, I know you love your son, just as you do, Sue. I know you both want what is best for him. But right now, Tom is at home, he can't get a job because of his drug addiction [deliberately chosen word], both of you are mad at each other because you disagree on what to do, and he's still

51

facing some very serious court charges. Bill, is this the good you want for your son? To go off to jail and then see his parents divorce?" In this instance, Bill was paying so much attention to what he intended for Tom that he could not see what was actually happening. The author's frame opened up a new reality for him and allowed Bill and Sue to begin constructing an effective strategy for actually helping Tom, which was a goal they both agreed on.

The sixth and final step in effective relabeling is responding to client feedback. Out right resistance is easy enough to spot. Rather than trying too hard to "sell" the new frame in the face of stiff resistance, the counselor should back off and try a different reframe. Beginning counselors should also beware of clients who either give polite agreement or who are overly enthusiastic about the reframe. Both behaviors are warnings that the counselor is being set up for a future "yes...but..." response. Polite agreement indicates the client will come back with excuses the next session why the reframe did not work. Over enthusiasm warns that the counselor has inadvertently been triangulated into a family problem area. Excessive questions constitutes another danger signal. Usually, non-verbals will help the counselor distinguish genuine attempts to understand the new frame from passive resistance. Relaxation, as shown by behaviors such as decrease in muscle tension and postural rigidity, eye contact and head alignment with the speaker, positive ("yes") head nods, and decrease in restless activity, serves as a positive indicator. The client likely accepted the reframe. On the other hand, signs of excitement (the opposite of all of the relaxation cues) when not followed by signs of relaxation usually indicate disagreement (L'Abate, 1986).

Making the Covert Overt

Coming, as I do, from a psychodynamically-oriented background, I am accustomed to making interpretations as a part of therapy. Evidently that is the expectation of culture, because in my years as a supervisor I have found that most interns seem to think they are supposed to be making interpretations, too.

Interpretations can be useful to therapy, but not nearly as useful as some people evidently believe. When I was receiving some clinical training at a very modern psychiatric center during my master's degree, I found many of the patients at the hospital who could explain in great detail why they had the problems they had. Knowing the "why" did not change anything for them, however. They still had the problems. That is why they were still in the hospital.

Every parent can understand that. I doubt there is a parent who has not demanded of a child who just misbehaved, "Why did you do that?" and received the answer, "I don't know." The real question is not why, but what's the function.

That is where interpretations are most useful. Clients behave as they do because they are trying to reach some goal. They may or may not be consciously aware of the goal for which they are striving. Indeed, they may hold one goal consciously and actually strive for a very different goal unconsciously. Going back to Bill and Sue, for example, Bill was very consciously trying to stay close to his son. The actual function of his behavior, however, was to put distance between him and Sue. If I had asked him, "Are you trying to put distance between yourself and your wife," he likely would have denied it. That was not his consciously held goal. Nevertheless, he could not argue that distance was the end result.

Therapeutic interpretations should be cautiously timed to build upon Front Stage awareness the client already holds. If simply telling a client what needs changing were effective, therapy would not be necessary. Change like that is strictly Front Stage, and is the province of advice-givers, either paid or free, solicited or self-appointed. As the therapist conceptualizes the case, the interpretations the therapist makes inside her or his own head change the therapist's reality. To that extent, they are useful.

Sharing these interpretations too soon, however, is worse than useless. If the client accepts the advice and it is correct, the client learns nothing. The client only goes away impressed at how "right" the counselor was. If the client accepts the advice and it is not correct, the client still learns nothing. The client only goes away thinking how "wrong" that counselor was (and perhaps how foolish it is to pay for such bad advice). Of course, if the client resists the advice, a win-lose contest of wills ensues. None of these options is beneficial for the process of therapy. Good therapy makes a very boring spectator sport. The process is seldom marked by blinding flashes of brilliant insight. Much more often process is measured in baby-steps of new growth tentatively taken by a client moving toward the new light the client discovers.

The same basic principle is true of uncovering secrets. The counselor certainly needs to try to discover what secrets are keeping a family stuck as part of the assessment process. When (or whether) to make those secrets overt is another matter. The counselor will need to make those decisions based on a) is this secret directly contributing to the problem(s) defined as the purpose of therapy, b) does this revelation directly move the client toward the client's agreed upon goals, and c) has the client demonstrated sufficient ability to use this new information constructively.

A client couple the author worked with illustrates the principle. Daniel was 24 years old. Donna was 23. Both had some college education, though neither was a college graduate. They came to therapy with the presenting issues of Daniel's "financial irresponsibility" (Donna claimed Daniel "made 35 dollars and spent 30" - "He ought to be saving a lot more."). Both had been previously married, and both divorces were particularly messy. That was the "reason," along with Daniel's "learning disability" (his term), for their frequent arguments. During the course of therapy, we did indeed discover that the "ghosts" of Greg and Rhonda, their previous spouses, still haunted this relationship. However, during an individual session with Donna we uncovered a secret that Daniel was not aware of. Donna had been physically abused by her father for the first six years of her life; her mother divorced her father on her sixth birthday. When she was 17, she was raped by her mother's youngest brother. Her mother told her she should just "forget it." Her mother's oldest brother was an alcoholic who died during coitus with a one-night stand. Since we had already discussed the "ghosts" of the past spouses and that made sense, talking about these "ghosts" made sense, too. Donna was able to understand how her secrets had kept her angry at men, and how this unacknowledged anger resulted in her being constantly critical of Daniel, who, in turn, responded in his typically passive-aggressive manner by "messing up the finances." We contracted together how to make this secret known to Daniel and in the next conjoint session the real process of healing began. Had we not found these ghosts from Donna's past haunting her marriage, we might never had been able to help them resolve their arguments about finances.

A safer way to make the covert overt is to focus on what is actually happening in the session by making process observations. All of us have scotomas, blind spots, to our own behavior. The patterns become so automatic that we are not aware of them. When the client consists of more than one person, having the various individuals talk directly to each other, rather than through the therapist, can reveal much more about the real process of interactions than simply relying on anyone's report. Another excellent method of generating process information is to stage enactments (see Chapter 10). Using process observations about what is actually happening in the session is always best, because it eliminates problems of faulty memory, scotomas, and arguable interpretations. In other words, I, the client, may argue that my being sexually abused as a child has nothing to do with my sexual difficulties with my partner, but I cannot argue with the fact that in this session I withdrew into silence right after my partner began talking about wanting more sexual attention from me.

Summary

Therapy is a process. Baking a cake is a process. Both require certain skills, yet the outcome of both therapy and cake-baking is more than simply the sum of the individual skills. Just as it takes experience to know when the cake batter is "right," it also takes experience to know when and how to apply the various process skills. Therapy can only be truly learned by supervised work with a trained supervisor.

Seeing therapy as a process means taking a longitudinal view rather than a cross-sectional or session-by-session view. That applies to the therapist's own work as much as it does to the development of the client's presenting problems. Keeping the focus of therapy on process involves becoming part of co-authoring with the client a new and different chapter in the client's life story. This new story builds on the client's life process up to that point, but it opens up previously unsuspected possibilities for wellness.

Living Into the Lesson

1. Assume you are working with a 23 year old male client whose presenting issue is daily marijuana use since age 12. This client is doing well in his college studies, but he cannot stop using marijuana even though he knows he should and says he wants to. Role play this with one other student. Let the first "counselor" work strictly from a behavioral perspective. Give each other feedback on how successful the intervention was. Then switch roles and let the other "counselor" work strictly from a psychodynamic perspective. After you have again given each other feedback, discuss: how was therapy different each time? Does the way the counselor frames the case actually affect the course of therapy?

2. Rigazio-DiGillio's framework suggests that the beginning counselor often predominantly uses the sensorimotor orientation, which, she claims, is similar to Piaget's sensorimotor and preoperational stages (roughly ages birth to age 7). Discuss with other students the attributes of the typical child during that age span. Be sure to include both the positive and the "negative" attributes. Does the analogy hold? Do you see similar attributes in your own beginning work as a therapist?

3. Clients operating primarily from a sensorimotor orientation will be prone to chaotic and impulsive functioning. Decisions are usually made by emotions rather than by logic. Family structure is usually so diffuse that even daily living creates problems. Working with a group of students, devise an intervention to a sensorimotor-oriented client family to gain control over the emotional life of the client system.

4. Clients operating primarily from a concrete orientation will tend to depend on a predictable set of rules and beliefs to maintain a sense of family identity, even when these rules or beliefs are no longer functional. Working with a group of students, devise a strategy to help concrete-oriented parents adapt to raising a rebellious teenager.

5. Clients operating primarily from a reflective orientation are able to identify and talk about their communication and behavior patterns, and they are capable of meaningful insight. However, seldom does anything ever change. Working with a group of students, devise a strategy to help reflective-oriented parents move from an

excessively cognitive approach to raising their adolescents to include emotional data in making plans for family change.

6.   Assume you are working with a client couple, both of whom are physicians. This couple is typical of systemic orientation clients in that they recognize the effects of multi-generational, intra-familial, wider cultural influences on their lives. They report feeling no sense of family identity, and they want your help. Work with a group of students to devise a strategy to help this couple get started creating a family identity.

7.   Go back through situations three through six. If the first time you attempted to move the client from one orientation to another, this time help the client move in the desired direction by broadening the client's competencies in that orientation. If the first time you went for broadening competencies, this time attempt to move the client up one orientation. How do these moves make the process of therapy different?

8.   In this chapter there is a segment of a conversation between Counselor Samuel Shmooze and Jane and Roger Bagodonuts. Roleplay that conversation, but this time have the counselor use linear questions. When the role play is finished, have the persons playing Jane and Roger describe their feelings during the process. How might this be different from what Jane and Roger felt when Counselor Shmooze used circular questions?

9.   One of the reframing skills is paying attention to the client's current frame. What non-verbal behaviors would tell you that your client comes from an authoritarian frame? From a laissez-faire frame? How would you match yourself to these client frames in joining with the client?

10.   Suppose you have a client with each of the following situations. Work with a partner to create an effective reframe for each:
    a)   The family has multiple problems and few resources. They have not been able to do any homework task successfully and are feeling discouraged.
    b)   The teenage daughter complains in a family session that her stepfather is "overbearing and insensitive."

c)   A husband whose wife had an affair complains that he cannot get his work done because he can only think about her and the other man.

11.   Suppose you have an adult male client who has come to you for help getting over his recent divorce. Work with another student to create a ritual which can help this client reframe his situation by creating a different context for viewing himself.

12.   You have a client couple who have been habitually conflicted throughout their twelve years of marriage. They are with you as a last ditch effort, but they do not really believe things can be different. Create an "as if" task ("Do this as if... were true") to provide them a more hopeful frame for looking at their relationship.

13.   The father in the movie "The Great Santini" was a Marine officer who took too much of his work home with him. Role play with another student how you would positively reframe the father's behavior in a way that would make sense to his son.

14.   The movie "American Beauty" is full of toxic secrets. We learn some from the father/husband, who narrates the film. What secrets do you think are at work in the mother/wife in the film? What data do you base you hunch on? If you were working with this family to improve their parent/child communication, how would you reveal these secrets? Or would you?

Chapter 4 - Administrative Skills

I have always thought the actions of men the best interpreters of their thoughts. - John Locke

John Locke would have appreciated the signs I frequently saw in offices during my years in the Air Force. The signs proclaimed, "The job isn't complete until the paperwork is done." In all of my years as a supervisor of therapy, I have never yet found a student who went into therapy for the expressed purpose of being able to do administrative tasks. Yet Locke is right. The way these administrative tasks are handled is often the best interpreter of the counselor's clarity and completeness of thought about a case.

Record Keeping Basics

Keeping sufficient, accurate records is an ethical requirement of all counselors and therapists (Pipes and Davenport, 1999). For example, the paragraph 3.6 of the AAMFT Code of Ethics (2001) explicitly states, "Marriage and family therapists maintain accurate and adequate clinical and financial records." Pipes and Davenport (1999) cite similar ethical standards from the American Psychological Association.

The primary ethical principle undergirding these formal statements is the fundamental belief that all professions exist for the benefit and welfare of the population the profession serves. Most codes of professional ethics recognize this principle by including a statement to this effect, often in the code's preamble. Good record keeping is simply an application of this general principle. To say the same thing in Locke's terms, the quality of one's record keeping is a concrete expression of the quality of one's care for the client.

The client will benefit from good records because the therapist will be able to access and use details of previous treatment to guide current treatment. In my first clinical training at St. Elizabeth's Psychiatric Center, I often saw five to ten patients a day. I hated going back to my room at night and typing out verbatim accounts of those interactions, but I have to admit in retrospect, doing so helped me remember what happened. One of those clients, I'll call him Wayne, was getting ready to be discharged from the hospital and go home for the first time in five years. Each time I saw him, he was pleasant and talked animatedly about his plans for going home. Everything seemed fine on the surface. However, something I could not specify began to gnaw at me. I began to read back over my previous encounters with Wayne and discovered that he was using different names for his mother and other family members. As I read the verbatims even more carefully, I found other evidences that Wayne was gradually decompensating. I presented my concerns and the evidence to the psychiatrist in charge of Wayne's care. After a careful investigation , he discovered that Wayne was not taking his medications because he was afraid to leave the safety of the hospital and go back to the community where his psychotic break had occurred five years previously. Once the care team understood what was happening, we were able to coordinate our efforts to help Wayne face his fears. He left the hospital almost on schedule, and as of the time I completed my training had successfully adjusted at home.

Another illustration of the importance to the client of good record keeping comes from another personal experience. I had seen Daryl and Cheryl for marital counseling. Cheryl had had an affair, but the two of them worked through the issues and formed a happier marriage than they had previously known possible. After we concluded our counseling, I lost track of them until one day, some seven years after the conclusion of our work, Daryl called and wanted an appointment. In the call he told me that Cheryl's mother had recently died and that had given them a set back. He wanted help getting back on track. A quick study of my records from our previous work brought all the family dynamics back to mind. When Daryl came in, we were able to review the skills he and Cheryl had previously learned and build on that with their new experiences. He felt so good at the conclusion of that interview that he felt no need for a follow up. About a month later, he sent an email to say that he and Cheryl were indeed back on track.

Beyond these ethical obligations, there may also be legal obligations to keep good records. Clients may voluntarily (e.g., divorce or child custody proceedings) or involuntarily (e.g., criminal charges) become involved in court proceedings. When they do, the counselor and the counselor's records may be subpoenaed by the court. Sometimes clients are mandated to counseling by the court, and almost always the judge giving the order will expect some sort of formal response about the progress of the counseling from the therapist. At times, the therapist might work with sexual assault or child abuse victims, or other crime victims. This form of interviewing, called forensic interviewing, normally requires specialized training and is beyond the scope of the beginning therapist. Still, it illustrates the range of activities which might make the therapist's notes a matter of record.

There is yet another legal reason to keep good records. We live in a litigious society, and people do sue their therapists for malpractice. Since malpractice is legally defined as a "tort," the standards of proof are not as great as the standards required for criminal prosecution (Huber, 1999).

Good records may be the therapist's best, and only, defense against charges of malpractice by a disgruntled client. This author's second supervisor of clinical work was fond of saying, "If it ain't written, it didn't happen." Courts could agree with that sentiment. If the therapist cannot document from records what happened and why, the court may well decide against the therapist. This is where the expectation of professional competence, and care, comes back in. The courts may hold the counselor to a higher standard of care because of his or her professional status.

Because of the possibility of becoming involved in a legal process, the counselor should maintain records at least as long as statute of limitations on filing malpractice suits, which varies from state to state. In the author's state, it is two years. Other states have longer statutes of limitations. In addition, some states may require that certain types of records be maintained longer. Every therapist, regardless of years of experience, should receive competent legal advice on this issue. Ignorance of the law is no excuse.

In summary, the quality of one's record keeping reflects on the quality of one's care for the client. Everyone benefits from good records. This said, the question then becomes, what constitutes "good" records?

Electronic verses Written. Traditionally, records were always written. Often that is still the case. However, in recent years there has been increasing interest in keeping records electronically. Computer-based records offer a number of advantages over paper-based records, not the least of which is the ability to rapidly search for specific bits of information. However, computer records are also more vulnerable to invasion by hackers, and they are more easily modified or falsified than paper records. These concerns have hindered the easy acceptance of any records which may be used as court evidence. This author performed a search of Medline.com, an online resource for abstracts and articles having to do with medical issues, in preparation for writing this text. The search yielded 70 articles on the subject of electronic record keeping. The only consensus in these articles was that electronic records may or may not be acceptable, but if they are accepted, they should at least meet the standards of paper records.

If the reader has an interest in using electronic instead of paper-based records, the reader should check with his or her clinical training supervisor before doing so. The supervisor should know, or be able to discover, the latest rulings about their acceptability in that state.

Informed Consent. In Chapter One, we used the metaphor of therapy as a blind date. That metaphor deserves some further development. A date assumes that both parties have the capacity to consent or decline to meet. Without that capacity to say no, the meeting is something other than a date. The same principle applies to therapy. The therapeutic relationship assumes that the client understands that she or he has the capacity to accept or reject the relationship. The few exceptions to this rule (e.g., involuntary commitment for treatment) only serve to prove the validity of the rule by the legal protections given to the client before the rule is waived.

The major mental health professional organizations all have statements which require the therapist to inform clients of their rights and responsibilities. For example, paragraph 1.2 of the AAMFT Code of Ethics (2001) states, "Marriage and family therapists obtain appropriate informed consent to therapy or related procedures and use language that is reasonably understandable to clients." The APA Code of Ethics (1992) has an almost identically worded statement. These requirements are based on the ethical principle that one must know what one is getting into, both the procedures and the foreseeable positive and negative outcomes, in order to give a truly informed consent.

Huber (1999) states that these ethical requirements mean that clients need three types of information to be able to make a truly informed consent about entering or continuing therapy. They need to know what will happen in therapy: the procedures used, the goals of the therapy, and the possible side effects of therapy. Further, they need to know the qualifications, policies, and practices of the therapist. This second type of information also goes to another ethical principle: that mental health professionals must accurately represent their qualifications (e.g., AAMFT, 2001, subprincipal 8.1). Third, clients need to know what other sources of help are available. This may relate to referrals, which will be dealt with in more detail later in this chapter, or it may relate to alternative approaches to therapy. No one therapeutic approach is always "right" for every client.

The Standard of Care mentioned in Chapter One is usually a summary of the informed consent document and may supplement, but not replace, the informed consent document. Usually, the informed consent requirement is met by a more complete document and may take the form either of a therapeutic contract or a professional disclosure statement (Huber, 1999). While the differences in these two types of documents are beyond the scope of this text, there are some basic similarities which should be in every counselor's informed consent document:

- A statement of the client's rights in therapy - what the client has a right to do and what the client has a right not to do. Among these rights are the right to see the client's records (and under what circumstances the client may exercise that right), the right to ask about why a particular process is being used, and the right to refuse any suggested treatment.
- A statement about client confidentiality - what matters are kept confidential and what the limits of confidentiality are. Some

examples of the usual limits of confidentiality are "duty to warn" situations, mandated reporting situations, compliance with court orders, and defending one's self against malpractice suits.

- The process by which the client may request a release of records to some other counselor or agency.
- A statement of the foreseeable consequences of therapy. Marriage and family therapists have some unique concerns in this area. For example, even the most skillfully performed marriage therapy may result in one of the partners deciding on a divorce while the other partner still wants to stay married.
- A statement of client responsibilities - what the client must do, or not do, in therapy. Among these responsibilities are making the promised payment for services, actively participating by carrying out the therapist's interventions, and responding to the therapist's moral or personal concerns about client goals. Therapy is a relationship, and the consequences of working toward goals either side considers unethical or unacceptable should be considered (Huber, 1999).

Constructing and using a good informed consent document helps both the therapist and the client. The client benefits by knowing the rules of therapy, and thus is better able to actively participate in the process. The therapist benefits by the client's increased ability to be active, and by being protected from false allegations of malpractice. As long as the informed consent does represent good care, as defined and accepted by one's professional peers, and the counselor acts in compliance with the informed consent document, the chances of being successfully sued for malpractice are relatively remote.

Treatment Plans. The treatment plan functions like a road map on the journey the counselor and the client are taking together - the journey from where the client is at the beginning of therapy to where the client wants to be at the conclusion of therapy. While it is true that many managed care companies require treatment plans before reimbursing for therapeutic services rendered, that is probably the worst reason to do them. Simply constructing treatment plans to satisfy an insurer's requirements can result in the plan being a meaningless exercise in paper work. A far better reason to consider the treatment plan is to further express the therapist's ethical duty to provide the best possible care for the client.

The treatment plan should include whatever information the therapist (or the therapist's employing agency) believes is essential for conducting good therapy. To some degree, the plan will be shaped by the purpose of the agency and/or the counselor's therapeutic orientation. As a good map, it should give all the details necessary to make the trip, though not all the possible details. The fine details will come in the case notes. Often treatment plans will give basic demographic information about the client (marital status, number of children, if any, age(s) of the client, educational attainment of the client(s), etc.). There should certainly be a place for the client's statement of the presenting problem and goals (L'Abate, 1986). Naturally, there should also be a place for the therapist's assessment or diagnosis of the client and goals for therapy. Some therapists will make a diagnosis using the five-axis format suggested by the *Diagnostic and Statistical Manual of Mental Disorders* (4th Edition) of the American Psychiatric Association [DSM-IV]. Others, notably marriage and family therapists, will focus primarily on relational dynamics such as emotional climate, problem solving, and organizational skills (Yingling, Miller, McDonald, and Galewaler, 1998).

However the counselor does the diagnostic work, the treatment plan serves as a "reality check" for the session-to-session work. In that sense, the treatment plan serves the invaluable function of keeping the therapist from chasing every new issue the client happens to present. Each new issue is measured by the questions, "How does this issue relate to our agreed upon focus of therapy? How will solving this issue help us reach our agreed-upon goals?" Unless the client and counselor explicitly contract for an additional focus of treatment, if the new issue doesn't meet the pragmatics of the treatment plan, the therapist must simply let the issue die from lack of attention.

Treatment plans serve another important function. By specifying in observable, behavioral terms what a successful outcome will be, the treatment plan makes measuring progress toward the goals possible. Suppose, for example, Counselor Shmooze is treating Juan for a fear of speaking in public which is keeping him from succeeding in his job. Their goal is that Juan will be able to make a specified business presentation without any physiological signs of panic or fear. Progress toward that goal can be measured by Juan's taking note of his sweating and pulse rate in previously uncomfortable situations, and noting the decrease in unwanted symptoms. By making these evaluations explicit, Counselor Shmooze helps reinforce Juan's changes and gives him a realistic basis for continued work in the desired direction.

Payment Records. In this author's experience, few therapists go into the mental health profession to be business people. Yet the reality is, therapy is a business. What we, the professional, have to sell is our time. If we do not consider our time valuable, our client's certainly will not.

Payment records are a normal part of any business' accounting practices. Accurate records of both income and expenses are essential to projecting profit or loss, and to making the required tax reports to the government. Counselors who work in agencies with support staffs may not need to worry much about this aspect of the business of therapy, but those who work in small agencies or private practice may have to do double duty. Fortunately, computers have greatly eased the process of accounting through numerous good software programs.

Those who operate on a fee-for-services basis can maintain their books on a simple cash flow basis. Those who accept third-party payment have additional concerns. They need to document how much is owed by each payer, and how much payment has been received to date. Since the actual date of payment may well be weeks or months after the date the service was rendered, there needs to be some way of matching which services have been paid and which bills are still due. If the therapist is self-employed, the Federal tax laws regarding self-employment are so complex that the therapist would be well advised to hire an accountant to at least assist with establishing procedures and filing the taxes.

Clients may also request receipts for their payment. These payments may, depending on the client's situation, be deductible on the client's income taxes. Clients have a right to request receipts of payment at any time for at least three years after the date payment was made.

Aside from these very practical issues, payment records serve another function. In our culture, we tend to value what we pay for. In the Christian scriptures, Jesus said, "Where your treasure is, there will your heart be also" (Matthew 6:21). That principle definitely applies to therapy. When clients invest their money in their treatment, they tend to be more emotionally invested in the process. When it costs them nothing, they tend to be less emotionally invested.

I learned this lesson in my own clinical practice. At first I did a good bit of *pro bono* (free) work with clients in financial difficulty. As my board of directors reviewed the records of my treatment success and failure, the payment record made one fact painfully clear. My highest rate of clients who simply dropped out of therapy, and my highest rate of treatment failures, were in the *pro bono* group. The board of directors insisted that I quit seeing clients *pro bono*. When I did, my rates of successful completion of treatment soared. Since the only thing that changed was the fact that all clients had to pay, it is reasonable to conclude that the clients were more emotionally invested in treatment and thus had better outcomes. A good payment record helped me help my clients by documenting this effect.

Process Notes

However lofty the counselor's personal notions of the profession, in the eyes of the law, therapy is a contract. Specifically, it is a *fiduciary* relationship between the therapist and the client. A "fiduciary" relationship is one based on trust in the therapist by the client, a trust based in the belief that the therapist will serve the client's needs in preference to the counselor's own needs (Huber, 1999). Process notes, then, become a means of documenting this care.

In the event the counselor becomes involved in some sort of legal proceeding, it is the process notes (along with other relevant, subpoenaed records), not the therapy itself, which will be admitted into evidence. The court will have no way of determining what actually happened in the therapy room. The only factual basis available to the court will be the therapist's records.

Good clinical records should have six attributes (Potter and Perry, 1997). First, they should have a factual basis. The record should contain objective information about what the counselor sees, hears, or smells. For example, instead of writing that the client "appears depressed" (which is a conclusion), the therapist should write something like, "the client sat in the chair slumped forward, with eyes focused on the floor. The voice was very soft with few inflections in volume or energy." If the client makes a statement the counselor wishes to record, the statement would be recorded as a quote: "Client states, 'I feel very depressed today.'"

Second, the records must be accurate. Regardless of whether the record is kept on paper or electronically, each entry must be dated. Any evidence that records have been altered or improperly destroyed (e.g., destroying records that have been subpoenaed to avoid having to produce them) could have exceptionally serious, negative consequences for the therapist. This is perhaps the most difficult part of accurate charting. Therapy is, by its very nature, a complex process. Accurately portraying the substance of a 50 minute interview in a few written lines is a challenging task. Nevertheless, it is exceptionally necessary.

That brings the third requirement - that all clinical records are complete. While lengthy notes are laborious to write and to read, sketchy notes may yield a false impression to someone else later on. There should always be enough information to clearly justify the therapist's conclusions and interventions.

Fourth, records must be current. One of the worst mistakes any counselor can make is putting off the necessary record keeping and then trying to catch up some time later. The only thing worse is to not catch up at all. Essential details may be forgotten, cases may be confused, the potential for inadvertent mis-representation is great. Counselors who do not keep their records current are inviting legal trouble.

Finally, records must be logically organized and they must be maintained in a confidential manner. Confidentiality is a special issue for those who work in agency settings, which is where most new counselors and therapists start. There is always a temptation to discuss case material with supervisors or colleagues. In itself, this may not be a violation of confidentiality. However, if the discussion takes place where persons without a valid need to know can overhear the conversation (such as walking down a hallway past the waiting room), or if the records are left where unauthorized persons could access them (a special danger with computers), the counselor is open to a malpractice suit.

<u>What to Include</u>. The issue of organizing notes brings up the practical question, "What do I include in my process notes?" At the end of this chapter there is a sample process note form that the author has used with some supervisees. It covers all the essentials and gives a consistent format to follow each time. It can easily be created as a template on a word processor and then filled in and printed out at the end of each session.

For those who prefer a more free-form style of clinical notes, one style that many health care providers use is called "SOAP" notes (Potter and Perry, 1997). SOAP is an acronym for the four required elements in each session's notes:

S   Subjective data. These are verbalizations made by the client. For example, "I am so worried my husband is going to leave me for another woman."

O   Objective data. These are data that the counselor actually measures (if using a formal assessment tool) or observes. For example, "Client wrung her hands almost constantly, shifted position in the chair every few seconds, and looked around the room the entire session. Little eye contact with therapist. Therapist observed tears as the client began to talk about living without her husband."

A   Assessment data. This is the counselor's diagnosis or assessment of the subjective and objective data. Ideally, the counselor should check each session's diagnosis against the initial diagnosis in the treatment plan to make sure therapy is on track to meeting the goals. For example, "Client's anxiety level is consistent with her initial complaint of having discovered husband is having an affair. Couple communication and problem solving remain poor. Wife states she has not yet confronted husband with her knowledge of the affair. As she gets closer to confronting him, her verbal and behavioral clues suggest she is feeling more anxious."

P   Plan. This is what the counselor proposes to do about the situation described. In other words, this is the prescription or homework referenced in Chapter Two. By this point there should be enough data that any therapist could read the notes and clearly understand the counselor's rationale for the plan. For example: "Homework: write a letter to husband detailing your knowledge of the affair. Do not give it to him and do not let him see it but do bring it to session next time for a role play to practice the confrontation."

Another, somewhat simpler, format for note taking is the "PIE" note. PIE is an acronym for Problem, Intervention, and Evaluation. The Problem portion of the note combines the data from the S and O of the SOAP note. The Intervention describes what the therapist actually did and why. Thus, the Intervention includes the A data, but also places emphasis not just on what the therapist thought but also on what the therapist did, including the P (Plan). The real benefit of the PIE style of note keeping is the Evaluation. The counselor evaluates both the proposed plan in terms of a risk-benefit analysis, and the client's ability to carry out the proposed plan (Gutheil, 1993). Going back to the example of the anxious woman dreading confronting her husband about his affair, the E section of the note might read: "Risks: greater anxiety, possibly to the point that husband will notice her inability to function and precipitate a confrontation before client is ready. Benefits: ability to objectify feelings, clarify thinking, gain control of emotions, increased likelihood that the confrontation, when it does happen, will be constructive rather than destructive to both parties. Client has demonstrated ability to deal with uncomfortable information in every session to date, and likely has the ability to pull this off."

Ancillary Records. Not all counselors and therapists use tests or other objective assessment tools. Those who do should keep the original test data with the other client records to serve as primary source data should the therapist ever be called upon to justify the conclusions reached about the course of therapy. Many family therapists will keep genograms or structure grams (see Chapter Eleven) on clients. These, too, belong with the objective data.

Some counselors also keep personal notes in addition to the formal case notes. This is especially true of those who work in agency settings, where the records are the property of the agency, not the therapist. That is acceptable. However, if the therapist's records are ever subpoenaed for any reason, these personal notes will almost always be included in the subpoena.

Finally, any worksheets or drawings or other work the client completes which would help document the client's problems or progress may be kept. A word of caution to the beginning counselor or therapist, however. Never ask for something you are not trained to interpret. It is one thing for a client to voluntarily bring in a drawing. It is quite another for the therapist to ask for a drawing when the therapist has no documented training or supervision in the use of artwork in therapy.

Referrals

"Dirty Harry" Callahan, the fictional movie police detective, always said, "A man's gotta know his limitations." The professional codes of ethics make a similar, though arguably more elegant, statement. Several subprinciples of the AAMFT Code of Ethics (2001), for example, make it clear that making a referral is an ethical obligation whenever it is clear that the client is not benefitting from the current therapy or whenever the client requests it.

From the Metasystems perspective, there are other reasons for making a referral which are just as important. Since Metasystems is a holistic approach to treatment, biological concerns are valid issues for treatment. However, unless the therapist is also a licensed medical doctor, a referral will be necessary to address those needs. Suppose, for example, worried parents bring their seven-year old son to Counselor Shmooze with the presenting issue of school and discipline problems. Counselor Shmooze carefully assesses the boy and concludes that he has Attention-Deficit/Hyperactivity Disorder, Predominantly Hyperactive-Impulsive Type. Naturally, Counselor Shmooze will want to continue to work with the parents and the boy to help them all learn, via behavioral interventions, how to help him control his impulsiveness. Yet Counselor Shmooze would be very remiss if he did not also refer the parents to a competent medical doctor who could prescribe an appropriate psychostimulant drug to assist the therapy.

Many clients present with spiritual or legal problems. Unless the counselor is theologically trained in the client's religious system, or is a member of the legal profession, these situations will also necessitate referral. Since no one can possibly know or do everything, the wise therapist will know his or her limitations and will have established referral resources to help clients who have needs the counselor cannot meet.

Those to whom the counselor refers should meet two specific criteria. First, the counselor should know the referral resource from first hand experience. Never simply pick a name out of the phone book. If referring to a lawyer, for example, be certain from previous conversations with that attorney that the attorney's area of legal expertise fits the client's needs and that the attorney's fees are within the client's reach. Second, make sure the referral resource will not be antagonistic to the work done by the therapist. Going back to our example of the parents with the son who has AD/HD, Counselor Shmooze would never refer to a physician who believed the only treatment necessary was medication and who would undermine the therapist's relationship with the parents. Counselors who work in a religious setting find it similarly important to refer to resources who are at least not antagonistic to the therapist's religious stance.

Conclusion

Some years ago there was a cartoon showing a tired physician talking with a grieving widow in the hospital emergency room. The physician said, "We did all we could, but the paperwork was too much." A standard joke among pilots is when the weight of the paperwork equals the weight of the aircraft, it is ready for takeoff. All of these kinds of jokes may have some ring of truth. Yet there is a greater truth. Administrative work, as unglamourous as it is, remains an essential component of good care. Professional codes of ethics require it. Laws may demand it. But more to the point, our clients deserve it.

SAMPLE OF A SESSION NOTES FORM:

CONFIDENTIAL CLINICAL SESSION NOTES

Case #:   **Session Date:**

Session #:   **Notes Written:**

Therapist(s):

Supervisor:

Present: H   W   S1   S2   S3   D1   D2   D3   O1   O2   O3   M   F

Age:

Detail all Yes on Back.

1.____ Referral Needed   4.____Diagnosis Change

2 ____ Suicide/Violence   5.____Treatment Plan Change

3.____ Significant Transference Issues 6.___ Possible Child/Sex Abuse _

Family Members and Descriptors: (age, gender, significant facts):

Statement of Problem: (Client: Presenting Problem)

Therapist: (tentative assessment)

Desired Outcome of Therapy:

Client:

Therapist (proximate/distant):

        Prox:

        Dist:

Present State: (how client(s) present today)

In session intervention:

Home work assignment:

Living Into the Lesson

1.   Take a position pro or con on the statement, "The quality of your record keeping reflects the quality of your care for the client." Hold a debate in class. Note the arguments on both sides. After listening to all the arguments, which is most persuasive to you? Why?

2.   One of the ethical issues in this chapter is client confidentiality. How do you maintain client records to allow you and only you easy access to the information?

3.   What do you think about electronic record keeping? Discuss the pros and cons as a class. You may want to invite someone who is very knowledgeable about computers to discuss methods hackers or others could use to gain unauthorized access to electronic records.

4.   In discussing the possibility of malpractice suits, the author states that courts may hold the counselor to a higher standard of proof than the client. Do you think this is fair? Why or why not?

5.   Pretend you are on a jury. Billy Bob Smith has accused Counselor Samuel Shmooze of malpractice, specifically, that Counselor Shmooze's therapy was ineffective and simply for the purpose of obtaining money from Mr. Smith. What facts would you as a juror need to help you reach a verdict? What can you apply to the issue of record keeping from this?

6.   Interview one therapist in your area. What written form of informed consent does the therapist use? Bring a sample to class to share. What questions would you have as a client that these sample documents do not answer?

7.   Obtain a treatment plan form currently in use in your area. Share this form with your class. What kinds of information

are included on the form? What do you wish were there?
How useful do you find this form?

8.   How do you feel about charging money for your time? Talk
honestly with one other person. If you feel uncomfortable
with the idea (most new counselors do), discuss where that
may come from. How do you maintain sound business
practices and still be compassionate toward your clients?

9.   The author makes a point that *pro bono* (free) services are less
effective because the clients tend not to value these services.
Do you agree? Why or why not?

10.   Watch the movie "Good Will Hunting." Make process notes
(your choice of style) of the filmed sessions between Sean
McGuire (Robin Williams) and Will Hunting (Matt Damon).
Compare your notes with at least one other person. How
similar are they? How do you account for any differences
which may exist?

11.   Suppose you are a brand new counselor. How would you
establish a referral network? What practical steps would you
take?

INDIVIDUAL COUNSELING SKILLS

C. Wayne Perry, D. Min, LMFT

Chapter 5 - Solution Focused/Problem Solving Skills

The indispensable first step to getting the things you want out of life is this: decide what you want. - Ben Stein

Like most other forms of brief therapy, solution-focused therapy has an innate appeal. We Americans do like things to be efficient. Why cook a potato in the oven for 50 minutes, when five minutes in a microwave will do? Both therapists and clients often apply the same sort of logic to therapy. Why invest years in psychodynamic, insight-based therapy, when six or eight sessions will do? While there are those who will argue that a potato cooked in an oven is better than one cooked in a microwave, and, similarly, that therapy based on depth of insight is better than a "band-aid approach to therapy" (as they call brief therapy), those arguments will have to be waged on other ground. This book's expressed purpose is to teach how, not why.

Yet from a Metasystems perspective, solution-focused approaches are not so opposed to a psychodynamic style of therapy as some believe. Alfred Adler was certainly psychodynamic in his theory, yet one of his fundamental tenants was that all human behavior was "teleological" - that is, it is aimed at some goal (Sweeney, 1989). Often Adlerian therapy takes the form of helping the client examine previously held goals in the light of experience as the client has actually lived it (as opposed to the client's private fiction of the way it "ought" to be).

What makes the solution-focused approach different from Adlerian therapy is the solution-focused approaches' attention to only the present (and, of course, the future the solution is designed to create). Adlerian therapy, by contrast, will pull data from the past as well as the present to help the client create a new future (Lundin, 1989). This difference in selecting the data that is relevant for therapy is grounded in the two world views, or epistemologies. Solution-focused therapy is one of the post-modern approaches. As such, it believes that "reality" is merely a socially constructed variable, with no external or objective existence (Nichols and Schwartz, 1998). Adlerian therapy, however, accepts "reality" as having an objective existence which humans can know (and distort) through a variety of means. This seemingly esoteric difference has one very major practical implication. If "reality" is merely socially constructed, one solution is as good as another. The only difference is in how efficiently the solution operates. On the other hand, if reality has some external existence, the therapist is justified in guiding the client toward a solution that conforms to reality, even if the client doesn't yet understand the connection.

The Metasystems model follows Adlerian therapy. However, the reader should make his or her own decision about which epistemology best fits his or her basic approach to life. For example, if the reader is an evangelical Christian, a post-modern approach to therapy will not be consistent with basic religious beliefs about the nature of this universe. The Adlerian approach will be more comfortable and consistent. However, if the reader identifies more with liberal religious beliefs, a post-modern approach to life and therapy will fit quite nicely. Adler will feel quaint, at best.

Defining Achievable Goals

It goes without saying that solution-focused therapy begins as all other therapies do - by joining with the client. These first few crucial minutes of any therapy session will look and sound very much alike, regardless of the counselor's theoretical orientation. The client brings in a list of problems, and the counselor listens patiently and carefully to the client's "problem-saturated story" (Walter and Peller, 1992).

What is not so obvious is the big shift that is going on in the therapist's mind. Instead of listening to discover what "caused" the problem, as Freud might have done, or listening to discover what maintains the problem, as Minuchin might have done, the solution-focused therapist listens for solutions that the client and therapist can jointly construct.

There are several basic assumptions inherent in this listening style. Obviously, the first assumption is that there are solutions and that they can be constructed. That follows from the basic epistemology of the solution-focused approach. Solutions are constructed, not discovered. Second, clients do not "resist" the therapist. Clients are showing by their actions how they believe change takes place. In this world-view the client, not the therapist, is the expert. Therefore, the counselor takes whatever the client gives as an honest effort to cooperate with the change process and uses that to help the client achieve the client's goals. Finally, solution-focused therapy assumes that small change is generative. That is, this therapy style believes that the client's small successes now can lead to more and bigger successes later (Walter and Peller, 1992). For this reason, solution-focused therapists totally reject the contention that their style of therapy is a "band-aid approach." To use a golf analogy, I do not have to learn anew how to putt on every single green I play. Once I have success at putting on one green, I can apply my success to other greens on other courses. I may need to adjust for other variables, but the basics will still serve. Indeed, as success builds on success, I become better at putting even on new greens.

The first noticeable shift in style comes when the therapist explicitly asks the client, "What change would you like to see happen?" The way I usually phrase this question to clients is, "Let's assume that this counseling is a total success, so much so that even ten years from now, you say to yourself 'You know, that was the best investment of time and money I ever made in my life.' Now, if all of that were true, what would be different?" However it is phrased, in my experience this question often catches the client off guard. It is one thing to complain about a problem. Most of us learn quite early how to do that very well. However, to actually specify what we want to be different requires a major shift of consciousness. In Metasystems' language, it moves us from the Victim position to a self-responsible position. Most clients will have some difficulty with the goal question, but those who are stuck in the Victim position will have the most difficulty. Their Back Stage message is that they do not believe change happens, or that change just mysteriously happens, and either way they cannot take responsibility for it. Later in this chapter we will look at how to deal with these situations. For now, it is worth remembering the solution-focused assumption that even Victims are cooperating as best they can.

Walter and Peller (1992) give criteria for a well constructed goal with which most solution-focused therapists could agree. There is no magic in the order of the criteria; all are necessary for an effective goal statement. The first is that the goal must be framed in the positive. Often clients will say, "Well, when therapy is a success I won't be depressed any more." The counselor's response is, "Great. That's a great goal. So, when you're not depressed, what will you be instead?" Push for as many specific, observable behaviors as possible.

C	I'll be sleeping better.
T	Fine. What does 'better' mean?
C	I'll be sleeping seven to eight hours, and I'll get up feeling refreshed.
T	Great. So what else will different when you are no longer depressed?
C	Well, I guess my appetite will be back to normal. Right now I just snack all the time, even when I'm not hungry. I've gained about 20 pounds. When I'm not depressed, I'll be able to go back to just eating when I'm hungry.

The second criteria for a well-defined goal is that it is in the process form. That means that it almost always uses verbs which express continuing action, verbs which end in -ing.

T	Okay, so you'll also be your old self, with your great sense of humor. How will you be doing that?

79

C   Well, folks have always told me I have a weird way of looking at the world. I guess I'll be back to seeing the funny side of everything, instead of only looking at the down side, like I do now.

The third criteria is that the goal has an immediate focus. Solution-focused therapists call this being "on track."

T   So, when you leave here today, what will you be doing differently, or saying to yourself differently, that will tell you that you are on track towards your goal?

C   Wow, that's hard. I guess I'll feel a little more hopeful about my situation.

T   And how will you be doing that? [Criteria Three]

C   Well, I guess I'll tell myself that I've made the hard step by coming here. This really was hard for me. If I could call for the appointment, and then actually walk through the door, I guess I can do anything.

T   Great. I can buy that. And when you're telling yourself that you can do anything because you have already done the hardest step, how will you be acting differently? [Criteria One and Two]

That last exchange illustrates the final two criteria of a well-constructed goal: the goal is under the client's control and in the client's own language. It also illustrates the circular nature of goal construction. Goals are not constructed in a linear, step-one, step-two, step-three process. The therapist never assumes what the client's goal "ought" to be or "probably is." Instead, the therapist loops back through the criteria as often as necessary to help the client hone the goal into one the client can actively visualize, one that engages the client's imagination and all the client's senses. Then the goal stands a chance of actually pulling the client toward it.

The criteria of having the goal under the client's control bears further comment. Often clients will frame a goal in terms of what someone else will do. Without realizing it, the client is slipping into, or maintaining, a Victim position. "Well, my husband won't yell at me any more. I'm going to stay depressed until he quits yelling. I can't help it." While this construction of reality may be logical (very few of us feel better after someone we love has yelled at us), it is not helpful. She cannot control her husband's behavior, so his behavior has no proper place in her goal. As long as she makes her behavior contingent on her husband's actions, she keeps herself locked into a belief system that says, "Change only happens to me. I cannot make it happen."

A subtle variation on this Victim theme is one that Walter and Peller (1992) mention. They worked with a woman who was trying to get off cocaine. She believed she had to get rid of her taste for cocaine before she could stop using it. Again, the belief appears logical, but it is not helpful. It was not in the woman's power to get rid of her taste for cocaine. That might eventually come as a side effect of treatment (not likely, but possible), but to focus on that as a precondition for starting change is to torpedo change before it can even begin. The tragic irony of maintaining a Victim position is that the more the Victim pursues solutions which are bound to fail, the more the Victim will see the goals as being out of reach, which in turn decreases the client's realistic hope, which in turn decreases the client's motivation to even try, and so on.

One common mistake that beginning solution-focused therapists are likely to make is not framing the goal in terms that are actually in the client's power to change. This is why keeping the goal specified in concrete, observable terms is so important. There is much in modern life we cannot control. We cannot control our emotions or preferences. We can control our behavior.

Exceptions; "Miracle Questions"

Even with skillful questioning by the counselor, often clients are unable to visualize a goal. Since solution-focused therapy does not believe in the concept of client resistance, the therapist simply assumes that the client needs a little assistance to be able to cooperate. One of the classic solution-focused techniques to assist clients is the "miracle question." Steve de Shazer (1988) first verbalized the "miracle question," and today many variations exist. This author's personal variation goes like this: "Let's assume that tonight when you go to sleep, a miracle happens. In this miracle, your problem completely disappears and you have the kind of life you really want. Now, this is a very quiet miracle. There is no thunder or lightening, nothing to wake you up. You sleep right through it. So when you wake up tomorrow morning, what would be your first clue that this miracle has happened?" Further questions help the client clarify and develop the full extent of the "miracle."

Another variation this author uses is "pixie dust": "Let's assume I have some pixie dust in my pocket [at this point I usually dig into my pocket as though retrieving something, and then make a sweeping motion with my arm as though spreading something in the air]. This pixie dust is magic, so you now have your problem completely solved. So what's different for you now? What has this magic done for you?" Notice that the "magic" is phrased in the present tense. That bit of grammar, plus the playful presentation, helps the client construct an alternative reality where magic really does happen and "logic" does not have to rule. That is the power of either variation on this theme. Miracles and magic move the client out of the old frame where "more of the same" is the only logical outcome and help the client construct a new frame "in possibility land" (as Bill O'Hanlon likes to call it).

Another solution-focused technique to help clients construct their goal is to look for exceptions - to situations when the problem either does not exist or is less severe. The assumption behind this technique is what the client experiences when the problem is not present or not as severe is what the client would like to experience more often. In other words, this absence of the problem constitutes the client's goal. The therapist's job is to take the client's negative statement (i.e., the absence of the problem) and make it a positive goal.

To illustrate this technique, assume that Counselor Samuel Shmooze is working with Sally, a 12 year old who recently attempted suicide, and her mother Alice, who came with Sally to therapy. Until very recently, Sally has always been a "good girl," according to her mother. Starting about two months ago, however, Sally had become increasingly distant, irritable, and negligent of her own appearance and of her younger siblings. Alice is a single-parent mother who works two jobs to make enough money to provide for the four children, so Sally had previously willingly taken on many of the parenting tasks for her younger siblings. Counselor Shmooze quickly assesses Alice as a loving parent who feels totally overwhelmed. They have come to counseling because they were referred by the attending physician who treated Sally's suicide attempt (she took a handful of aspirin), but in the first session neither was able to verbalize any goals they had for the therapy.

T   Okay, so, tell me, Sally, what is it like when you don't feel like killing yourself?

S   I feel happy. I like me. I like to take care of my baby brother and my sisters.

T   Great. So when you're better, you feel good about you and you express that by doing good things for others.

S   Right.

T   Okay, so when was the last time you felt like that, even a little bit?

S   I don't know. I can't remember. It's been a long time.

T   Alice, how about you? When have you noticed Sally taking care of her baby brother and her sister the way she - at least, doing some of what she used to.

A   She does it all the time. I couldn't get along without her.

T   Oh, so Alice, you see Sally taking care of the other kids all the time, and she really makes a difference to you? (Sally looks straight at Alice for the first time in session, as though genuinely surprised).

A   That's right. Sometimes she seems like she's just going through the motions, but, hey, I do that, too. I just appreciate the way she gets all the kids ready for school so I can get myself ready to go to work. And that's only part of what she does.

T   Sally, you looked surprised. Did you know you were making this much difference to your mom?

S   No. I figured it didn't matter.

Counselor Shmooze uncovered some exceptions to the problem (Sally feeling like killing herself) that were happening all the time, but without Sally noticing it. In the process, the therapist discovered Sally's real goals. She wanted attention from her mother, and she wanted to feel good about herself and to express that by helping others. Sally's mistaken belief was that she had to feel happy in order to do anything good. What Counselor Shmooze helped her create was a new reality where she can indeed do good things even when she is not happy. Her mother's words of appreciation were critical elements in helping Sally create this new reality.

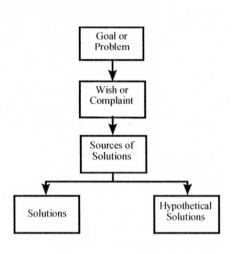

Figure 5.1

Figure 5.1 summarizes the various pathways the therapist can use to bring the client to "possibility land." Rarely, the client will come in with a clear statement of a goal. If that's the case, the client and therapist can begin to simply and quickly problem solve (see the next section) and work on solutions. More often (at least in this author's experience), clients will arrive with a wish or a complaint. The therapist can then take the direct path (i.e., "What would you like to be different?") to solutions, or can explore a more indirect path via exploring exceptions to the problem. An alternative which is especially effective when the client is highly emotional or tightly locked only onto a problem frame is to use one of the "hypothetical solution" paths - the "miracle" question or the "pixie dust" (or some variation on those themes).

<u>Getting Beneath The Presenting Problem</u>

Whichever pathway the client and therapist follow, constructing the client's goal will often take most if not all of the first session. It naturally follows that the homework assignment at the end of this session will be to actually do at least a bit of the goal-solution.

The second (and each succeeding) session opens with the question, "What's going better for you now?" or "What is different for you this week?" That question clearly communicates the counselor's expectation that change will occur between sessions and that it is within the client's power to make it happen. However, clients will often have at least as much trouble answering this question as they do the original goal question. In this author's experience, the most common response is, "Nothing is different." Since therapy is what happens in the therapist's head, if the therapist truly believes that change can happen, the therapist will creatively dig for exceptions to the problem.

Whether the client spontaneously identifies an exception, an instance where the goal-solution actually happened, or has to be prompted by the counselor, the counselor's next question is, "That's great. How did you do that?" Again, client's will often say, "I don't know." In doing so, they are communicating that they believe change simply "happens" mysteriously without any effort or control on their part. The logical response of a solution-focused therapist is to press the client, usually (in this author's experience) with humor and/or genuine puzzlement, to actually own what they did, to experience their own power to create change.

An example of this process is Counselor Shmooze's meeting with Sally for a third session. Although she no longer reported feeling like killing herself, she said she still felt depressed and worthless.

T	So, Sally, what was different for you this week?
S	Nothing. It was the same old stuff. I'm not any worse, but I'm not any better.
T	Did you take care of your brother and sisters at least a little like you used to?
S	Yeah, but that's nothing new. I've been doing that.
T	That's great. How did you do that?
S	I don't know. I just do it.
T	Yeah, I know you do it. That's what amazes me. You have all this stuff going on in your life, you have more responsibility than many adults, and yet you're just 12 years old and you're doing a great adult job. [Shmooze is deliberately painting the problem in very dramatic terms - a technique solution- focused therapists often use to force clients to acknowledge their problem "isn't that bad"]. How do you do it?
S	Well, mom is paying more attention to me. I guess that helps.
T	Oh, I see! So you're getting more of your mom's attention, and that's helping make a difference for you?
S	Yeah. I guess so.

Once the client and counselor have identified some changes in the past week, the questioning turns to what new piece of the solution the client would like to work on. In this sense, every session is just like the first. The counselor and client jointly use the same basic techniques to co-create new slices of the goal. The counselor's main function is usually "cheerleading" the client's past successes and (very importantly) helping the client identify new goal steps in concrete, behavioral terms. One of the surest ways to set a client up for failure in solution-focused therapy is to leave the goal statements vague and undefined. An old cliche states, "The road to hell is paved with good intentions." Real change requires specifics, not just good intentions.

When Clients Are Stuck

Sometimes, even the most skillful solution-focused therapist gets stuck. Clients may be so discouraged from multiple failures in the past that they find it hard to really try any of the solutions. Very frequently, clients present with multiple problems. Forces outside the control of either the client or the therapist may hinder the solutions. For example, one couple I was working with following an affair found great difficulty healing because the person with whom the wife had the affair attended the same church they did - and continued to come and stare at the husband and the wife as they sat in the church choir. At other times, the problems will be like some forms of bacteria and prove resistant to the best normal techniques. Solution focused therapy offers a few extra techniques for times when a counselor may feel stuck.

"Scaling." Scaling is a rather simple solution-focused technique that has multiple uses. One very common way I use it with couples is to ask, "If you were to visualize your current relationship on a one-to-ten scale, with *ten* being the kind of relationship you have always dreamed you would have and *one* representing about the closest thing to hell on earth, where is your relationship right now?" That illustration gives the essential components of the scaling technique. You ask the client to visualize their stated goal on a one-to-ten continuum (one-to-ten seems to work best; one-to-five is a bit too compressed, and one-to-100 is a bit overwhelming), with ten representing the goal is totally accomplished and the person feels completely happy about that level of change, and one represents either the total lack of the goal (as in my illustration) or where they are now - their starting point. You then ask the client to state where they are on that continuum and why they rated their level of goal accomplishment at that point.

Incidentally, in working with couples or families, the counselor will need to explicitly tell the client (all persons in the room) that the answers may be different for each person and that the difference is okay. In fact, the difference becomes very important information for the client, as each person involved can see for him or her self the differences which need to be accounted for in constructing their common solution.

In science there is a concept called the "just noticeable difference." In essence, the "just noticeable difference" is the smallest amount of change that can be detected by available measurement methods. That concept illustrates the next step in the scaling technique. After the client has rated the goal accomplishment on the one-to-ten scale, the counselor asks the client what will be necessary to move one-half step closer to the goal (e.g., from a "5" to a "5.5"). Again, if there are several members of the client in the room, each person specifies what that "just noticeable difference" will be for her or him. As always, these changes must be clearly stated in observable, behavioral terms which are under the individual's control.

There is a variation on the scaling technique which is particularly helpful for "stuck" clients. In addition to asking the client to rate the goal accomplishment right now, the counselor also asks the client to rate the relationship at various times in the past. Going back to my example with couples therapy, I often ask the couple to rate the relationship now, and then I ask what is the best it has ever been and then I will ask what is the worst it has ever been. At each point, I ask what made it a "3" or an "8" or whatever rating the person gives.

If Counselor Shmooze were using this technique with Sally, he might phrase it like this:

> T   So, tell me, Sally, if you were to rate how depressed you feel on a one-to- ten scale, with ten being the depression totally gone and you feel your old self, and one being you are so depressed you can't even get out of bed, much less function, where are you now?
>
> C   I'm about a 3.
>
> T   What makes it a 3 for you?
>
> C   Well, I can get out of bed and I can go to school most of the time, but I don't enjoy anything and I really have to force myself to do anything at all.
>
> T   Okay, and what is the most depressed you have ever been?
>
> C   Oh, I've definitely been a 1. Maybe a 1. That's when I tried to kill myself.
>
> T   Okay, and on that same scale what is the least depressed you have been?
>
> C   Definitely a 10. That's the way I am most of the time. Or, at least, I used to be.

What makes this technique so powerful with stuck clients is that they get to see from their own experience that they have not always been a "3" (or whatever they gave their current rating). They see from their own experience that the problem has come and gone in the past. That gives a realistic basis for hope that this current situation can change. Asking about "the best it has ever been" also gives the counselor a basic for assessing the prognosis for change. While clients may occasionally do better than they ever have done before, returning to their previous highest level of functioning is certainly a reasonable goal in most cases.

Whether the counselor accepts, with solution-focused therapy, the post-modern belief that clients construct their own reality, or whether the counselor accepts, with Metasystems, the Adlerian belief that people live according to their own life script, scaling works by giving the client a way to make the seemingly impossible present more manageable. Whether used as a snap shot in time or as a view of change over time, scaling reduces the problem from "King Kong" size to something mere mortals can conquer.

"How do you keep it from getting worse?" Occasionally, clients will be so stuck in their problem-saturated stories that scaling or other techniques do not help. In that case, the therapist can shift gears and go with what the client is presenting. Remember, solution-focused therapy does not believe in client resistance.

Counselor Shmooze was working with Linda, a married mother of teenaged children. She was a compulsive shopper and felt totally out of control. Linda had run up more than $10,000 in credit card debts, and would have run up more but all of the credit cards were at their credit limit. Since Linda payed the bills, her husband knew nothing of this, and she was terrified what might happen if he found out. So far, she had managed to make the minimum payments each month, but she came to therapy when she realized that she either was going to have to get her compulsion under control or she would be discovered.

Linda was able to state her goal of getting the shopping under control, but she was totally unable to verbalize any concrete specifics of what "under control" would look like. She stated that she felt like this compulsion (a word she used and freely accepted) just overwhelmed her. When Counselor Shmooze asked her to scale how bad her problem is currently, Linda readily rated herself as a one. She agreed that she had been a 10 back in high school, but she attributed that to not having any money of her own. In her life-script, any money she had MUST be spent. She stated she truly wanted to change, but she felt hopeless that she could.

T   So, tell me Linda, it sounds like things have been pretty bad.

C   Pretty bad? It's been <u>awful</u>! It's been like living in hell, trying to keep my husband from finding out, trying to save my marriage, trying to pay all the bills... (begins to sob gently).

T   (After several seconds of silence) Linda, I can see from what you say that it has been awful for you. So, how did you keep it from being even worse?

C   (Looking up, surprised) Huh?

T   Yeah, really. I mean, you've been under an awful strain, I can see that, but some how you managed to pull it off. Somehow you managed to keep all the bills paid, and you kept your husband from finding out. How did you keep the spending from getting even more out of control than it was?

C   I don't know. I just did it.

T   You sure did. I'm surprised. Not many people could pull off something so difficult. But you did it. How did you do that?

C   Well, a lot of times I couldn't [retreating to problem-saturated talk].

T   True, that's why you're here. But you didn't have any of the things you fear most happen, so you did something to keep it from getting that bad.

C   Well, I guess when I felt like I just had to spend and I knew I couldn't, I'd just tell myself that I couldn't. And I'd go over to Susie's house and play canasta so I wouldn't be tempted to go shopping.

T   Great. So what has worked, at least a little bit, is telling yourself that you have to control your urges, and distracting yourself by having fun with a friend.

C   Right.

Counselor Shmooze succeed in helping Linda identify a way out of her problems by patiently going with what she presented and then taking that to a logical extreme. He did not try to talk her out of her feelings to tell her how illogical she was being. Instead, he put her into the position of having to say, in essence, "Well, it really isn't that bad." That is the real power of the "How did you keep it from getting worse?" technique.

Summary

Solution-focused therapy is very positive and respectful of both the client and the therapist. Therein lies one of its major appeals. However, there is a down side to this approach. It requires the therapist to work in a

89

very positive, hopeful manner with clients who are often very discouraged. As anyone who has ever worked with truly discouraged people can tell you, there is a real pull downward into discouragement and/or depression for others in the discouraged person's relational system, which certainly includes the therapist. To successfully use this style of therapy, the therapist must be very self-assured in her or his own ability to maintain a positive, hopeful attitude no matter what the client may present. For those who can do so, solution-focused therapy can be a powerful, dramatic avenue for client change.

Living Into the Lesson

1.   Stage a debate with classmates. Have one group take a pro stance and the other group a con stance on this statement: "Resolved: all reality is merely socially constructed." After the debate, discuss your true feelings. Which epistemology discussed in this chapter is most attractive to you? Why?

2.   Test the assumption that change is generative in your own experience. What parts of your own experience either conforms or refutes this assumption? Be sure to go into details. Based on the weight of your own experience, do you buy this assumption?

3.   Several schools of therapy talk about dealing with client resistance. Solution-focused therapy, however, does not believe in that concept. Instead, solution-focused therapy believes that clients are always trying to cooperate. Do you agree? Why or why not?

4.   Work with another student to practice constructing effective goals for each of the following client complaints:
        a.   A 14 year old male complains of being so anxious he cannot go to school. He can, however, go to church and other activities.
        b.   A 23 year old woman complains of being depressed so depressed she cannot concentrate on her college work, even after taking the anti-depressant medication her physician prescribed her, because her husband is "angry all the time."
        c.   A 38 year old man complains he is depressed because his wife spends all her free time on the computer and neglects him.

5.   In what one area of your life would you like to see a change? Construct a "miracle" for that change. Then take your "miracle" statement and carefully construct a goal statement for this change. Now read your goal statement. How do you feel? How is looking at your goal statement different for you than simply wanting the change?

6.   Pick another area of your life you would like to change, but this time construct an "Exception" statement. Use that to construct your goal statement and repeat the rest of the process from Number 5.

7.   If clients really are not resistant, how do you explain the reality that so many clients have difficulty in the beginning stages of therapy identifying change that is happening?

8.   On the 11th session (scheduled to be the final), Bubba did not show up. Bubbette was furious with him. The identified goal of therapy was to end the husband's uncontrollable fits of rage at his wife, during with he frequently grabbed (but never hit) his wife. The goal had been accomplished. Now Bubbette was angry. Role play the situation (remember Solution-focused therapy doesn't care "why" something happens) to help Bubbette construct a final session goal which will help successfully terminate therapy.

9.   Go back to the change you wanted to happen in your own life in either number five or six of this section. If ten represents complete goal accomplishment, and one represents you haven't even started, where are you now? What will it take for you to move a half-step closer to your goal? What will you be doing differently when you are a half-step closer?

Think of the most negative person you have known. Role play that person, while another person works with you on "How did you keep it from getting worse?" Then switch roles with your partner and you play counselor. After the role play, talk about how you felt in both roles. What did you do in your counselor role to keep from getting discouraged?

Chapter 6 - Cognitive Therapy Skills

We are what we think. All that we are arises with our thoughts. With our thoughts, we make the world. – Buddha

When the student turns to cognitive therapy, things quickly get pretty complex. Cognitive therapy is often associated with behavioral therapy (See Chapter 7). While cognitive therapy certainly contains a behavioral emphasis, as it is currently practiced it stems primarily from the work of Aaron Beck and Albert Ellis. Although Beck and Ellis are both, as of the date this is written, still alive and still producing practical and theoretical work, the field of cognitive therapy certainly has not been static. Other thinkers have moved cognitive therapy into a richly diverse theoretical and therapeutic arena. Purists from the various camps within this large, diverse movement hold to the superiority of their particular variation on the theme.

What they all have in common is a belief that cognition is the key to understanding psychological disorders (Alford and Beck, 1997). While the various schools of cognitive therapy may use different terms, they all also agree that humans are meaning-making creatures. Some times the meaning is created deliberately (i.e., consciously), while other times it is created pre-consciously ("automatic thoughts"). Whether consciously or pre-consciously developed, these cognitive meaning structures ("schemas") give rise to emotions. For example, cognitive therapy would claim that Jim does not feel depressed because his wife left him. Jim feels depressed because of the meaning he assigns to the fact that his wife left him.

Cognitive therapists believe that cognitions, that is, the meanings both consciously and preconsciously associated with events, must change for behavior to change. In turn, behavior must change to reinforce the new and more productive meaning systems the client acquires via therapy (Nichols and Schwartz, 1998). Because of this emphasis on changed behavior as evidence of changed cognition, cognitive therapy has been perhaps one of the best researched styles of therapy. Its emphasis on observable data makes scientific study relatively easy, and thus this style of therapy is among the most well-documented as effective for a variety of psychological problems. As one example, the Beck Institute's web site references a meta-analysis of some 325 different studies which indicate that cognitive-behavior therapy is superior to moderately superior over a variety of other treatment modalities, including pharmacological approaches and supportive psychotherapy (Beck Institute, 2000).

Because of the weight of objective data, many therapists, in this author's experience, would allow for some influence of cognitive therapy on their own practice. This includes those who would not specifically identify themselves as cognitive therapists. Some are more influenced by Beck and his disciples, while others find Ellis more helpful, and still others are much more interested in one of the emerging integrated approaches. This text will make no attempt to distinguish between these competing therapies in summarizing cognitive therapy techniques. Students who find this approach particularly helpful should do more work on their own to add breadth and depth to this all-too-brief summary.

Clients with Whom this Therapy Is Appropriate.

Proponents of cognitive therapy claim that this style of treatment is effective with a wide variety of presenting issues, ranging from mood and anxiety disorders to severe personality disorders, such as borderline personality disorder. Albert Ellis (1997) himself, in his usual inimitable style, holds that his style of cognitive therapy, Rational-Emotive Therapy, works for almost everyone except "(1) autistic children; (2) low-grade mental defectives; (3) schizophrenics in a catatonic state or otherwise severely withdrawn; and (4) manics or manic-depressives while they keep acting in a highly manic way." He also grants in that same article that certain people will not be helped regardless of the style of therapy employed. Aaron Beck is no less enthusiastic about his style of therapy. It would appear that one could not go wrong simply by learning one or both of these styles of therapy and employing them with every client.

In this author's experience, life in the therapy room is not that simple. These are excellent treatment modalities, and they have much in common with the Metasystems approach. In more recent years, cognitive therapy, like other therapy systems, has moved to a more integrated stance, finding much common ground with more traditional psychotherapeutic modalities (Alford and Beck, 1997). This chapter, however, will focus on the more typically unique aspects of cognitive therapy, not because cognitive therapy is necessarily actually practiced that way, but because it is easier for the beginning counselor to learn the techniques that way.

Cognitive approaches can work well with people who are comfortable with a mathematical style of logic (e.g., "All A is B. All B is C. Therefore, all A is C"). These people find the work of analyzing dysfunctional thought patterns comfortable and natural. Many others not so inclined can also learn to do this sort of work. However, in this author's experience, it takes a little patience and persistence on the part of the therapist to teach the necessary skills.

People who are much more comfortable with immediate, here-and-now experience tend to have a little more trouble with cognitive therapy. It seems for them too distant, too bloodless, too abstract to be meaningful.

Whether this is a problem or not depends on the client. I have, in my practice, found some people, who are very much locked into feeling and emotional logic, helped by forcing them away from their comfort zone and into a more cooly abstract style of logic. For these clients, it is the very strangeness of the cognitive therapy style that is its biggest asset - having to do something very different slows down their automatic reactions and helps them to gain control of their situation.

With other here-and-now, feeling types of people, I tend to stay with their strengths. The criteria for me tends to be whether the immediate access to emotional material has proven to be a help or a hindrance to the progress of therapy thus far.

One fact should be very obvious. Whether the counselor is using "pure" cognitive approaches, or some integrated style of cognitive therapy, cognitive therapy is at its essence very directive (Dattilio and Bevilacqua, 2000). That is, the function of the counselor is to listen carefully to the client's situation, analyze the situation, and then prescribe some behaviors (including cognitive behaviors) for the client to do. Note the word "prescribe." The model of operation is not unlike what one experiences going to a physician.

This fact brings up one caution in using cognitive-behavioral therapy. People who do not accept an authoritarian environment, however benignly it is presented, will not do well. A good example is a client of this author's. Mirabelle was a 39 year old divorced mother of two teens. She had lived in an emotionally abusive marriage for 14 years, and had come to therapy to "heal" from the after effects of the abuse. She started therapy two years after the divorce was final, and almost three years after she and her now ex-husband separated, but when she talked about the emotional abuse it was as though she were still there. Mirabelle was an intelligent woman, a college graduate with a business degree, so by all rights she should have been an excellent candidate for cognitive therapy. However, she was so overly-sensitive to any sort of control that I quickly found that any directions, even homework prescriptions, on my part simply generated resistance on her part. We worked instead in an Adlerian fashion, allowing her to tell her story with all the emotional data intact, and allowing her to both analyze her story themes (her "private fictions") and create her own homework assignments for her own continued growth. While Mirabelle is, admitted, a somewhat extreme example, she does illustrate one of the dangers in trying to force all clients into any one box.

Defining Dysfunctional Thoughts.

Cognitive therapy totally agrees with the principle stated by Buddha at the beginning of this chapter - we are what we think. Dysfunction comes from holding beliefs that are either false or are inappropriate to the given situation. Like behavior therapy, the goal of therapy is to shift the client's interactions (behavior) from a ratio of predominately unsatisfying to predominately satisfying interactions (Beck 1979). The student should note that "behavior" explicitly includes emotional behavior for both Beck and Ellis.

Ellis makes this simple with his famous "ABC" structure (more recently expanded into ABCDE - Derrington, 1999). A stands for the actual events - what happens in the "real" world. The C stands for the consequences of the events. B stands for the beliefs about the events (A) that determine the emotional reaction (C). This is a key point of Ellis' therapy - and cognitive therapy in general. There is no direct connection between what happens to us and how we react. The reaction is mediated, for better or worse, by our beliefs.

People learn these connections between events (A) and outcomes (C) early in life, and often these beliefs (B) become codified into fixed, unconditional cognitive structures of meaning referred to as "schemas" (Dattilio and Bevilacqua, 2000). Schemas keep the person experiencing these past connections as though they were present. In other words, when Janie Sue has a sensory experience that is even remotely similar to a situation-response connection which was codified into a schema (meaning), she will experience the same emotions she did in the original experience, whether that is appropriate in this situation or not. The schema produce this automatic response by automatic thoughts - thoughts or sensory images which flash in the person's mind and produce both emotions and behavior. For example, it is true that this author played intermural soccer in college. I played left wing - normally a responsible position for a good player, but in reality, I was a terrible soccer player. Still, my friends and I had a great time. Thus, if I were to see a soccer ball, the automatic thought most likely to hit me would be of my friends and I having fun on the soccer field. From that automatic thought, it is reasonable to expect that I would feel happy or playful upon seeing a soccer ball now, and that the playful feeling might even give rise to my going over to the soccer ball and dribbling or kicking it (at least in my mind) "for old time's sake." Naturally, the automatic thoughts which bring people to therapy are not so benign, but the process is essentially the same.

In therapy, the automatic thoughts are typically based on one of a number of cognitive distortions. Ellis tends to label the distortions in more colorful terms than does Beck, but they are essentially the same in both schools of cognitive therapy. Among the more common ones that Dattilio and Bevilacqua (2000) list are:

- Arbitrary Inference - conclusions made in the absence of supporting evidence. For example, the husband comes in and sees his wife working late on the computer and concludes "She doesn't love me any more."
- Over Generalization - conclusions based on an isolated incident or two which are taken as universal laws. For example, after a bitter divorce from the only woman he ever dated, one client concluded "I'll never date again. All women are just castrating bitches."
- Magnification ("horriblization" for Ellis) or Minimization - Taking an incident as having either greater or less significance than it objectively deserves. For example, one client couple described how, when the husband's check bounced (something that happened rarely) the wife would carry on for hours about their "ruined credit rating" and the police coming to take him to jail for bad checks. A different client, a woman, illustrated minimization by referring to her husband's multiple affairs as "his hobby."
- Dichotomous Thinking - drafting everything in either/or, black/white terms. Everything is either all good or all bad. Clients stuck in this cognitive distortion interpret every suggestion as a put down, and every comment for improvement as evidence "you think there is something wrong with me."
- Mind Reading - assuming, without verbal communication, that one knows what is going on in the mind of someone else. For example, a client may say, "I know what she thinks. She thinks I am stupid" when no such verbal communication has ever been made.

One of the key skills of any cognitive therapist is to elicit these automatic thoughts and to help the client discover and correct the cognitive distortion. Beck (1979) provides a "Daily Record of Dysfunctional Thoughts" to assist with that process. The first column of the record is for the date and time of the event. The second is for listing what was actually happening at the time the thought occurred. Together, these two columns help the therapist, and the client, discover what is triggering the automatic thought. The third column is for the emotion as experienced. One of Beck's techniques is to have the client scale the emotion, from 1 (just barely noticeable) to 10 (extremely intense). It makes a big difference, for example, if a client feels anxious in a new social setting at a three or at an eight.

The next column is for recording the automatic thought. In actual practice, this author usually recommends that clients complete this column first, as soon as possible after the client becomes aware of the automatic thought. This is because automatic thoughts are so brief and so perishable, that unless they are written down very quickly they will likely be forgotten. Once again, the client rates the intensity of how "real" the thought appeared at the time on a 1 (not at all) to 10 (totally believable) scale.

The fifth column is for recording the alternative response. This is where the client and therapist work together to identify any cognitive distortions which may be at work. Among the key questions the therapist will need to help the client answer are: What is the evidence the automatic thought is true? What is the evidence it is not true? Are there other explanations which account for the data at least as well as the automatic thought, but which produce more desirable emotional reactions? What is the worst that could happen if the automatic thought is true? What is the best that could happen? What is most likely to happen, based on the evidence? How is this automatic thought actually affecting how I act and feel? What would be the effect of my changing this thought? What am I willing to do about it?

Once the alternative explanation is created, the final column on the thought record is for recording the outcome of the client's use of the alternative explanation. Using the same one-to-ten scale to rate emotional intensity, the client can easily see if the undesired emotion has disappeared or decreased in intensity.

"Action Research".

While it is very true that cognitive-behavioral therapy is directive, it is never (once the actual process of therapy has begun) simply didactic. Merely telling someone "That's not a helpful way to think" is itself not a very helpful intervention. The odds are, the client had already come to that conclusion prior to beginning therapy and still stayed stuck in the same old dysfunctional patterns of thought (and therefore emotion and action). When the counselor begins the process of disputing the client's irrational beliefs (the D in Ellis' ABCDE formula), the counselor will need to find a way to help the client experience the new data for her or him self. One way to do that is through skillful questioning.

Another useful way to help the client discover that a particular way of thinking is a cognitive distortion is by assigning the client a research project to accomplish. Jonathan was one such client. Jonathan needed to fly from our city to Los Angeles for a business meeting. The company was paying all travel expenses and even allowing a very generous expense account because the trip was so vital. The only problem was, Jonathan had never flown in his life because he was terrified of flying. In our introductory session I guided Jonathan in picturing going on his business trip as a means of accessing his automatic thought. Even in the guided imagery, Jonathan became increasingly agitated as he "walked" closer to the "aircraft," until once inside the aircraft his anxiety hit a "ten." He had no trouble at all describing his automatic thought: "Here I am, helpless in this big metal tube, and something awful is going to happen." His helplessness in the face of near-certain disaster paralyzed him.

I assigned Jonathan a research project. He was to go to the local airport and go down the concourse to where the flights come in. Then he was to select at random 25 passengers coming off at least three different flights and ask them questions about the flight they just arrived on and about their history of flying. After Jonathan committed to a certain day and block of hours he would be willing to devote to this project, I called the airport manager to inform him what Jonathan would be doing and why. As I expected, the airport manager was very cooperative (this step was necessary to ensure Jonathan did not have any difficulty with airport security; however, an unspoken agenda in doing this for me was building in some accountability so that Jonathan would not be able to "forget" doing the research).

There was another, also unspoken, agenda in my selecting this task for Jonathan. By having him actually go to the airport and be in the area from which he would have to leave, I was applying a behavioral therapy principle known as "progressive desensitization." I already knew from our visualization that merely the thought of being in an airport would trigger anxiety at about a "four" for him. By putting him in a previously threatening environment but with no fear-producing stimuli (i.e., he knew he was not going to have to fly this time), he was able to associate his feelings of confidence and/or curiosity with the airport building rather than associating anxiety with that location.

The next session Jonathan brought in the results of his research. He was positively astounded. He had interviewed 39 different passengers and had stayed an hour longer than planned to catch passengers off a fourth flight because he was so totally surprised by what he found. Not one of the people he interviewed (including a few flight crew members) had ever had a terrifying experience. A few had reported some flights that were "pretty bumpy" and a few others had recalled one or more that were "uncomfortable," but no one ever reported feeling in fear for his or her life. "From the news reports, I thought planes fell out of the sky all the time," he stated.

T   Well, aircraft do occasionally crash, so your automatic thought is not totally crazy. Do you have any idea how common these crashes are?

C   I thought you'd ask that. I was so totally blown away by what I found that I went to the National Transportation Safety Board web site [www.ntsb.gov/aviation/] to look up the stats. No wonder no one I talked to had ever had something bad happen to them! In 2000, there were only three fatal accidents for scheduled airlines in over 17,000,000 hours of flying!

T   (Smiling) So, what's the rational conclusion from your research?

C   That I have been the victim of a cognitive distortion?

T   Okay, since you know enough to use that term, which one?

C   Magnification. It's got to be.

Creating Alternative Explanations.

Once Jonathan had identified the automatic thought and the cognitive distortion, he was in a position to begin to create an alternative explanation or an alternative response. While he easily identified the "worst that could happen" (he would be trapped helplessly in the aircraft as it fell to the ground) and just as easily identified the strength of his terror in that situation as a "twenty" (on the one-to-ten scale), because of his research he was able to say that the best that could happen would be a totally uneventful flight, and the most likely thing to happen would be "a few bumps here and there, but nothing I can't handle."

Since Jonathan had an active religious faith, I asked if he believed that prayer made any difference. He eagerly stated he strongly believed in the power of prayer to make a difference.

T   Since one of the things you said terrified you most before was being totally out of control, how does prayer fit into that picture for you?

C   Oh, yeah, I hadn't thought of that. I can always pray. That way I'm not out of control. I can't fly the plane, but God can certainly help the guys that are.

T   So, on our one- to- ten scale, how much control does prayer give you?

C   Since I don't have to worry about me, just the guys flying the plane, prayer gives me about a seven or eight.

T   Even if they don't believe in God? I mean, do you believe God will help them even if the pilots don't believe in God?

C   Oh, sure. God helped me all the time before I became a believer. I didn't know it at the time, of course, but I can sure see it now.

T   In other words, your alternative response, praying instead of just being terrified, already fits with your past experience. Your past experience already shows that makes sense to you.

C   Absolutely.

We spent the balance of the session walking through the visualization we had used in the first session to create alternative responses to feeling "a little anxious" at the ticket counter, "a little more anxious" going through security, "feeling pretty bad now" coming to the waiting area, etc. Jonathan's homework was to practice his alternative responses (in his case, self-talk statements) as often as he could to prepare for our "flight" in the next session.

Testing Alternatives.

Our final session consisted of a repeat of the visualization of Jonathan's flight. This was a crucial test, because Jonathan was to actually take the flight the next day. I instructed him to do precisely what he would do tomorrow, except that for our session he was to speak his thoughts aloud instead of keeping them to himself. We started with his loading his bags in his car at home, kissing his wife goodby, and driving toward the airport. We concluded with his meeting his business associates in Los Angeles and walking out of baggage claim with his bags in hand. Throughout the experience, the worst anxiety Jonathan reported was "about a three" when he was getting on board the aircraft, and again when he felt the wheels "bump" into the well on take off. Both times he was able to get his feelings under control without any visible signs of distress.

In our final five minutes of conversation we talked about this experience. He reported it was very "real" for him. He was able to use what he had seen while doing his research to help him build the scene very vividly. The fact that it was so "real" gave him confidence that the actual flight would also go as well. We terminated our therapy with Jonathan not exactly looking forward to flying, but at least very confident he could make the flight.

(Jonathan did email me from Los Angeles the next day. He had indeed made the flight, and, despite some rather rough weather in the Dallas-Fort Worth area, where he had to change planes, he was able to make it and keep his anxiety under a "four" the whole time. He stated he and his wife had prayed together before he left, and he was convinced that is why he sat next to very experienced travelers the whole trip - those persons' relaxed confidence helped reinforce his own use of alternative responses whenever his anxiety would start creeping up.)

Jonathan's case illustrates one central truth of cognitive-behavioral therapy: Not all schema are dysfunctional. He was able to use his schema about the power of prayer to positively influence human events to help him overcome a dysfunctional schema, "I must be in control. If I am not in control, something awful will happen." The therapist does not necessarily have to share Jonathan's schema about prayer (or any other schema a client may have) to be able to use it.

His case also illustrates another central truth of cognitive-behavioral therapy. One need not worry about the cause of the dysfunctional thought to remove it. While it is doubtless true that Jonathan's fear of flying (or of being out of control) has its roots in his past, what was paralyzing him was his fear in the present. That was the proper focus of therapy. "Although we cannot change the past, *we can change how we let the past influence the way we are today and the way we want to be tomorrow*" (Ellis, 2001).

Living Into the Lesson

1.   As the author indicated, cognitive therapy is one of the most solidly researched styles of therapy, and research does seem to confirm its effectiveness. Take a position pro or con on this statement and debate it with classmates: Cognitive therapy's emphasis on behavior makes change easier to measure, but not necessarily more effective, than emotionally-focused therapies.

2.   One of cognitive therapy's prime convictions is that changing one's thoughts is both necessary and sufficient to change behavior. How do you respond to the client who doubts that? Role play explaining cognitive therapy to a doubting client.

3.   Keep a diary or journal of all your activities for the next week. How did you actually spend your time? What does this actual use of time say about schemas (meaning systems) which are operating in your life? How do these schemas fit with what you believe out "ought" to do?

4.   Think of someone you know (it could be a friend, a relative or a client) who would be, in your opinion, an excellent candidate for cognitive therapy. Now think of someone you know who would be, in your opinion, a poor candidate for cognitive therapy. What do these people have in common? In what ways are they different?

5.   Cognitive therapy is essentially a very directive style of therapy. What are the advantages for the client of such a directive approach? What are the advantages for the therapist? What disadvantages do you see for the client and for the therapist?

6.   The author states that the primary goal of cognitive therapy is to shift the ratio of client interactions from predominantly unsatisfying to predominantly satisfying. What happened to "cure"? Shouldn't therapists try to "cure" their clients? Discuss.

7.   The author cited one example of an automatic thought he experiences - the sight of a soccer ball triggers happy feelings associated with fun on an intermural college soccer team. Identify at least two automatic thoughts of your own. How did you identify them? What process helped you "catch" something so fleeting and

perishable? Do you think your techniques could be helpful to your clients? Why/why not?

8.   Of the cognitive distortions listed in this chapter, which do you find yourself using most often? Where did you learn this distortion? How was it reinforced in the past? When is it not functional (i.e., accurate) for you now?

9.   Going back to the dysfunctional thought you identified in Question 8: What emotion did you feel the last time you experienced that thought? On a one-to-ten scale, how strong was it? After you have completed this exercise, reflect on how helpful this process was.

10.   Staying with that same dysfunctional thought, create an alternative explanation which accounts for the facts at least as well as the old thought. What process helped you created this alternative explanation? On a one-to-ten scale, how much do you believe it?

11.   Role play with another student this situation: Your student-partner has been arrested for domestic violence. He/she attacked and physically beat her/his spouse when the spouse refused to go to the store as asked. The couple had been verbally sparring all day over many different issues. You are the therapist. How do you begin cognitive-behavioral therapy with this client? How do you respond if the client sees no need to change? How do you respond if the client claims to feel guilty about the assault and says, "I never want to do that again"? If possible, have a third student observe and make suggestions at the conclusion of the role play.

12.   Discuss: How would you use cognitive-behavioral therapy to treat someone who was in a major depression? Do you believe antidepressant medications have a place in cognitive-behavioral therapy? Why or why not?

Chapter 7 - Behavior Therapy Skills

It is necessary for us to learn from others' mistakes. You will not live long enough to make them all yourself. - Admiral Hyman G. Rickover

Behavior therapy has its roots in the laboratory experiments on learning that Ivan Pavlov first published in 1903. Most people know that Pavlov, a Russian physiologist, observed that when a dog is fed at the ringing of a bell, the dog would salivate at the sound of the bell when no food was present. However, this fact is not merely of academic or historical interest. The applications of that very simple observation continue to influence all sorts of events in the world around us. From this simple beginning grew classical and operant conditioning (the basis of much of behavior therapy), social learning theory, and, of course, cognitive-behavioral therapy. These theories, in turn, shape our modern approaches to education, business, and even advertising.

Take, for example, a common ad for a sleek sports car. The car will usually be presented along with an equally sleek, beautiful woman. By pairing these stimuli, the advertisers are hoping to elicit a conditioned response much like Pavlov's dog - male car buyers will "salivate" to some degree over the sports car as readily as they do the beautiful woman, and female buyers will see themselves as desirable as the model in the ad. A totally different example comes from modern education. Many companies offer computer assisted learning for various subjects ranging from foreign language to flight instruction to computer instruction. These computer assisted learning programs are normally based on operant learning theory. The examples go on and on.

Of course, behaviorism remains a mighty force in the mental health world, too. Because it had its roots in a laboratory, behavior therapy shares with cognitive therapy the distinction of being one of the most well-researched of all of the methods of therapy. Its effectiveness is also among the best documented, largely due to work published by proponents such as Neil Jacobson. Cognitive theorists like those cited in Chapter 6 and social learning theorists like Albert Bandura add to the weight of evidence. Since the fundamental assumptions of behavior therapy differ in some significant aspects from other forms of therapy, however, before moving to applying behavior therapy techniques we need to take a brief, practically-focused look at the theory undergirding all of this work.

Brief Review of Behavior Theory

Pavlov and others who followed him employed "classical conditioning." Classical conditioning begins with an unconditioned response to a stimulus. In Pavlov's work, of course, the stimulus was food presented to a dog that had been deprived of food for some hours, and the unconditioned response was the dog's salivating. Using that pairing, the therapist (or experimenter in Pavlov's case), then presents a new stimulus (the conditioned stimulus) at the same time the unconditioned stimulus is presented. In Pavlov's case, of course, the conditioned stimulus was the sound of the bell. Soon, the presence of the conditioned stimulus alone was enough to elicit the unconditioned response (salivating).

Since Pavlov had deprived the dogs of food for some hours, and since the dogs ate the food as soon as it was presented, Pavlov assumed that the food was reinforcing. That is, Pavlov assumed that giving the dog food made the response (salivating) more likely. Because the dog also got to eat immediately following the sound of the bell, the food reinforced the response of salivating to the bell. This brings us to a crucial difference between all forms of behavior therapy and many other forms of therapy. Behavior therapy believes that behavior is determined far more by its consequences than by its antecedents (Nichols and Schwartz, 1998).

This is often difficult for the beginning counseling student to grasp practically. Our culture is saturated with the assumption that the cause of behavior is in our past. For example, many would assume that Margie has a bad temper because her parents verbally abused her. For behavior therapy, however, "What caused Margie's temper?" is a meaningless question. The correct question from the behavioral perspective is "What consequences make a given behavior more likely (or less likely) to happen?" In other words, a behavior therapist would be much more interested in observing what actually happens when Margie acts in an angry manner. Likely, if this were a common behavior for Margie, the therapist would observe that when Margie acts in an angry manner, others give in to her demands. What is essential for the beginning student to understand, however, is that her parents' behavior did not "cause" her temper. Her temper is a conditioned response which is reinforced, however unwittingly, by others' response to her - in this illustration, by giving in to her when she displays that temper.

This leads to another key component of behavior therapy. Because behavior therapy is not interested in the past, only the present, behavior therapists must be skilled at careful, methodical observation and analysis of current behavior sequences. "Analysis of behavioral sequences prior to treatment, assessment of therapy in progress, and evaluation of final results are the hallmarks of behavioral therapy" (Nichols and Schwartz, 1998, p.

271). This does not mean that behavior therapists deny any role of past experiences. They just believe that the past cannot be measured or evaluated, while present behavior sequences can.

There is another very sound (from a behavioral perspective) reason for ignoring the past. Behavior continues only if it is reinforced. Returning to the illustration of bad-tempered Margie, for example, if Margie had gotten her way with her parents by throwing temper tantrums but found when she got to college that every time she threw a temper tantrum people walked away and left her alone, eventually the conditioned response (temper tantrum) would be extinguished. That is, it would cease to exist because it was no longer reinforced. Alternatively, if when she became angry her friends laughed at her instead of simply leaving her alone, the response would still disappear. This would be an example of "punishment" - applying a reinforcement (usually an aversive stimulus) which makes the behavior less likely to happen. Either way, behavior therapy assumes that the response continues to be reinforced, at least intermittently, or it would not continue to be present, and therefore an accurate focus on present behavior sequences is all that is necessary to produce real change.

Joseph Wolpe built on these classical conditioning tenants and introduced a still-widely used technique called "systematic desensitization" or "counterconditioning" (Hall, Lindzey, and Campbell, 1998). Wolpe gave some laboratory animals shocks in a certain box and conditioned (via classical conditioning) a fear of the box in those animals. Then he put them into a box that was somewhat similar to the "shock box" and fed them. When they could eat comfortably in that box, he moved them to one that was a bit more similar to the "shock box" and so on until the animals could eat and carry on comfortably with no observable signs of fear or upset in a box exactly like the previously-feared "shock box." Chapter 6 contains a clinical application of Wolpe's theoretical work - Jonathan's assignment to conduct his survey of airline passengers at the airport terminal in the gate area was designed to expose him to a previously-feared situation (being near aircraft) in a situation which was safe (i.e., he knew he was not going to fly that time). This technique is often used to treat a variety of phobias and anxiety disorders.

B.F. Skinner took the principles of classical conditioning to the next level. He believed that all behavior is not only lawful, in the sense of following observable stimulus-response sequences, it is determined (Hall, Lindzey, and Gardner, 1998). In other words, like balls on a billiard table, human behavior occurs in response to forces acting on the person. Choice has nothing to do with it, any more than billiard balls "choose" to move around the table. From this core belief, Skinner set out to develop schedules of reinforcement that make the control of behavior easier to accomplish.

Unlike classical conditioning, however, Skinner did not start with someone doing something to the subject. Skinner's theory is called "operant conditioning" because the subject has to operate or initiate something. Going back to bad-tempered Margie, Margie most likely learned her temper through operant, not classical, conditioning. That is, she displayed the temper first, and then it was reinforced, rather than having someone deliberately teaching her to relate getting her own way with a display of temper.

Again, unlike classical conditioning, which relies mostly on continuous reinforcement (e.g., every time the bell rings, food is presented), operant conditioning often employs interval or ratio reinforcement. A very common example of interval reinforcement is pay day. Most workers expect to receive a pay check at a certain interval (weekly, bi-weekly, monthly, etc.), and as long as they receive this reinforcement at the expected interval, they will continue the behavior (i.e., doing the work they are paid to do). School grades are another form of interval reinforcement (though whether they are reinforcing or punishing will depend on the grade the student earns!). Ratio reinforcement does not depend on time, but rather on the number of behaviors the subject initiates. Gambling devices pay off on a ratio schedule - every so many times the device is operated the machine will pay off (usually this is a variable ratio, rather than a fixed ratio. This makes predicting the exact number of plays before pay off more difficult, and therefore increases the number of tries before extinction starts to set in). One key principle to note is that intermittent reinforcement, especially variable ratio or variable rate reinforcement (in that order of effect), makes a learned response more resistant to extinction than continuous reinforcement (Hall, Lindzey, and Gardner, 1998). The practical application of this law of behavior is that humans are seldom perfectly consistent about anything. Therefore, most human behavior is intermittently reinforced, and thus is harder to extinguish than might at first appear. This is especially true because, as modern behavior therapy and social learning theory recognize, the reinforcers may be remote from the immediate situation. A common example is parents' trying to extinguish (by some form of punishment) a behavior that is reinforced by the child's peer group. This only emphasizes the need for a complete assessment of the total situation before setting out on a course of behavior therapy.

Types of Clients for Whom Behavior Therapy is Appropriate

Like cognitive therapy, behavior therapy is highly directive. Persons who are uncomfortable submitting to the expertise and directions of the behavior therapist will likely either drop out of therapy or not successfully complete the tasks. That said, behavior therapy has demonstrated effectiveness with a very wide range of presenting problems and a very wide range of clients. Naturally, the behavior therapist will still apply the same skills of creating a therapeutic alliance, displaying empathy, and employing good communication skills (including problem-solving skills) as any other psychotherapist (Nichols and Schwartz, 1998).

Given that these techniques can work with almost any situation, there are a number of types of cases which, in this author's opinion, seem to be ideal for behavior therapy. They work well where the client is either not motivated or not able to do insight-based work. Often this author receives court-mandated clients. Seldom are these clients interested in "navel gazing." They want something which will get the courts off their backs. This author has also successfully resolved (using techniques discussed in this chapter) marital difficulties with clients whose intellectual functioning was definitely at the low end of average.

Behavior therapy also works well in cases where insight is not necessarily an issue. One common example of this latter condition in my practice is families who have a child with some form of attention-deficit disorder. Once the child is so-diagnosed, a physician will normally prescribe a psychostimulant such as methylphenidate (Ritalin) or Adderall. Unfortunately, many parents assume that the pill will "cure" the problem, when nothing could be further from the truth. The child, and the family, could tremendously benefit by adding behavior therapy to the drug therapy. The goal of family therapy would be to teach the child how to manage his or her behavior (e.g., tricks the child can employ to stay task-focused on tests in school).

Another very common use of behavioral therapy is helping parents gain control of children with conduct disorder or oppositional defiant disorder. In these cases, the child is seldom motivated to change or explore any intrapsychic "causes" of the behavior, even if she or he had the intellectual ability to do so. Techniques such as using a "token economy" (for example, poker chips) to provide immediate reinforcement for desired (e.g., cooperative) behaviors can produce real and relatively rapid change in these children - as long as the parents are consistent in applying the reinforcing and extinguishing (e.g., ignoring) behaviors.

Following the lead of Masters and Johnson, many sex therapists also use behavioral techniques for treating sexual dysfunction. Even in this era when former presidential candidates can tout the use of a pill to treat erectile dysfunction, the reality is that the vast majority of men and women with sexual dysfunctions can respond very positively to behavioral treatment (Nichols and Schwartz, 1998).

This author also uses behavioral therapy techniques as a part of an overall substance abuse treatment program in his outpatient clinic. The client and I jointly explore the conditioned stimuli for the substance use, and then employ a carefully designed regimen to help extinguish the old responses and condition new, more healthy responses to stimuli such as "Friday night" or "party" (two common triggers for substance abuse in many people).

Defining Change in Behavior Terms

The goal of behavior therapy is easily stated: To increase the number of desirable behaviors (as defined by the client) while eliminating the undesirable behaviors. Very closely related to this is altering the reinforcement schedules operating on the client by fostering positive behavior exchange, and reducing or eliminating aversive or coercive reinforcement (Nichols and Schwartz, 1998). These two statements point to a key skill the beginning behavior therapist must master - being able to state the client's goals in positive, rather than negative terms.

Often married couples, for example, will present themselves with behaviors they want their partner to stop doing. Ultimately, such a strategy will prove unsatisfying, even if successful, because it only eliminates the dissatisfiers in the relationship without simultaneously building in any new satisfiers. That is why change must always be defined in observable behavior terms, and in terms of what the client wants to experience rather than what the client wants to avoid.

Basic Behavior Therapy Techniques

Behavior therapy begins with carefully listening to the client's story. One difference from ordinary therapeutic listening, however, is that the behavior therapist is often more active. Since behavior therapists believe that symptoms are learned responses (often acquired and reinforced without deliberate effort), the counselor does not listen for any supposed underlying causes. Instead, the therapist guides the client to describe the problem in terms of stimulus (or trigger) and response (including reinforcement of the conditioned response behavior) (Nichols and Schwartz, 1998). Contrary to the stereotypes of detractors, behavior therapists may well be very empathetic and warm in their interviewing techniques. The simple reality is that they, like all other therapists, teach clients what is "important" in therapy by the questions they ask and the data to which they pay attention. As a part of this overall problem-defining phase of therapy, the therapist may ask the client to complete one or more assessment instruments to help further clarify the stimulus-reinforcement-response (S-R) sequences.

In behavioral terms, the overall analysis of S-R sequences is known as a "functional analysis of behavior," and it is one of the most crucial steps in the entire process of behavior therapy. Working with the client, the counselor carefully explores both the antecedents to and the consequences of the target behavior (the behavior to be changed). In other words, the counselor defines in observable terms the response to be modified, the stimuli (or triggers) that produce that response, and the reinforcers that maintain that response.

Once the counselor completes the functional analysis of the target behavior, the counselor and client establish a behavior contract to change that behavior. In this contract, the counselor defines what behaviors the client is to perform and what the reward (reinforcement) is to be for successful accomplishment. If the client is a couple or a family, the contract may well be in the form of contingency contract (Jacobson and Margolin, 1979). For example, Counselor Samuel Shmooze was working with Bill, Betty, and Ben, a family concerned about Ben's (the 10 year old's) after-school behavior.

T	So, our goal is that Ben will come home, and go out to play for no more than 30 minutes. At the end of 30 minutes, or before, and without being asked or reminded, Ben will come inside and start studying his school work until you call him for supper, Betty. This will apply even when he does not have new homework. Is that what you all agreed would help?
H, W, S	(in unison) Yes.
T	And how will you know you are studying correctly, Ben?
S	I guess I can read my science, history and English, and I can work problems in my math. I usually do that, anyway.
T	And Betty and Bill, will you accept that behavior as evidence that Ben is studying?
W	Oh, sure. I'd love to see him crack a book without having to threaten him.
T	Great. And when Ben successfully plays and comes in without being called, then studies until supper time, what will his reward be?
H	Betty and I have talked about this since last week. Ben really likes to play on his Play Station. So every

	night he does this he'll get an hour on his Play Station.
S	(Excitedly) On a school night! Like, wow!
T	And what happens if he does not successfully complete his assigned behavior?
H	We talked about that, too. In keeping with your suggestions last week, Betty and I will just ignore it. But no Play Station. He can try again the next day.

Counselor Shmooze and the family then continued to play out various "what-if" scenarios to help Ben learn the new, desired behavior sequence. Based on these "what-if" scenarios, the original contract may be modified to include more or different reinforcers. In addition to positive reinforcers (i.e., reward for desired behavior appearing), the contract may use negative reinforcement (i.e., reward for the target behavior not being present - such as giving a spouse who normally would verbally explode in a given situation a kiss for not verbally exploding in that situation) or punishment (i.e., aversive stimuli applied when the undesired behavior appears, such as a client who wants to stop smoking and who hates vacuuming the house agreeing to vacuum the entire house every time she/he smokes a cigarette). What is essential here is that all parties involved agree the reinforcers are appropriate for them and that they will abide by the contract.

Once the behavior contract is established, behavioral therapists may well employ cognitive and/or social learning techniques in moving client towards desired behaviors. Regardless of the specific intervention techniques, each session of behavior therapy will be marked by the therapist's careful analysis of the effectiveness of the intervention (always measured by actual, observable changes in behavior). Equally necessary is a re-evaluation of the original functional analysis of the target behavior to ensure the plan of therapy accurately conceptualizes both the antecedents and consequences of the target behavior. Once necessary changes are made to the treatment plan, the therapist then assigns new tasks to further the behavioral change. Therapy ends when the client achieves contracted-for behavioral goals.

Schedules of Reinforcement

Because behavior therapy believes that the consequences of behavior are far more influential than the antecedents, creating effective schedules of reinforcement are crucial for effective therapy. To be truly effective, these schedules of reinforcement must conform to two key principles of behavior therapy. First, as already mentioned, the reinforcement must be positive.

That is, it must provide something the clients want, not merely remove something they do not want. Helping clients frame their goal(s) in positive terms is absolutely crucial to effective behavior therapy.

The second key principle is that the schedule of reinforcement is tied to the individual client. That is, each schedule is unique. The reason for this is quite simple. Human behavior is, by all accounts, multiply determined, and thus what is reinforcing for one person may not be effective for another person. For example, Jane Bagodonuts may find being able to take a candlelight bubble bath with soft music very reinforcing while her son, Roger, would find that experience very boring. However, Roger would do almost anything to be able to spend a Friday night with his friends at the local shopping mall, while Jane would find a Friday night at the mall only slightly more desirable than a root canal. Obviously, this makes creating effective behavior contracts for couples or families a complex process, because each individual must have his/her own uniquely designed schedule of reinforcement.

There must also be provisions in the contract for reward given for progress toward the goal. In behavioral terms, this is known as "shaping behavior." Simply put, at the beginning the person receives a reward for even approximating the target behavior. As therapy progresses, the person must more and more closely perform the goal behavior to receive the reward until, at the end of therapy, the person is correctly performing the goal behavior. The schedule of reinforcement contained in the behavior contract must specify when (in behavior terms) each of these incremental milestones is reached and thus when a new level of behavior is necessary to receive the reward. In this author's experience, this is especially crucial in working with children. If they do not have very clear guidelines for "success," they will usually perceive the entire process as "unfair" and become uncooperative.

Conclusion

Conceptually, behavior therapy is very straightforward and simple. The most difficult part of using behavior therapy for the beginning counselor is listening carefully enough to accurately define the right stimuli for the current behavior, and then determining what reinforcement to apply to help extinguish the old response and condition the new response. Students who wish to dig a bit deeper will find a helpful summary in "Behavioral Family Therapy" by I.R.H. Falloon and "Behavioral Marital Therapy" by A. Holtzworth-Munroe and N.S. Jacobson. Both articles are in *Handbook of Family Therapy* edited by Gurman and Kniskern (1991).

Living Into the Lesson

1.   Assume you have a 12 year old only very recently diagnosed with Attention-Deficit Hyperactivity Disorder. The child is taking the medication as prescribed. Work with a group to design a behavioral training regimen the parents could implement and use. Use your own imagination about what might be reinforcing for this child, but make the stimulus-response-reward sequence logical and consistent.

2.   Assume your own eight year old child is refusing to do homework. Work with one other student to design a "poker chip reinforcement schedule." Decide what behaviors you want to reinforce, and what behavior will be required to receive a red, a white, or a blue chip. Then decide what these chips might be redeemed for.

3.   All behavior therapists agree that behavior is lawful, but not all would agree with Skinner that all behavior is as determined as the movement of billiard balls on a table. Take a position pro or con and stage a debate: Human free choice is merely an illusion. Be sure to state the empirical evidence for your position, pro or con.

4.   Interview someone who smokes at least 1 pack of cigarettes per day. Determine when they smoke and what they subjectively enjoy about the experience. Then, with a group of fellow students, determine a behavior therapy program that could help this "client" stop smoking (You do not have to actually have this person agree to stop for this exercise).

5.   One of the principles of behavior therapy is that employing a positive reinforcer is more powerful than simply removing punishment (an aversive stimulus). Discuss why this is so from your own experience.

6.   Assume that 10 year old Ben has test anxiety - that is, even when he has studied well he "freezes" on tests and fails the test because he cannot write what he knows. This test anxiety is not confined to one subject area in Ben's case. Design a schedule of systematic desensitization to help Ben be comfortable enough in test-taking situations to be able to write what he knows.

7.   Work with a colleague to design a schedule reinforcement for this marital therapy case.   During arguments Sean is often physical (pushing and grabbing, never hitting) with Jennifer, and Jennifer has occasionally responded in kind.   Most often, Jennifer simply shuts down and will not respond at all.   This only causes Sean to escalate his behavior in an attempt to connect with her.   Their goal is to solve problems more effectively.

8.   What makes "shaping behavior" work?   Why doesn't the person simply stop at the lowest level of behavior that produces a desired reward?

9.   Role-play with another student.   One of you is a client with a sexual dysfunction, the other is a behavior therapist.   Together, perform a functional behavior analysis of the dysfunction.   When you are satisfied you are finished, come out of your roles and discuss the process - what was helpful and what was not.   Then switch roles and repeat.

10.   One of this author's professors claimed, "Physical punishment is always the least effective means of producing [behavior] change.   However, some times it is the only way to produce change."   Do you agree?   Why/why not?   What might be the basis for this claim?

Chapter 8 - Depth Counseling Skills

If you hate a person, you hate something in him that is part of yourself. What isn't part of ourselves doesn't disturb us. - Herman Hesse

Psychotherapy has its roots in depth analysis. As any student of counseling and therapy knows, Sigmund Freud developed psychoanalysis, a style of therapy that dominated the field for nearly half a century. Jung, Adler, Erickson, Honey, and Sullivan are just a few of the greats whose styles of therapy relied on discovering the underlying, usually unconscious, dynamics of human behavior. In more recent years, Object Relations therapy has taken up this cause.

Yet depth psychotherapy has also fallen from favor in recent years, primarily for two reasons. First, there are few if any studies which verify the superiority of this style of therapy over other styles of therapy (Hall, Lindzey and Campbell, 1998). The concepts of all of these theories are framed in terms which make empirical verification difficult if not impossible. For example, Jung's concept of archetypes may make intuitive sense, but it is very difficult to measure with scientific precision. Similarly, all of these theories hold that attaining some form of insight is a necessary condition to being set free from the unconscious restrictions to healthy interaction (Nichols and Schwartz, 1998). Attaining insight is difficult to operationally define (i.e., define in observable terms) and therefore is difficult to measure. Given the current emphasis on empirically validated therapies, depth therapies seem weak at best.

As even their proponents will agree, depth psychotherapies often take years to achieve their results. That brings up the second reason they have fallen from favor. The modern domination of health care by managed care concerns dictates that therapy take place as quickly and efficiently as possible. In other words, managed care dictates that therapy end as soon as the immediate crisis is resolved. By contrast, depth therapies are just getting started at that point.

Despite these difficulties, some clients, in this author's experience, continue to expect and want to do the demanding work of depth therapy. Some of the newer therapies, such as Depth-Oriented Brief Therapy (DOBT) created by Bruce Ecker and Laurel Hulley (1996), make possible doing depth-oriented work in far less time than Freud, Adler, or Jung would have believed. Metasystems, too, builds on Adlerian therapy to create a brief depth-oriented therapy. For that reason, this chapter will begin with some Adlerian techniques, as an example of traditional depth therapy, and then conclude with the unique modifications offered by the Metasystems paradigm.

Types of Problems For Which Depth Counseling Is Best Suited

The founders of psychotherapy employed depth-oriented techniques with clients who had all sorts of disorders. Harry Stack Sullivan (1964), for instance, focused much of his work on people with schizophrenia. Freud documented work with a wide variety of clients, as did Adler and Jung. Kohut, a leading object-relations therapist, worked with "narcissistically disturbed" clients (Hall, Lindzey, and Campbell, 1998). On the surface, then, it would appear that depth therapy can work with almost anyone.

In this author's experience, it is not so simple. Depth psychotherapy is real work for the client and the therapist. Whatever the client's presenting problem, he or she has to be genuinely motivated toward change to do this much emotional work. A client of this author's expressed it well: Good depth psychotherapy is "like pulling tape off a hairy man's chest." Like birth pains, the end result may be worth it, but still it is not the sort of experience one will undertake casually. As already stated in this text, many people today are simply not that highly motivated. They want to solve the current problem, and then get back with everyday life. Before beginning a course of depth therapy, the counselor must clearly contract with the client that they want to face material they have not been willing to face up to this point. For example, this author's informed consent document warns all clients that even properly performed psychotherapy may "arouse feelings or memories that are uncomfortable and/or unpleasant" and that it may produce change "in unintended directions."

Depth therapy clients also need at least an average level of intelligence and ability to think abstractly. The second part of that clause is especially important. People who, for whatever reason, cannot or will not think abstractly will have a difficult time with the sundry projective and/or imaginative methods of depth therapy. The reason for this caution will become more clear as this chapter progresses.

Finally, the various codes of ethics require that clients understand the implications of their decisions about therapy, and that includes financial implications. Depth therapy, at least as it has traditionally been practiced, is not cheap. The client will need to feel comfortable about the financial obligation they may be incurring by setting out on a course of therapy which may well last a year or more.

Early Recollections

Adler believed, as did Freud, that many influences on personality, and thus on behavior, come from a person's early experiences in family (Hall, Lindzey, and Campbell, 1998). For that reason, one's earliest recollections of family life are often very helpful for the therapist's looking for the sources of the major themes of life (one's "style of life" in Adlerian terms - more on that later in this chapter).

Unlike traditional Freudian psychoanalysis, which relies on free associations to uncover unconscious materials and reveal psychic themes, Adlerian psychotherapy relies on skillful, detailed questioning about the person's earliest memories. Counselor Samuel Shmooze was using Adlerian therapy when he interviewed Pedro during this first session.

T   Tell me, Pedro, what's the very first thing you can remember?

C   About what?

T   Anything, anything at all. Just go as far back in your memory as you can and describe the first scene that pops into your mind.

C   [Long pause.] Well, the first thing that pops into my head is when I was about 5 years old. I was visiting my next door neighbor and I had this balloon, this helium-filled balloon, with me. I don't remember who gave me the balloon. Anyway, I was at the neighbor's house and I walked out on the front porch and the boy I was playing with told me to let go of the balloon. So I did. And when I saw my balloon fly away up into the sky I started to cry. I don't have a clue why I remember that.

T   So when you started to cry, what happened next?

C   Oh, I don't know. I probably went home and cried some more in my room.

T   Okay, and what happened next?

C   I don't remember.

T   It's okay. If you don't remember, tell me what you think probably happened.

C   Well, I guess I probably stayed in my room feeling really lousy, like a fool for letting go of my balloon. This is really silly.

T   No, Pedro, you're doing great. Please, keep going.

C   Well, I guess I probably cried myself out and then came out of my room and started playing again.

T   So no one ever came into your room to check on you or comfort you? You just had to take care of yourself?

C   Yeah, that's probably right. That's the way it usually was.

Two key points come from Counselor Shmooze's interview. First, in good Adlerian fashion, Shmooze is very respectful of Pedro. In fact, mutual respect between therapist and client (and within the client system) is the hallmark of Adlerian therapy (Sweeney, 1989). Specifically, Shmooze manifested this respect by accepting whatever Pedro wanted to offer. He let Pedro set the agenda, and then simply helped him fill in the details.

Secondly, Counselor Shmooze did not worry when Pedro could not remember. Probing for early recollections is not a search for truth in an absolute or forensic sense. Searching for the client's truth is all that counts. What matters is what the client remembers, not whether it ever objectively happened. In other words, it does not matter whether the balloon incident ever happened to Pedro. He "remembers" it, and therefore it is significant to him. It reveals a part of his basic assumptions about life.

This point is especially crucial for the therapist whose client may be presenting early recollections of sexual or physical abuse. Often clients who were abused as young children will not fully remember the incidents. They may have only vague, unformed images and feelings. For legal and ethical reasons, the counselor should never try to lead the client in recovering these lost memories by "filling in the blanks" (e.g., "Oh, did he come into your room and touch your privates?"). Like Shmooze did with Pedro, the counselor can only say, "That's okay. What do you think happened?"

Just as important, the counselor should never encourage the client to act on these early memories, even if they are clear and well formed. The many legal cases arising from the so-called "false memory syndrome" should caution any therapist, especially one with no specific training in resolving in adults the issues arising from being abused as a child, that memory can be unreliable as evidence in court. For effective Adlerian therapy, it does not matter if this abuse really happened. If the client believes it did happen, or it may have happened, the counselor simply focuses on the client's style of life - the client's living "as if" the events truly happened.

These early recollections are, for Adlerian therapists, both a means of joining with the client and a step in the assessment process. They constitute a very large part of the first stage of traditional Adlerian therapy (Sweeney, 1989). Depending on the course of therapy, in sessions after the first, the counselor may simply allow the client to begin with whatever early recollections jump to the front of consciousness at the moment, as Counselor Shmooze did with Pedro in this illustration, or the counselor may ask for more details and build up previous early recollections. Either way, at this point the counselor simply accepts and notes what the client presents, without adding any interpretation. That comes much later.

Family Constellation

Another part of the first stage of therapy is exploring the client's family constellation, and genograms (see Chapter 11) make an excellent tool for this task. Although genograms were not developed until decades after Adler's death, the theory behind them is consistent with Adler's insight that a person's place in the family constellation influences (NOT determines) the patterns of interactions which will affect his or her development.

Walter Toman (1993) is among those in recent years who has clearly delineated these influences. However, the beginning (and even advanced) therapist will do well to remember that these influences are exceedingly complex. Toman himself gives a formula: each person holds one of $n*2^{n-1}$ possible positions in his sibling configuration. For example, this author's wife was one of six children in her family of origin. She occupies one of $6*2^5$ (= 192) possible psychological positions in her family based on various arrangements of age and gender. In other words, real life is always more complex than the generalizations given in any text, including this one.

Generally, the oldest child is "king (or queen) for a day." At first they are the undisputed masters of the household, holding both parents' attention with every whimper. They tend to relate well to adults, because adults were their primary contacts very early in life. They also tend to strive for perfection as a goal. Whether this is a healthy or unhealthy striving will depend on many other factors.

Second children find someone is already in place when they arrive. No matter what they do, someone is older, bigger, smarter, and more privileged than they. Typically, second children will choose not to compete with the oldest child directly, but rather indirectly. For example, if the oldest child is a gifted athlete, the second child will perhaps excel in music or art. The second child's motto is like the old auto rental company's commercial: "We try harder."

If the second child becomes a middle child, she or he gets the worst of both worlds. They tend to become more independent, rebellious, sensitive, and overtly demanding of their parents attention (Sweeney, 1989). This is because the middle child still feels the competition of the older child before, and the arrival of the younger child who has stolen the favored position of "baby."

Youngest children do tend to stay the "baby" of the family. They know they have protectors in the form of older siblings and parents to care for them. This gives them the courage to try things out. Of course, the "baby" will often test this out by starting something with the middle child, and then watching the older sibling and/or parents run to protect the youngest.

Only children have no sibling position (Toman, 1993). Oldest children, of course, start life as an only child, but they are eventually dethroned. Only children never face this change in family constellation. They continue to enjoy the focus and attention of their parents. As a result, they relate well with adults (and thus, later, authority figures) but much less well with peers.

In examining the family constellation, the counselor will note the age differences and the genders of the siblings. The parents' birth order is also a factor. Generally speaking, a parent will relate best to the child whose birth order is the same as the parent's. For example, this author is the older brother of a sister. My father was the oldest brother of brothers and a sister. Our similarity of birth order meant he could relate well to both my sister and I, because he had experienced something very similar while growing up. By contrast, my mother was an only child. She could never understand either of us, because she had never experienced living with siblings.

In determining sibling influences, two generalities can be helpful. First, children who are closest in age will have the most influence on each other. This is true even when they do not particularly feel close. The influence may be one of reaction instead of attraction. Second, children who are more than six years apart should be considered as though they were separate sibling groups. For example, this author had a client who was the youngest brother of sisters and brothers (five siblings in all). However, his next oldest sibling (a sister) was 10 years older, so in reality he could be considered as though he were an only child.

Developing the family constellation is just one way to use early recollections. The counselor might ask the client who taught him or her about sex. If the client is female, a very important issue is who taught her about menstruation. Who ate with whom? Who in the extended family was significant, and in what ways were they significant? Who could the client always count on - in both the positive and the negative sense of that phrase? What losses or changes were there in the family constellation? At least for many middle class families pets should certainly be considered under changes in the family constellation. I know one client who always felt she played second place in the family to the family dog. These are just some of the relevant issues a counselor can explore via the client's early recollections.

Lifestyle Analysis

The second stage of Adlerian counseling consists of interpretation. All during the first stage the therapist has been gathering data which will help uncover the unconscious. Often formal questionnaires or other instruments are used to help focus the material from the early recollections, especially material about the family constellation. In addition, Adlerian therapists use direct observation of the client, especially if "client" happens to be a whole family.

Based on all of this data, the Adlerian therapist can move deductively from the specifics to the underlying unconscious style of life which has motivated the person's behavior. Adler believed that most people form their basic life position, their basic life style, by age six (although Adler also believed that people could change their life position whenever they became aware of the need to change and were sufficiently motivated to do so) (Sweeney, 1989). For example, some people become "Getters." They believe that they belong (one of the basic psychological needs, according to Adler) only to the extent that they can "get" from others. These people live by the motto, "What's mine is mine and what's yours is mine." Some get by manipulation or seduction, while others (obviously this would include criminals) get by force and other threats.

Some people are "Victims." They believe, unconsciously of course, that this world is a hostile place, that it is a dog-eat-dog existence. They need someone to persecute them to "prove" what a dangerous place this is, and therefore to justify why they have not done more in life (i.e., why they have short-circuited the drive for superiority). Victims will unconsciously repeatedly put themselves into harm's way. If they cannot find someone who will persecute them, they will set someone up to fulfill that role. Many substance abusers operate from this life position. Their motto is, "It's not my fault. It's _____ fault. If it weren't for _____ I would have....."

Other people are "Martyrs." Martyrs find meaning in their suffering, too, but in their case it is accepted and chosen. Spouses of substance abusers are often Martyrs. Like Victims, Martyrs have short-circuited the normal drive for superiority, but in their case instead of opting for helplessness they opt for an attitude of "I suffer better than thou." Also like Victims, Martyrs need someone to play the role of persecutor. That makes distinguishing these two lifestyles difficult at times. One helpful way this author has discovered is to look at the major life tasks (work, friendship, love, and spirit). Martyrs are often functioning at least acceptably in most areas, confining their suffering to specific tasks, while Victims tend to be more global in their ability to "snatch defeat out of the jaws of victory." In other words, Martyrs still seek superiority, but they seek it via suffering at someone's hands, while Victims avoid superiority all together.

These life positions are only illustrative of the possibilities. The skillful Adlerian therapist will assemble all the facts, build a case, and present it like a good detective. When the client can say, with a sudden burst of insight, "Yes! Yes! You understand! That's me!", the therapist knows the interpretation has been successful.

Private Fiction; "Fictional Finalism"

One of Adler's most basic concepts is the unity of the personality (Lundin, 1989). This is true both in terms of the personality as it exists now, and as the personality exists across time. One of the functions that keeps the personality unified is the person's "private fiction." The person's private fiction is the set of unconscious beliefs which both create the unconscious life position, and which generate the person's day-to-day actions. Adler called these beliefs "fiction" because it does not matter if they are objectively true or not. For example, many people believe "Crime does not pay." Despite the fact that some criminals do profit by their crimes and some even escape punishment, these people continue to act "as if" their belief were true and are therefore genuinely surprised at disconfirming data.

Obviously, there are many similarities between this part of Adlerian psychology and the core beliefs of cognitive therapy. Some Adlerians, such as this author, would even claim that Adler is the unacknowledged father of cognitive therapy. Whatever the case, the similarities between the two allow many of the techniques of cognitive therapy to be easily adapted and used by Adlerian therapists to uncover the person's private logic.

One major difference, however, is the Adlerian emphasis on teleology, on goals. Adler believed that all behavior is goal-directed, and thus what the person is moving toward is far more influential in determining behavior than the past "causes" of the behavior (Lundin, 1989). A practical implication of this difference is that Adlerians will spend much more time interpreting the current private logic and its future consequences than trying to uncover "schema" or "core beliefs" (to use Cognitive terms).

Counselor Shmooze continued his work with Pedro. After ten sessions, he interpreted to Pedro his style of life: "I am no durned good. I deserve all the bad that happens to me because I am flawed to my very core." They spent all of session eleven looking at that interpretation and testing it against Pedro's experience, both the data that Pedro had revealed in the previous sessions and the new data Pedro added. By the end of the session, Pedro was able to see how he had lived his life by that script and agreed that Shmooze's interpretation was accurate.

123

Session twelve was a transition session, a session moving from interpretation (the second stage of Adlerian therapy) to reorientation (the third and final stage of therapy). Shmooze wanted Pedro to see how his private logic influenced his goals.

> T   Pedro, I'm puzzled. You really have done very well this week thinking about your life position. How does your obvious success fit with your position that you have proven so often that you're no good?
>
> C   Well, I'm not stupid, man.
>
> T   I know you're not. You've proven that to me every time I have met you. But I have also heard you tell me how you managed to "snatch defeat out of the jaws of victory" repeatedly in your life. You didn't do that this week. How did you do something so different?
>
> C   I guess I'm just tired of feeling bad about me.
>
> T   Good. So what would you have to believe about you to start feeling tired of feeling bad?
>
> C   I don't know. I just don't want to feel bad any more.
>
> T   I understand that. But we have already seen that your life position made it absolutely essential that you do things to make you feel bad about you, no matter how much you hated it. So what's going to have to change for you to start acting differently, to start acting like you like you, at least just a little?
>
> C   I guess if I really liked me, I'd quit not going to work just because I got mad at the boss. That's gotten me fired several times. If I liked me, I wouldn't need to get myself fired to prove how no- good I really am.
>
> T   Great work. So what would you do instead?
>
> C   Well, if I liked me, I'd go to work even if the boss is a -- hole.

Shmooze continued working with Pedro to help him define his goal and to make his new script, his new private logic, explicit. A part of this process was helping Pedro identify people he can use to help him reinforce his new private logic and support him in his new goals.

The Metasystems Variation

Since Metasystems is grounded in Adlerian therapy, the various techniques of Adlerian therapy are very appropriate for this style of therapy.

One of those is the technique that Shmooze employed in making his interpretation to Pedro - a technique traditionally known among Adlerians as "spitting in the soup" (Sweeney, 1989). This technique is especially appropriate for self-defeating behavior such as Pedro's. Pedro had operated from a Victim life position, and thus blamed all his problems on everyone else - cruel father, unreasonable boss, nagging wife, etc. Shmooze simply revealed his underlying private logic. As the name of the technique implies, making the covert overt does not prevent the client from continuing the behavior, but it certainly does make it less enjoyable.

Another Adlerian technique Metasystems frequently employs is antisuggestion. Decades after Adler, the Strategic school of family therapy called this "paradox" or "prescribing the symptom." This works well for many social and goal anxieties. The therapist may set up a role play in session, for example, and invite a client with test anxiety to get as anxious as possible and come into the next session to take a test. The unspoken message of the antisuggestion is, "This behavior is completely under your control." Most clients get it, and are then ready to explore the private logic which makes their past behavior necessary and reasonable.

Where Metasystems parts with traditional Adlerian therapy is in using a variety of Gestalt techniques to access the private logic and life position much more rapidly than early recollections, dream interpretation, or life style analysis. There is certainly no incompatibility between these newer techniques and the traditional Adlerian theory, so they integrate very well and allow Metasystems to join other modern theories like Depth-Oriented Brief Therapy (Ecker and Hulley, 1996) in producing deep change very quickly.

Essential to any of the Gestalt techniques, and therefore the Metasystems' adaptation of Adlerian therapy, is creating a direct experience of the private logic, rather than simply talking about it. Shmooze in working with Pedro used early recollections and dream interpretation to talk about his past and therefore uncover Pedro's private logic. He could have, for example, had Pedro talk directly to his father by talking to an empty chair and have Pedro imaginatively speak out loud the conversation. One caution the beginning therapist must be aware of is that the client using this technique will often slip out of the direct experience and flip up into their head. Often, they will start using phrases such as, "And then I would say..." or "And then they would say...." The therapist has to bring the person back to a direct experience: "Don't tell me what you would say. I'm not here. Tell him."

Often clients will find a direct confrontation, even one that happens only in the imagination, too threatening. In those situations, this author often uses the "television technique." I have the client imagine a television set in the room and have them look at the television. Playing on the television is a movie of their life. I have them describe the action on the screen. The power of this technique should be obvious. How often do sports fans, for example, watch a game on the television set and jump and cheer (or boo and hiss) as though they were actually in the stadium participating in the event? How often do people watch an action adventure movie and jump (at least internally) when something jumps out at the hero? Just as watching a television movie keeps us, the audience, one step removed from the action on the screen, imagining one's life as a movie on television provides the client one step of emotional distance, and thus makes viewing the life script safer.

Still another very powerful technique for uncovering private logic is the sentence completion. The key to effectively using this technique is peeling away the various levels of logic from the conscious down to the deeper levels of the unconscious by following up each client statement with another sentence completion. If Counselor Shmooze had used this technique with Pedro, the conversation might have gone something like this.

C   I don't know. I try, but it just seems like I can never do anything right.
T   So, you can never do anything right. Try this for me, please: Even though I try, I can never do anything right because...
C   ...Because I manage to mess up.
T   Good. Keep going. I manage to mess up, even though I try not to, because...
C   ...Because I guess I just can't do anything right.
T   Great. Keep going. It's important for me to believe that I can't do anything right because...
C   ...Because if I believed I could do something right, I'd have to start doing it.

One key to making this technique work, other than the therapist's persistence, is the therapist's using the clients own words and images, with no interpretation. The purpose is to reveal the client's logic in the terms that fit the client's own experience. This technique also reveals the goal-directed nature of the client's behavior directly, without the therapist ever having to "teach" any theory. The direct, experiential access is what is so powerful, not the "head stuff."

A final Metasystems adaptation (for this chapter, at least) of Adlerian therapy is what Ecker and Hulley (1996) call "utilizing unexpected resistance." As already stated, the hallmark of Adlerian therapy is its

126

respectful stance, so Adlerian therapy accepts so-called client resistance as actually just a coherent expression of the client's life style. When a client who has been working well suddenly hits an emotional wall (sometimes accompanied by bodily sensations) or simply slips into a "fog" of unknowing, of remoteness from the material, the first step for the therapist is to simply state what she or his is observing.

C   Uh, I don't know. I just don't seem to be able to go there.
T   Okay, so all of a sudden you have sorta entered a fog and you just don't seem to be able to go any further.
C   Right. I don't know why.

The second step is to encourage this dissociation and actually encourage the client to do some more of it. This is a good place to use the television technique or some variation. Whatever technique the therapist chooses to suggest, the therapist wants to very clearly, perhaps even explicitly, acknowledge that the client knows the dissociated state is for the client's own safety, and that they will look at the threatening material only from that position of safety until the client is ready and able to move on. For example, the therapist might ask the client what they were going to experience if they had not gone into the dissociated state. Or the therapist might encourage the client to stay safe behind their wall, but to climb up a ladder (or use a periscope, depending on how much threat the wall is protecting the client from) and look over the top to see what the threat is. The third step comes when the client is able to identify the experience she or he was trying to avoid. Then the therapist asks, "What makes it so important to avoid ...?" Therapy continues from that point using any of the usual techniques.

Conclusion

All forms of depth therapy are interested in the client's early experiences, and all forms of depth therapy believe that the client's emotional experiences provide as valuable data as the client's cognitive insights. Traditional forms of depth therapy, like Freudian, Adlerian, and Jungian, use dream analysis among other techniques to access this emotional material. Newer forms, like Metasystems and Depth-Oriented Brief Therapy, rely on creating experiences in the therapy session. However one does it, doing depth therapy is hard work for client and therapist alike. By definition this style of therapy uncovers unconscious ("Back Stage" in the Metasystems language) material which is so important to the client that it had to be hidden from view. That makes bringing it out on "Front Stage" for the client to look at under the glare of the "klieg lights" of the therapy process uncomfortable at best.

The point of doing so is, of course, that depth therapy, like all forms of therapy, aims at changing the behavior of the client. In fact, as I teach my supervisees, any process which does not result in behavior change is entertainment, not therapy. The various styles of therapy differ in their beliefs about how change is produced, but they all agree that is the measure of success.

Those who want to work in Adlerian therapy must be comfortable working with emotional issues from a very respectful, democratic stance. Students who want to learn more should find a supervisor skilled in Adlerian therapy. Reading about Adlerian therapy is like reading about being pregnant. The cognitive data may be totally correct, but it still does not do justice to the experience.

Living Into the Lesson

1. Take a position pro or con this statement and stage a debate: "Depth therapy has not been scientifically proven effective, and therefore has no place in modern mental health." Research the evidence for your position, whatever it is, and bring that to the debate.

2. Think of one person (a client or simply someone you know) who you believe would be a candidate for depth therapy. What makes this person a suitable candidate? Now think of a person who you believe would <u>not</u> be a suitable candidate. What makes them unsuited for depth therapy?

3. Get with one other student and take turns. Go as far back into your memory as you possibly can and come up with the first very early recollection that pops into your head. Tell the story to your partner, and then give your own interpretation of how this illustrates at least part of your private logic. While you are talking, your partner is to actively listen but provide no interpretation. When you have finished, swap roles.

4. Create a genogram of your family of origin (see Chapter 11 if you need help). Get with one other person and use the material in this chapter to analyze your style of life. What were the family secrets? What were the gender, sociocultural, and family rules? What were the family rituals? What "ghosts" influenced your family for better or worse?

5. Using Toman's formula, calculate the number of possible sibling positions in your own family of origin. How did you come to occupy your unique place in your family constellation?

6. Taking the material from question four, how are you different from the "you" in your family of origin? How are you similar? How does your experience fit with Adler's concept of the unity of personality across time?

7. Do you believe that memories, especially traumatic memories, can be lost to conscious awareness and then later come back? Why or why not? How does Adlerian therapy, with its emphasis on early memories, deal with this issue?

8.   What goals have you striven for in your past? What goals are you working on right now? Speculate how your life might have been different if you had chosen other goals. How does your experience prove or disprove Adler's contention that behavior is more determined by what is before us (i.e., teleology, our goals) than by what is behind us?

9.   List some of your core "Front Stage" beliefs - your conscious private fiction. As you look at your list, what themes do you see? What do these Front Stage beliefs reveal about your Back Stage private fiction? How does this fit with the results of your life style analysis you did in question four?

10.   Think back to some time when someone "spit in your soup." How did you react? Did you change your behavior, did you try harder to prove your previous position, or what?

11.   Role play this situation with a partner. You are very nervous with the opposite sex. After you are firmly in your role, have your partner give you an antisuggestion. What happens?

12.   Use the television technique to visualize changing one part of your life you would really like to change. Be sure to get into your "movie" - get emotionally involved.

INTERPERSONAL COUNSELING SKILLS

Chapter 9 - Psychoeducational Approaches

"When you believe in yourself, the power behind you is greater than any task in front of you."
- Richard L. Weaver II.

In my years as a supervisor of therapists, I have found that most new counselors and therapists tend to gravitate toward psychoeducational approaches. That is quite understandable. These approaches tend to replicate, at least to some degree, the student's own academic experience. The commercially available approaches often have books for both leader and participant, lesson plans and learning objectives for the leader, and teaching resources (e.g., video tapes, handouts, etc.). The beginning, middle, and end of the process is very clear-cut.

Certainly these are very useful approaches. Indeed, there is a growing movement among some segments of the mental health community which believes that mental health professionals ought to be doing much more preventive therapy and spend less time "picking up the pieces" after people have developed problems. For example, Diane Sollee, a marriage and family therapist, "dropped out" of the therapy movement to found the Coalition for Marriage, Family, and Couple Education, an organization totally dedicated to providing psychoeducational interventions. Many renowned researchers have joined the Coalition and push their materials at annual conferences for therapists who want to provide their clients researched-based psychoeducational interventions. Students who want to learn more about these approaches, including the many which are not included in this chapter, will find the Coalition web site, www.smartmarriages.com, a good starting point.

Since many of these programs are commercial products, one disclaimer seems in order. This author is making no attempt to evaluate or rate any of these programs. I am including here only programs with which I am personally familiar, so inclusion does not imply endorsement. Other programs may be just as good or even better. These programs are included in this chapter simply to illustrate the types of programs which are available and the way they work. Most, if not all, of these programs require specialized training to be able to use them. Therefore, students who wish to add psychoeducational approaches to their own toolbox should investigate the many options and select the ones they feel most compatible with.

Types of Situations Where These Are Appropriate

Sometimes all a client needs is a little information or some new skills. These clients are obvious candidates for one of the numerous intervention programs. In addition, many couples or individuals could potentially benefit from one of the myriad prevention programs. These people do not yet have conflicts, and may, with proper instruction, never develop problems. Indeed, as the old saying goes, "An ounce of prevention is worth a pound of cure."

The medical profession typically distinguishes three levels of prevention. Primary prevention aims at deterring the development of some sort of disorder. One example of a primary prevention program might be a parenting education program for new parents. The goal would be to teach the new parents the skills they will need to do an effective job of parenting long before problems develop. Secondary prevention seeks to reduce the harmful effects of a disorder that have already developed. Most traditional therapy would fall into this category, as would most of the psychoeducational intervention programs. Tertiary prevention focuses on chronic disorders and provides resources to help the person cope effectively with the disorder. In this case, the goal is to prevent either a reoccurrence of the crisis phase of the disorder or the development of secondary problems related to the original disorder. Support groups such as Alcoholics Anonymous and NAMI consumer groups would be examples of tertiary prevention from a mental health perspective (Thomas, 1997).

One key to using the psychoeducational materials effectively, then, is to decide at which level of prevention you, the counselor, are trying to focus your efforts. That will tell you who should be included. One common problem, for example, is that couples with troubled marriages often seek out marriage enrichment or marriage encounter programs, and then they go away dissatisfied with the lack of results. The real trouble may not be with the program itself but with the couples' expectations. Couples with troubled marriages require secondary prevention, while most marriage enrichment or marriage encounter programs are structured to be primary prevention. So, first the counselor will need to carefully screen group participants to ensure that the needs of the participants and the structure of the group are a good fit.

A second pre-group activity is to decide whether the group is to be primarily a task group or a process group. While it is true that most of the commercially available psychoeducational programs are already slanted one way or the other, the counselor will need to know what she or he is trying to accomplish to select the most efficient materials to help meet the desired goal. Task groups are, as the name implies, aimed at achieving some task.

The task might be the mastery of a certain set of skills or the development of a new set of behaviors. Process groups, on the other hand, tend to be more open-ended. These groups are about process - about the interactions among the group members. This author often uses debriefing groups to help local emergency responders (police, fire, ambulance) process their feelings following a particularly disturbing disaster, such as a house fire where children are killed. These groups are process groups, because the responders do not learn new skills, they "just" get to talk.

A third pre-group activity is for the counselor to study group dynamics. Groups, like families, often behave with a life of their own. Unlike families or other ongoing groups, however, the vast majority of psychoeducational groups come together for a specific purpose and for a fixed period of time. Theses differences make the dynamics of groups very different from typical family functioning. While a full discussion of group dynamics is far beyond the scope of this text (and is, very appropriately, often the subject of a full semester's course), a very cursory review of the normal development of any group seems in order.

The first stage of most groups is "forming." At this stage group members are relying on safe, well-rehearsed behaviors. They are getting to know each other and the expectations of the group leader. The second stage is "storming." Conflict may develop over any of a number of presenting issues, but the real issue (from a Metasystems perspective) is the group members' trying to discover what it takes to belong to this group. The group leader must be prepared for this development and model both effective listening and effective problem-solving skills. The third stage is "norming." At this stage group members are beginning to trust one another. Creativity tends to be high because members tend to feel good about their relationships with one another. The fourth stage of development is "performing." Not all groups reach this stage, but those who do are exceptionally productive. The final stage is "adjourning." Group members have to dissolve the interpersonal bonds they formed and part company (Tuckman, 1965).

Prevention Programs

Since the 1970s, numerous studies have consistently shown that distressed marriages are overly reliant on negative communication styles. In other words, distressed couples are more likely to send negative messages to each other and to perceive their partner's behavior as negative. True to a systems understanding, these same persons are more likely to respond to a perceived-negative message with a negative message of their own. Thus, distressed couples create a vortex of negativity which can quite literally suck the life out of the relationship (Levy, Womboldt, & Fiese, 1997). Most of the prevention programs for couples build on this wealth of data and assume (with good empirical support) that changing the negative communication and conflict resolution style to a more positive one will create a healthier and more satisfying relationship.

Howard Markman and Scott Stanley, professors at the University of Denver, and their colleagues applied these findings to develop PREP (Prevention and Relationship Enhancement Program - see www.prepinc.com for more information). PREP explicitly aims at both primary and secondary prevention. For primary prevention, PREP would be useful for premarital couples or for marriage enrichment/marriage education programs. For secondary prevention, PREP can be taught and employed with individual couples as part of the course of therapy.

In looking at the factors which predict relationship distress and divorce, Markman and Stanley make a distinction between "static" factors, which are difficult if not impossible to change after marriage (factors such as having divorced parents, living together before marriage, being previously divorced, having children from a previous relationship, and marrying at a very young age), and "dynamic" factors, which can be changed if the couple is willing to work at it (factors such as negative styles of talking and fighting, difficulty communicating well, trouble handling disagreements as a team, and unrealistic expectations about marriage). PREP specifically addresses the dynamic factors through twelve hours of mini-lectures, discussions, and skill practice sessions.

For example, one of the skills PREP teaches couples is identifying four key warning signs of relationship trouble: dismissing the partner's ideas, discounting the partner's personhood, defensiveness in relationships (as evidenced by expecting a negative interaction and reacting to the expectation as though it were reality), and emotional withdrawal (e.g., giving the partner the "silent treatment"). Then PREP teaches couples a specific speaker-listener technique during which the one speaking literally holds a small piece of linoleum tile ("the floor"). When the speaker finishes, he or she literally "passes the floor" to the listener, who then summarizes what she or he heard the speaker say. After the original speaker confirms that the message was correctly heard, the former listener assumes the speaker role and the process continues.

In addition to teaching communication and conflict resolution strategies, PREP includes material on forgiveness, religious beliefs and practices, fun, and expectations. PREP is one of the few programs this author is familiar with to offer both secular and Christian versions of its material [Dr. Susan Heitler's "The Power of Two" (www.therapyhelp.com) is the only other program to offer both versions I am aware of].

One example is a case from the author's own practice which illustrates the power of PREP. Jim and Kathy had been married about seven years and had lived together for three years prior to that. Their relationship was satisfactory, according to both their reports, during the years of cohabitation, but shortly after they married they began to bicker over almost every topic. When they came to marital therapy, they were both very discouraged about the future of their relationship because, as Jim expressed it, they could not even talk about the weather without starting a fight.

I taught them the speaker-listener technique and we practiced that technique in session. For a short while, things seemed to be getting better. They even decided to go out to eat as a "date," the first time they had "dated" each other in years. Unfortunately, at the restaurant things began to unravel very quickly, and their old relationship patterns came roaring back. Jim became so angry he got up and left the stunned Kathy sitting in the restaurant with no meal, no money, and no way home. Jim jumped in his car and, according to his report, "peeled rubber" out of the restaurant parking lot headed he did not know where. He had only gone a few blocks when he realized what he was doing, so he turned the car around, returned to the restaurant, and walked back to the table where Kathy was still sitting, trying to stifle her tears. Jim sat down quietly, picked up the menu and handed it to Kathy, and softly said, "You've got the floor." That was the break through. They talked through their problems and ended the evening with some of the best physical and emotional connecting in years, according to Kathy.

Couples Communication Program (www.couplecommunication.com) is one of the oldest and best researched programs currently available. Dr. Sherrod Miller and his associates at the University of Minnesota Family Study Center developed the concepts and began marketing the program in 1972. Since then it has been updated and revised as new research and teaching methods became available.

Originally, Couples Communication was grounded in general systems and communication theories. The current version makes extensive use of constructionist theories, as well as insights from psychology about perception and cognition. Like PREP, it is extensively researched and empirically verified as useful for its clients. The primary difference is in emphasis. Markman and Stanley were impressed by the negative impact of conflict resolution on marriage, so they concentrated on an effective means of problem solving and dealing with anger. Miller and his associates, grounded as they were (and continue to be) in communication theory chose to emphasize basic communication skills. Both programs do an excellent job of presenting the full range of skills necessary. Again, the difference is primarily in emphasis.

Couples Communication is best known for the Awareness Wheel, a means of visualizing (and with some of the new teaching techniques kinesthetically feeling) the various processes involved in an issue's becoming conscious in our awareness. The Awareness Wheel also helps couples learn about and apply modern psychological insights concerning emotion and motivation. The Listening Cycle, which teaches "active listening", a skill similar to PREP's speaker-listener technique, gives couples tools to build empathy and a helping relationship, rather than an oppositional one.

Couples Communication is taught in two modules, Couple Communication I (CC I) and Couple Communication II (CC II). CC I usually involves four two-hour sessions. CC II, which builds on and expands CC I, takes five two-hour sessions. While the Couples Communication material is designed for primary prevention use, this author can testify that it can indeed be used for secondary prevention.

As an illustration of using the CC material in therapy, this author was working with Barbara, a single-parent mother, and her son, Scott, a 10 year old boy diagnosed with Attention Deficit Disorder. Since the CC material includes mats with the Awareness Wheel and the Listening Cycle on them, I had used these mats to teach skills to the mother and her son to help them with their communication problems (the presenting issue for therapy). In every session, I got the mats out and placed them on the floor, whether I planned to use them or not. One session Scott was becoming particularly frustrated with his mother. There had been a problem at school, and Barbara was more inclined to believe the teachers than her son. In frustration, Scott spontaneously jumped up and began stomping around the Awareness Wheel mat, pausing at each division of the wheel to talk about that part of his awareness of the problem. When he finished with his intentions, he stopped and looked at his mother. Barbara sat looking blankly at Scott for several minutes. Finally, she stood up and moved to the Listening Cycle mat. As she stepped on the Summarizing line, she did a masterful job of paraphrasing all that Scott had said. They continued to "dance" around the mats for the rest of the session, and ended the session with no further intervention from me but well satisfied with the solution they reached.

A different type of prevention program is needed for parenting skills. Since the Metasystems model is grounded in Adlerian therapy, quite naturally this author gravitates toward Systematic Training for Effective Parenting (STEP - published by American Guidance Service Company [800-328-2560]). STEP materials are based in the classic book by Rudolph Driekurs, *Children: The Challenge*. Driekurs was the man who popularized Adler in the United States, and whose theoretical work undergirds many parenting programs today.

Based as it is in Adlerian thought, STEP teaches a mutually respectful style of democratic parenting. Like PREP and the other programs, it uses a series of mini-lectures, discussions, videos, and skill practice sessions to help parents learn the various skills required to make mutually respectful parenting a reality. Although there is some flexibility in the schedule, usually this author follows a six-week format, with each session taking two hours. Like PREP, STEP comes in both secular and Christian versions.

There are two key concepts in STEP (and STEPTeen, the version of the material which uses illustrations drawn from typical teenage behavior which often provides challenges for parents). The first key concept is the four mistaken beliefs which underlie all misbehavior. Adler taught that belonging is an essential psychological need in all humans. These mistaken beliefs are distorted notions about what it takes to belong: I only belong to the extent that I get attention; I only belong to the extent that I have power; I only belong to the extent that I can get revenge; and I only belong to the extent that I can play helpless and get people to wait on me.

Once parents become adept at identifying which of the mistaken beliefs is motivating their child's misbehavior, and how their response is unwittingly making the undesired behavior worse, parents move on to the second key concept: applying natural and logical consequences. STEP does not believe in punishment, that is, applying some deterrent to undesired behavior. Instead, STEP teaches parents to allow children, to the maximum extent possible, to learn from experiencing the consequences of their own choices. Instead of fighting with children over meal time (or bending one's self to fit the children's whims about meals), STEP coaches parents to allow children who refuse to come when called or who refuse to eat what is served to learn from the natural consequence of hunger. Instead of battling with children who can not seem to get ready for school on time, STEP coaches parents to allow them to learn from the natural consequence of going to school with teeth unbrushed or clothes not fully put together.

One of the real strengths of a STEP group is that the parents help teach each other. As each parent experiences some successes and shares those with the other parents in the group, the group members become excited and begin to creatively think of new options for their own situations. Group leaders should realize that STEP is intended to be primary prevention. However, in this author's experience, few parents volunteer to come to a parenting class until they have begun to have problems. Therefore, the group leader should be skilled at and prepared for doing group therapy. Fortunately, the Adlerian background makes transitioning from teaching and coaching to doing therapy relatively easy.

Intervention Programs

As this chapter has already indicated, most, if not all, of the prevention programs can be used as part of a therapeutic intervention. In addition to these, there are a number of psychoeducational approaches which are specifically intended to be part of an intervention. Therapy games are very common examples of this type of tool. The author's counseling center employs a number of these games, primarily with elementary aged children and others for whom verbal communication is difficult. A favorite with my staff is "The Anger Solution Game." As players move around the board, they are faced with various situations. Through their decisions, they learn to choose solutions to anger-provoking situations which can lead to success (defined as not getting stuck in the Victim Cycle or in an anger cycle). Another favorite is "My Positive Change Card Game." This is a card game designed for oppositional children. Cards depict common challenges and offer some behavioral and cognitive coping strategies. By discussing the situation and contrasting the proposed solution with the child's own normal solution, children learn to recognize their negative thoughts and behavior. Then they can come up with more constructive solutions to difficult situations. A game junior high and high school age clients can relate to is the "Imaginiff Game." This game gives players an opportunity to explore their feelings and preconceptions about people they know well - their parents, for example. The player who gives the most popular answer gets to move his or her game piece to the center of the board.

Many therapy groups are, at core, psychoeducational. A common style of doing substance abuse groups, for example, is to begin each group with a mini-lecture about a particular aspect of the substance abuse. The rest of the time the group members apply the cognitive material to their own situations.

This author recently conducted a smoking cessation group in conjunction with a local physician. The physician managed the anti-anxiety medications that many members required and prescribed nicotine patches if necessary. She also tracked their physical improvement through other aspects of the program. I conducted eight group sessions, each with a specific focus. The first, for example, introduced the concept of stimulus-response conditioning to the group. That filled twenty of our 90 minutes. The balance of the time group members identified their "triggers" for smoking and made plans to eliminate those triggers. At a later session I discussed relapse prevention, and again group members had to talk about times they had lapsed, or been tempted to, and what had actually happened during those times.

Another group therapy series this author conducted was for parents facing divorce. The purpose of this group was to teach the parents the effects of the divorce on their children and some behaviors the parents could employ to minimize the harmful effects. In this particular group, the educational content was dominant. The application came, for the most part, through private journaling and other home work because, by definition, those in this group were too angry with their spouse to have a constructive conversation.

Tertiary prevention can bring big benefits, but these are hard to measure because at least some damage is already done. It is hard to empirically verify that the intervention "made less" some damage which has not happened yet. Still, tertiary prevention measures are useful.

A classic example of this kind of prevention is Alcoholics Anonymous (www.alcoholics-anonymous.org). Membership in AA is open to anyone who believes she or he has a problem with alcohol; one need not be medically diagnosed as "alcoholic." Some meetings are open meetings, that is, they are open to therapy professionals and others who want to see what an AA meeting is all about. Other meetings are closed meetings, that is, they are open only to AA members. The local AA service center will gladly provide any therapist a list of local AA meetings, including place, date, and time, and whether the meeting is open or closed.

All AA groups follow the Twelve Steps, and most follow the Twelve Traditions. One of those Traditions is that AA groups are strictly non-sectarian. Another is that AA groups are strictly self-supporting. This non-sectarian stance has given rise to numerous off-shoots which define the Higher Power in specifically religious terms. This author is familiar with Christian, Buddhist, and Muslin variants.

Of course, many other support groups exist. Narcotics Anonymous is patterned after AA and has as its mission assisting those with a drug abuse problem. Weight Watchers, TOPS and other weight-management groups help many people struggling with their weight. NAMI (the National Alliance for the Mentally Ill) offers separate support groups for "consumers" (those diagnosed with a mental disorder) and for family members. Of course, these are only a very few of the possibilities. The bottom line is each therapist should learn about the options in his or her own area and use these resources to extend the power of the therapy room into places the therapist often cannot go.

One final example of intervention programs for this chapter is ENRICH (Evaluating and Nurturing Relationship Issues, Communication & Happiness) and MATE (Mature Age Transition Evaluation), both from Life Innovations (www.lifeinnovations.com). Both, along with the other tools in the PREPARE/ENRICH series, have been subjected to numerous studies and found to have exceptionally high levels of reliability and validity (in the .80 to .95 range, depending on the study). Both also share very large

(100,000+) national norm groups. While these two tools are part of the PREPARE/ENRICH series of preventive tools developed by Dr. David Olson and his associates, ENRICH and MATE work especially well as intervention instruments.

Couples who are very discouraged and contemplating divorce are ideal subjects for an intervention building on ENRICH. The couple takes the 165-item inventory, and then discuss the results with a trained counselor. The counselor will use the data provided by the 15 page computer print out to help the couple gain an objective look at their relationship in each of the eleven relational areas measured by ENRICH - their strengths and their growth areas. Based on that data and the couple's responses, the counselor then designs an intervention specifically tailored to maximize the couple's strengths while working on the growth areas. In this author's experience, it is not uncommon for these discouraged couples to be very surprised that there are any strengths in their relationship. That knowledge alone is sometimes enough to motivate them to begin to do the hard work of rebuilding. Even if the couple should decide "the gain ain't worth the pain" (as one client put it), at least they have an objective basis for that decision.

MATE offers a different potential for intervention. One of the tenants of modern psychotherapy is that transition times are inherently stressful, especially for relationships. Since many transitions do affect those over age 50, MATE offers the therapist a tool to help the couple navigate the transition. One example from this own author's experience shows the need (MATE was not available at the time of this incident). One of my long-term friends is a Japanese-American couple. The husband had worked as a research chemist all his life. His bride, as the dutiful Japanese wife, stayed at home. He looked forward to his retirement, eagerly planning on raising a bonsai garden in his back yard. A few months after his retirement, I dropped by for a visit, and sure enough, he was in the back yard happily working away. As I sipped tea and talked in the kitchen with his wife, she looked straight at me and said, "You know, I married that man for better or worse, but not for-home-for lunch!" Obviously, there were some transition issues this couple had not yet worked out. MATE would have been excellent for them.

Conclusion

Psychoeducational approaches have many attractions. Most are empirically verified. All are easily learned and applied (although many require specialized training and/or certification to use). Even better, while traditional therapy can normally deal only with one client at a time (whether "client" means a single individual or a single couple or family), many of these psychoeducational approaches work well for groups of six or eight clients, or more. That gives an efficiency of scale.

For all of their advantages, these approaches do have limitations. Some clients are simply not willing to participate in groups. The rise of self-help "chat" rooms on the internet has made driving to a group meeting even less attractive. Some clients are not willing or able to do the intellectual work required by all psychoeducational approaches. And, of course, not all clients' needs will "fit" a particular program. All approaches will require some degree of flexibility and adaptation on the part of the counselor employing them. Still, for many counselors, their benefits may well outweigh their limitations.

Living Into the Lesson

1.   Take a position pro or con and debate this statement with classmates: "Psychoeducation is not real therapy." Defend your position with material from this text and other material you choose to bring in.

2.   Very few insurance companies pay for primary prevention programs. Why should or should not therapists be involved in offering primary prevention programs?

3.   Suppose you had several women in your practice who had been recently diagnosed with breast cancer. You have diagnosed each of them as having an adjustment disorder with anxious and/or depressed mood. What kind of preventative group might you design for them? Would it be a task group or a process group? What resources would you need to lead it? Share your plan with at least one other student.

4.   Bruce Tuckman's model of group development referenced in this chapter is more than 35 years old. Is this model still valid? Why or why not?

5.   Pick a partner and practice the speaker-listener technique as taught by PREP. The speaker holds an object ("the floor") and speaks for a MAXIMUM of 3 minutes. Then the speaker passes "the floor" to the listener, who paraphrases the verbal and non-verbal content of the speaker's message. Repeat the process until the first speaker verifies that the listener correctly understood the message. Then the listener assumes the speaker role. Go through at least 2 cycles of this process. The first speaker may pick any topic, but it should be something real he or she would like some help with.

6.   Process your feelings after doing the previous exercise. Did you find the process frustrating, liberating, or what? How do you think couples will find this experience? What could you say to help encourage them if they want to resist the technique?

7.   The first three components of the Awareness Wheel are Sense Data (i.e., which of the five physical senses was stimulated by the issue at hand), Thoughts (both interpretations of the sense data and unconscious "automatic thoughts" to use the language of Cognitive

Therapy), and Feelings. Use those three parts of the Awareness Wheel to discuss some issue in your life with one other students. Have your partner respond with active listening. How does this structure help you talk about your issue? What limitations do you see?

8.   Assume you are a single parent of a two-year old who throws temper tantrums. Use the material on STEP in this chapter to design an intervention to break this pattern. Now discuss your solution with other students in your class. What did you learn? Estimate from this experience whether it would be easier to construct effective consequences as a single parent or as a two-parent dyad.

9.   Search the internet. See how many sources of therapeutic games you can find. Bring to class a report of two not listed in this chapter which interested you.

10.   Make a list of support groups you would be most likely to use as a referral resource for your clients (or, if you are not yet actively counseling, for the clients you believe you will be most likely to serve). Then make a contact list of those resources in your area. Share your list with your class mates.

Chapter 10 - "Get Them On Their Feet"

We should take care not to make the intellect our god; it has, of course, powerful
muscles, but no personality.
- Albert Einstein

In mid-May 2001 a message started circulating around the Internet. According to this message, Larry LaPrise, the Detroit native who wrote the song the "Hokey Poky", died earlier that month at age 83. It was especially difficult for the family to keep him in the casket. They put his left leg in...well, you know the rest.

There is something about the physical humor in that joke that strikes a cord with most of us. As wonderful as the human gift of language is, there are times when physical movement speaks more loudly and accurately than any number of words.

Educators have recognized this for some time. Some people are indeed verbal learners, that is, they learn best when hearing the material. Others are primarily visual learners. They need to see to be able to absorb and integrate new material. Still others are primarily kinesthetic learners. They learn best by moving and doing (Keefe, 1987). While education and therapy are by no means synonymous, it is reasonable to assume that since therapy often includes learning some new skills or gaining some new insights, the same basic styles of learning will apply. For that reason, the rest of this chapter will focus on techniques which will appeal to those who respond best to visual or kinesthetic stimuli.

Situations Where Kinesthetic Techniques Are Appropriate

In one very real sense, there is almost no therapeutic situation where using some form of kinesthetic learning is not appropriate. Since the brain is a living system, and since the brain/mind and body are dynamically connected, and since complex learning is always enhanced by access to as many parts of the system as possible, getting clients to do something as well as talk about it makes learning new behavior more likely (Living Systems, 2001). As the old saying goes, "Tell me something, and I forget. Show me something, and I remember. Let me do something, and I learn." The good news for therapists is there are lots of ways to "get them on their feet." Because learning always involves conscious and unconscious processes, and because learning is developmental (that is, it builds on all previous experiences), the "do something" may involve actual movement, such as that described later in this chapter, or it may involve only imagined movement such at that employed in Gestalt therapy techniques like "empty chair," etc (Living Systems, 2001).

Even so, there are clearly some therapeutic situations which cry out for the use of movement. When doing therapy where pre-school through early adolescent children are involved (as is often the case in family therapy), acting out feelings and relationship patterns enables the children to be active participants. Children of that age do not yet have the verbal capacity or the abstracting ability necessary to simply talk about their experiences. Using any of the techniques about to be described puts them on an equal footing with their parents and indeed plays to the children's natural strength - learning by doing.

Of course, this is not just an issue for children. Some adults simply do not have the verbal skills to effectively use talk therapy alone. That would certainly be the case if the adult is on the lower end of the "normal" range of intelligence. Socio-cultural factors are also important. For example, when I was supervising beginning therapists in San Antonio, Texas, many of the clients my supervisees saw came from the *barrio* areas. These clients were often quite intelligent and remarkably resilient. However, many of them were high school drop-outs because of social and economic pressures. They were so accustomed to working with their hands (being *manoceros*) that working purely in the world of words and insight was difficult if not impossible. It was just too alien to the way they lived day-to-day. Allowing them to work things out physically allowed them to use their strengths, too.

Less often, but just as important, the therapist may notice that issues in the room are too painful to be verbalized. In that case, acting the pain out may allow the speakable to be "said." For example, Joy and Steve had come to Counselor Samuel Shmooze for marital therapy. Both were Christians, and both believed strongly divorce was wrong. They presented as having a basically good relationship which just needed "a little work" to make it better. They were both college-educated and very verbal. However, nothing Counselor Shmooze tried made any real difference in the relationship. His intuition gnawed at him, so he had Joy and Steve stand in the middle of the therapy room back to back with their backs touching. Counselor Shmooze instructed them, "I want you to imagine that the space of this room represents the emotional space of your marriage. Where you are right now represents the goal you say you want - lots of closeness. Now, I want you to move anywhere in the room to show how you actually feel the closeness to your partner. When you're ready, nod. When you are both ready, I'll have you turn and face each other." Steve stayed where he was and nodded. Joy, however, walked to the far wall as close to the wall as she could get. When Counselor Shmooze told them to turn around and both saw their reality, they both cried and rushed to hug each other.

This kinesthetic variation of the scaling technique (Chapter 5) was a breakthrough for Joy and Steve. Physically seeing what both had previously only felt provided a stimulus painful enough that they could no longer maintain their usual "make nice" exterior. Their relationship system's rules had to change. "Getting them on their feet" often allows clients to actually see when unspoken rules are operating and what the effect of those rules are.

Sculpting

Sculpting is an active style of metacommunication, that is, a style of communicating about one's style of communicating (Nichols & Schwartz, 1998). Conceptually, the process of sculpting is quite simple. The family members arrange themselves as a living tableau. Some times this tableau will be a "snapshot" in time. Other times the therapist may have the tableau act out some process by having the family members move in some way.

In addition to the general advantages of all forms of kinesthetic/visual therapy, one of the very real advantages of sculpting is that it makes very clear that therapy is a collaborative process. No one can simply sit back and let the therapist (or even the therapist and other family members) do all the work (L'Abate, Ganahl, & Hansen, 1986). Because of its power, sculpting can usefully be employed at almost any point. Sculpting can be a technique for assessment of family interactions, and it can be a technique for intervention into those interactions.

While sculpting is an exceptionally flexible technique, it should never be pointless. The first step in sculpting, then, is for the therapist to clearly decide what the goal of the exercise is. Note the singular "goal" in that sentence. Each instance of sculpting should be aimed at only one goal. If the therapist would like to accomplish more than one goal, more than one instance of sculpting will be necessary. Once the therapist's goal is clearly in mind, the family's involvement can begin.

Often, the best way to prime the family for the activity is for the therapist to say something like, "I'd like to have us act out something. Are you willing to try something with me?" When the family agrees, the counselor will have them stand up, with permission to move around the room as they wish while the counselor explains the process and assigns the roles.

There are two basic roles in the many variations of sculpting: "Michelangelo" and "Play-Doh". Michelangelo is the sculptor. "Play-Doh" is everyone else. The therapist may assume either of those roles, or the therapist may choose to sit outside the family process and observe or coach, depending on the therapist's goal for the exercise. If the therapist wishes one of the family members to be Michelangelo, he or she may ask for volunteers or the therapist may select someone. Often, in this author's experience, it is easier to select a family member (usually a child, since they tend to be more ready to play and thus to be less inhibited) for the first time sculpting is used. After the first time, other family members will more frequently volunteer.

Let's assume that Counselor Shmooze is working with the Jenkins family: Dan and Martha, the parents, and Billy (age 10) and Jim (age 9). Once Counselor Shmooze has the Jenkins' on their feet, he may explain the process like this:

> Now, I want us to do something that I hope will be helpful and fun for all of us. Billy, would you be willing to help me out? (Okay. What do you want me to do?) Well, once upon a time there was a very famous sculptor named Michelangelo. He was able to take clay and make it really look alive. So I want you to be Michelangelo and I want all of the rest of us to be your Play-Doh, okay? (Okay!). I want you to make us into a statue that represents the way the family talks to each other most of the time [Shmooze's goal for this sculpting - to visualize their communication patterns]. You can pose us any way you want. You can put us anywhere in this room you want. After all, you're Michelangelo, and we're Play-Doh. I'll play you, so you put me the way you believe you normally feel about the way the others talk to you, okay? (Okay! This'll be fun!)

Depending on Shmooze's goal for the exercise, he may have given more specific instructions to Billy. For example, he may have labeled one side of the room as the "cold" side and the other as the "warm" side and have Billy place people in the room according to his perception of whether they were "cold" or "warm" toward him. As with the scaling exercise, the distance would indicate how cold or how warm he felt they were. A more elaborate variation on the theme would involve the use of props, such as stuffed toys, to represent pets, relatives, and other emotionally significant relationships which are not physically present in the room (L'Abate, Ganahl, and Hansen, 1986).

From within the sculpture the counselor might have to help Michelangelo sharpen the focus of the sculpture. For example, the counselor might ask, "Where are we supposed to be looking?" "What are our hands doing?" "Do our eyes meet?" "Do we all have the same expression on our faces?" A few thought-starter questions such as these are usually sufficient to help Michelangelo make the sculpture come alive.

Occasionally, the family members will interfere with or resist Michelangelo. When that happens, the counselor must quickly step in to encourage the family members' cooperation with Michelangelo and to assure them they will have time for any rebuttal they may want to make later. If the therapist has been a part of the sculpture, this may very well mean that the therapist will have to literally step out of the role and into the counselor role, and then literally step back into the Play-Doh position given by Michelangelo.

Once Michelangelo announces she or he is finished with the sculpture, the therapist has a choice. The therapist may, from within the sculpture, ask Michelangelo to explain the meaning of the sculpture. Most often, the counselor may ask each member of the sculpture to express how his or her role in the sculpture feels. This is the place for rebuttals (e.g., "Whoa, if this is how Billy thinks his family talks to him, no wonder he stays in his room all the time. But I certainly don't feel like this at all."). Once each person has expressed his or her subjective experience of the exercise, then they can derole and talk about the meaning. Another alternative the counselor has is to invite Michelangelo to put the sculpture into motion. Of course, there are variations on this theme. Michelangelo may move among the static members of Play-Doh and interact with them one at a time, or Michelangelo may put the whole thing into motion like a "Rube Goldberg" machine before the family talks about the process. Indeed, repeating the motion may be a means of visualizing and enacting the family's "stuckness" in a given pattern. The down side of using motion is that it does increase the emotional intensity, and therefore should be used cautiously and only with families who are ready to deal with that much intensity.

However one does it, processing the meaning of the experience is crucial to sculpting. Ideally, each person in the sculpture should be able to express his/her feelings and meaning from the direct experience. Once everyone has had a chance to talk, the counselor may move out of the sculpture and ask the family members to rearrange themselves into a more ideal relationship. Or the therapist may ask another family member to sculpt the family from his/her point of view. Or the therapist may become Michelangelo and sculpt the family into an alternative ways of relating. "In general, the sequence should be to derole, debrief the immediate and subjective experience, and then process it..." (L'Abate, Ganahl, and Hansen, 1986, p.185).

One further caution applies to this technique as well as the ones which follow. Insight is more powerful when it comes from the client than when it comes from the counselor. If the counselor became part of Play-Doh, the counselor may fruitfully talk about his/her subjective experience in that role, but the insight and interpretation should come from the family members themselves. If the counselor stayed outside the sculpture, she/he may make descriptive statements (e.g., "Martha, when Billy posed you running away from Dan, I thought I saw a tear on your cheek" or "Jim, the look of surprise that Billy sculpted on your face was priceless! You really seemed to get into this"), but again, leave the meaning and interpretation to the family members.

Role Play

Like sculpting, role playing offers the counselor many variations, which allows this technique to be adapted to almost any therapeutic situation or need. I have used role playing in individual therapy for presenting problems ranging from alcohol or drug abuse to anxiety disorders to relatively uncomplicated parenting problems. However it is used, role playing has its roots in psychodrama developed by Moreno and his followers, and it has become a staple of family therapy at least since the work of Chloe Madanes in the early 1980s (L'Abate, Ganahl, and Hansen, 1986).

Sculpting can often be diagnostic for which families can effectively use role playing. Unfortunately, very intellectual or very rigid people, who could potentially benefit most from the role play, often find role playing exceptionally difficult (L'Abate, Ganahl, and Hansen, 1986). If someone is unwilling or unable to participate in a sculpting experience, they are highly unlikely to be willing or able to make good use of a role play. Conversely, those who find sculpting helpful will likely also find role play helpful.

While role play can be an excellent therapeutic tool, the counselor should be aware of a few cautions. Young children can often effectively participate in sculpting, especially as Play-Doh. However, experience shows that children must be at least school age to assume and maintain a specified role during a role play. In addition, this tool does not work effectively for families who are actively chaotic or paranoid, or are in an active crisis which feels to them overwhelming.

There are four fundamental variations of role playing. Within each type, the subvariations are limited only by the counselor's imagination and the needs of the client.

Role playing. Although "role playing" is a general term which can, and often does, refer to all four of the fundamental types of role play, when used in its specific sense, "role playing" is more like psychodrama. Each person in the role play assumes a simulated or hypothetical role and pretends to become that role. Many of the "Living Into the Lesson" exercises at the end of each chapter of this book ask that the students role play, that is, that they assume a hypothetical persona and experience the skill under study.

151

There are many advantages of using role play like this. One major one is, it allows clients and trainees to experience situations which would be too dangerous or too threatening in real life. For example, one of my favorite role plays with student therapists is "the Client from Hell." Depending on the size of the supervision group, I may either have some students play the client who is every student's nightmare, or I may play that role, and I allow other student therapists to function as the therapist in trying to deal with this horrible situation. While this does get fairly intense at times, the fact that it is totally imaginary and we can call "Time out!" at any point keeps a certain safety net under the process.

When the sculpting went very well, Counselor Shmooze decided to use a role play with the Jenkins family. They had recently all seen the movie "Castaway" together, so Counselor Shmooze had them pretend to be marooned on a desert island. He had them crawl across the floor to act out crawling out of the ocean and onto the beach. Then they had to decide how they were going to survive. For the next 30 minutes, they struggled for power and control. Billy and Jim, because they were Cub Scouts, thought they ought to be in charge because they knew more about the woods than their parents (neither of whom had ever been camping before). Dan thought he ought to be in control because, after all, he was the man of the house. Martha basically stayed out of the discussion, though all the men tried to get her on their side.

At the end of 30 minutes, Counselor Shmooze called time and had each person process the experience. Being in this hypothetical survival situation enabled them to experientially understand some of the power struggles that were at the root of their communication problems.

Role assumptions. Role assumption is a specific type of role play where the roles are clearly specified. In other words, role assumption is deliberately not as open-ended or free-flowing as a pure role play.

One common type of role assumption is to have various members of a family assume each others' roles. One family I worked with, the Marshalls, found this very enlightening. Steve and Peggy Marshall, the parents of two teens, were very frustrated by Roy's, the 15 year old son's, "Goth / Grunge" appearance and his resistance to any instructions they gave. Shelby, the 14 year old daughter, played the "good girl," who stayed out of trouble and did what she was told. I had Steve assume Roy's role, Peggy assume Shelby's role, and the kids assume their same-gender parent's role. At first "Steve" (Roy in role) tried to parent "Roy" (Steve in role) the way he said he wanted to be parented. Both "Peggy" and "Shelby" stayed out of it. But "Roy" quickly escalated the confrontations, and "Peggy" began to step in to assist him (interestingly, the only time Shelby would become vocal and active in therapy was when she was playing Peggy's role). Things quickly escalated to the point that I had to step in and call a halt to process what had happened. Although he was not ready to admit that his parents had any validity to their case, Roy did have to admit he was saying he felt just like Steve often said he felt. Steve enjoyed the experience so much that the next several sessions he brought some "goth" props with him to put on when he assumed Roy's role, and he and Peggy frequently requested the role assumption. This bit of playfulness even got to Roy, and the family slowly began to actually work together.

A variation on the role assumption is to assume a more generic role. In an alcohol recovery group I directed, I often had group members assume the Victim, the Rescuer, and the Persecutor roles. When they had been in a role for a few minutes, I would have them switch to a different role.

Still another variation came as a part of a workshop at an AAMFT national conference. During this workshop I and the other participants were told to assume the role of some famous person. Then we were to wander around the room as though we were at a cocktail party and "meet" the other people there. An interesting bit of subjective learning for me came from observing how quickly we each sized the other up and decided who had the more status. The higher status person usually controlled how long the interaction took place. Had I been doing the same behavior but in my own role, I might well have missed that insight.

Role rehearsal. Role rehearsal involves the person staying in their own normal role, but rehearsing for some future situation. The goal is to enable the client to play the new situation with greater comfort and ease.

There are many opportunities for using role rehearsal. Faye had come to Counselor Shmooze because she had felt devastated when Harry told her he didn't love her any more. She had tried for several weeks to cope with Harry's emotional distance, but found that the less she invested in the relationship, the less Harry also invested. She tried all of the potential solutions she and Counselor Shmooze worked out, and none of them brought about a change in Harry. Yet Harry also stated explicitly that he was happy and he had no intentions of moving out, even for a trial separation. So Counselor Shmooze allowed Faye to rehearse her telling Harry that she was going to need to see some small, specific behavior changes or she was going to go to a lawyer to begin divorce proceedings. During this rehearsal, Shmooze played Harry, and offered all the objections that he had learned Harry was likely to offer.

This is just one example of a role rehearsal. During premarital counseling I always have couples rehearse the roles they will need to play to resolve the inevitable conflicts in a healthy way. I also give them structured opportunities to rehearse goal setting and negotiating change in the family rules. Where step-parenting is an issue, I usually have them first assume their partner's role in a "touchy" child discipline situation, and then rehearse the same situation from their own role with the skills we have previously practiced.

Individual counselors often use role rehearsal, too. A shy client may rehearse with the therapist asking for a raise. An adult man may rehearse telling his mother that she is too intrusive without "blasting" her or retreating from her. An adult woman with social phobia may rehearse the speech she has to give at a business meeting. And so on.

Role reversal. In role reversal, the person plays the opposite role from the one they normally play. Counselor Shmooze noticed from the "Castaway" exercise that Martha frequently played the Martyr role in the family, while Dan usually played the General role. In the session following the "Castaway" role play, Counselor Shmooze asked Martha to play a Persecutor and Dan to play a Victim. Then they were to plan a weekend outing. Billy and Jim were assigned the roles of observers, to assess how accurately Dan and Martha stayed in the assigned roles. Both really got into their roles, to the extent that Dan's body language began to portray the characteristic Victim slump of the shoulders and bowing of the head so as to avoid eye contact. He had to break it off shortly after that.

Dan	(looking directly at Martha, speaking quietly but intensely) Do I really do that to you?
Martha	(almost a whisper) Yes.
Dan	I had no idea you felt like this. How can you love me after I've treated you like this all these years?
Martha	I do love you, though.

Billy and Jim sat in silence as their parents began to talk honestly and openly for the first time in years. All Counselor Shmooze had to do was sit and smile at the healing taking place before his eyes.

Naturally, whatever the particular form of role play the therapist employs, the same basic sequence required by sculpting still applies: derole, debrief the immediate and subjective experience, and then discuss insights gained from the experience. Just as with sculpting, the insight is most powerful when it comes from the family, not from the therapist. Hopefully, the therapist, like Counselor Shmooze in the above case example, gets to just sit and smile. Most often, a little therapeutic guidance will be necessary before the smiles can come.

Enactments
==========

Enactments are one of the hallmarks of Structural family therapy. Structural therapists do not talk about the family's functioning. They get the family to functioning, and then directly observe and modify the functioning as necessary. Indeed, one of the major critiques of other forms of psychotherapy by Structural therapists is that others frequently label or relabel a client's behavior, but do not directly intervene to help the client change the behavior. Structural therapists do, and they do by enactments (Nichols and Schwartz, 1998).

There are two basic types of enactments. One is spontaneous behavior sequences. This requires no effort from the counselor to start. Instead, the counselor simply picks up on a sequence of behavior the clients bring into the session.

In my work with the Marshall family, the repeated spontaneous behavior sequence of Steve lecturing Roy in session led to the use of the role plays already discussed. Therapy continued after the role plays with my directly intervening when the old sequences reappeared.

Steve	(to Roy) Well, if you'd get rid of that crowd of drug- using friends of yours you'd be a lot better off.
Roy	Get off my friends. They have nothing to do with it.
Therapist	Ouch! Ouch! (Long pause while everyone looks at me like I have lost my mind again.) Well, you two decided to trade verbal blows again, so I thought I would say "ouch" for you.
Steve	Okay, I get it. So what should I have said?
Therapist	Well, think back to the role play. What did you find helpful when you were playing Roy?

That got the conversations back on track. Steve and Roy were able to talk to each other in mutually respectful terms and come to an agreed upon solution.

Another type of enactment comes from the therapist setting up some sort of situation. This can be accomplished by almost any of the previous techniques already discussed in this chapter. The one caveat is that the therapist should never leave the therapist role when directing an enactment. This is because of the necessity of being ready to intervene directly and immediately if and when the role play or the debriefing starts to go awry. Most often the role plays encourage each person to stay in his or her usual role so that the shift to rehearsing a new behavior sequence happens more naturally. However, this is not a hard and fast rule. Enactments can be successfully staged with family members assuming roles other than their normal one, especially when the therapist is trying to get the family members to see their own role from a different perspective. That in itself can be a powerful intervention.

Conclusion

As a holistic approach, the Metasystems paradigm makes extensive use of all of these kinesthetic techniques. All of these engage several senses, and all of them allow clients to directly access emotional data from a present-tense experience. That multi-sensory experience greatly facilitates insight, and it makes consolidating the new behavior a bit less challenging. Which parts of the experience are most important to the individual client is irrelevant. The counselor provides a rich smorgasbord of sensory input by employing kinesthetic techniques. This frees the client to organize the experience in a way that is most helpful.

Living Into the Lesson

1. Think back to your own educational experience. How do you learn best? Are you primarily verbal, visual, or kinesthetic? How about other members of your family of origin? What do these differences (if any) tell you about doing therapy?

2. The author indicated that some adults of even average or above-average intelligence may respond best to a therapy or learning style which allows them to physically work things out. What support for this assertion do you find from your own experience?

3. Counselor Shmooze used a kinesthetic variation of the scaling technique in this chapter. Get with at least three other students (or other adults) and use this to act out your support for or disagreement with a mutually-agreed upon political issue. State the issue positively (e.g., I believe every terminally ill person ought to have the right to die when and how they wish). The center of the room represents total agreement with the stated position. When you have taken your places, talk about why you chose the distance you did and how it feels to visually see the distance.

4. In the exercise above, you were to discuss how the use of physical distance felt. Did you discuss the feelings, or keep it on a more cognitive level? How did you decide to do what you did? What do you think would make it easier for clients to discuss their feelings? What would make it more difficult? What help could the therapist be to the client?

5. The author refers to the two roles in sculpting as "Michelangelo" and "Play-Doh." What are the advantages of using playful terms like this? What are the disadvantages?

6. The author introduced the Jenkins family in the discussion of family sculpting. Get with three other students and agree on your family roles. Once you know your roles and the presenting problem, the one playing Billy will sculpt the other family members into those roles. Discuss how being in the sculpture feels different from the earlier discussion about those roles. What new insights does the sculpture provide?

7. Sculpting is a means for metacommunication - for communicating about communicating. From your experience with these class exercises, are experiential techniques for metacommunication more helpful than verbal techniques? Less helpful? Explain.

8. Brainstorm some situations where you would want to introduce movement into the sculpture. What types of situations would you not want to move? Be ready to explain.

9. Get with a partner and sculpt "loneliness." Then come out of your roles and discuss. Now reverse roles and sculpt "longing". Again, come out of your roles and discuss.

10. Assume you are working with the Jenkins family and you want them to participate in a role play. Further assume that Dan Jenkins thinks this is a silly idea and doesn't want to go along. Practice with a fellow student how you would win him over to the idea.

11. The author states that role play "does not work well for families which are actively chaotic or paranoid, or are in an active crisis which feels to them overwhelming." Why would this be so? Why can't these types of families benefit from role play?

12. Get with another student. Each of you will assume the role of your parent that you know best (it could be the same or the opposite gender). From within that role, try to decide on which movie you will go see together. What does this role assumption teach you about this parent you know so well?

13. Assume you have been laid off from your job due to corporate downsizing, and this will have a very major impact on your family finances. Get with another student (who can assume the role of therapist or best friend) and rehearse how you will give your spouse this news. How "real" was the experience for you? What helped? What got in the way?

14. In the next social gathering you attend, assume a role exactly the opposite of the one you normally play. Notice how people respond to you differently. What pulls do you experience to "get back where you belong"? How can you use this experience to help your clients who are experiencing similar pressure to "get back to where they belong"?

15.   Role play this enactment with two other students: One of you is the therapist. One is a harried parent of a child with attention-deficit disorder, hyperactive type. The third person is the hyperactive child. The child should start bouncing around and acting out, and the mother should respond by trying to coerce the child into sitting still. The challenge for the therapist: intervene directly into this sequence and have the parent do something different. When you are all satisfied the enactment is complete, derole and discuss. How was this different for the usual technique of telling the parent what she/he should do?

Chapter 11 - Diagraming Interactions

"The difference between fiction and reality? Fiction has to make sense." - Tom Clancy

There is an old saying, "A picture is worth a thousand words." This is especially true in relationship therapy. To the non-systemically trained person, the concepts can appear very vague and purely theoretical, with no practical consequence. Even highly intelligent people may find fundamental concepts like circular causality and recursion puzzling because they are so different from the normal linear thinking in Western culture. For all these reasons and more, a picture of a relationship truly is worth a thousand words.

Because diagraming paints such a clear picture, my normal process of using cases drawn from my own clinical experience is too risky. There is too much danger of a client's identity being revealed no matter how carefully I try to disguise and protect that client's confidentiality. For that reason, most case material in this chapter will come from the Book of Genesis in the Hebrew Scriptures. Most of these stories are accepted as scripture by Christians, Jews, and (with some modifications) Muslims. Those readers who do not accept these stories as historical can still readily access the basic "clinical data" by reading Genesis Chapter 12 through the rest of that book. I encourage readers who are not familiar with these stories to read them in order to meet the families we will be dealing with throughout the rest of this chapter.

Types of Situations Where Diagraming Is Appropriate

Sometimes the most effective way to hide something is to put it in plain sight. Tom Clancey's quote which heads this chapter makes somewhat the same point. "Reality" does not always make sense the way a fiction novel does because sometimes the cues we need to understand real life are hidden in plain sight. When a client does not seem to be able to grasp relationship structures or themes that are very obvious to the counselor, a good diagram can help make the client make sense of her or his reality.

For example, a former client (I will call her Barbara) could not understand the role that drugs had played in her life. She had been arrested for abuse of prescription drugs and had not seen that she had a problem until the police took her to jail. Barbara and I began our third session together by constructing a genogram of her family. Evidently there were few secrets in Barbara's family, because she readily related the necessary details of family history. However, when I handed Barbara the completed genogram for her inspection, she looked positively shocked. "I never realized there was so much alcohol abuse in my family!" Barbara was the only person in her family to abuse prescription drugs, but a high percentage of others abused alcohol or illegal drugs (mostly marijuana). Seeing generations of drug and alcohol abuse on both sides of her family brought her to the realization that she was simply living out her family's unspoken creed: "Pain is unbearable and must be anesthetized as quickly and often as possible." Armed with that bit of understanding about her reality, she could begin to make changes to break the family history, and her personal cycle, of substance abuse.

Of course, not all theories of therapy pay attention to family of origin or historical data. Other types of diagrams can reveal current structures or larger system influences. These, too, can help both the counselor and the client make sense of reality the way a good outline helps make sense of a fictional novel.

As the previous chapter stated, some people primarily process data visually. This is a second major reason for using diagrams. With a well-constructed diagram for guidance, visual learners can efficiently combine new insights with old learning to create the desired new behavior. The key word in that sentence is "efficiently." While visual learners might be able to reach the same goal by purely verbal means, giving them visual data makes it possible for them to get an accurate perception more quickly. The therapist's task is to decide if a diagram or other visual learning (such as the role plays discussed last chapter) would be most helpful for this particular client, and, if so, precisely what type of data will best help the client reach specified goals.

Genograms

Monica McGoldrick (1999) is one of the most renowned authorities on genograms. Students who wish to go into more depth with this tool should study her text carefully. This chapter will give only some of the fundamentals of genogram use.

In essence, a genogram is simply a structural diagram of a family's relationship over three generations (L'Abate, Ganahl, and Hansen, 1986). Genograms grew out of Bowen's family systems theory, though other approaches (such as the Metasystems paradigm) which value family of origin data also find them very valuable for collecting and organizing data. The key to using genograms effectively is to understand that they organize data that has developed over time. While, of necessity, a genogram is always a "snap shot" of a particular point in a family's developmental history, other tools are more effective for revealing influences which are more "here and now."

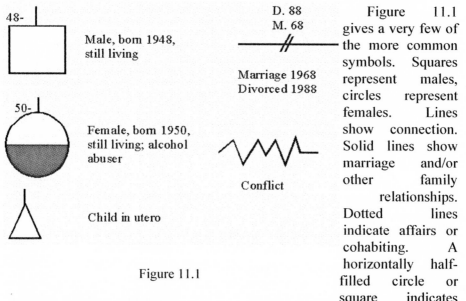

48- Male, born 1948, still living

50- Female, born 1950, still living; alcohol abuser

Child in utero

D. 88
M. 68

Marriage 1968
Divorced 1988

Conflict

Figure 11.1

Figure 11.1 gives a very few of the more common symbols. Squares represent males, circles represent females. Lines show connection. Solid lines show marriage and/or other family relationships. Dotted lines indicate affairs or cohabiting. A horizontally half-filled circle or square indicates substance abuse. Normally this is understood as alcohol abuse unless otherwise noted. A vertically half-filled circle or square indicates serious mental illness. A zig-zag line usually indicates a conflicted or abusive relationship, and often an arrow indicates the direction of abuse (e.g., spouse abuse). Some practitioners place the age of the person inside the circle or square. Others follow the example given here by placing the year of birth to the left of the connection line and the year of death to the right. A large X drawn across the square or circle indicates the death of a family member.

Besides the basic factual data of dates of birth, death, marriage, and divorce, other information can be added to the genogram to make it more complete. L'Abate (1986) suggests several, among them:

1. Physical location of family members (i.e., city and state of residence).
2. Communication patterns (who talks and does not talk with whom; who is the family "switchboard").
3. Toxic issues (e.g., sex, money, religion, etc.) - anything that stimulates problems in this particular family system. Gaps in genograms frequently point to toxic secrets.
4. Health issues (i.e., noting what caused the death of those who died; noting serious, non-fatal illnesses (e.g., diabetes)).
5. Nodal events (i.e., job changes, moves, crises, catastrophes, etc.).

This list is merely illustrative. Each counselor should add information to the basic genogram based on her or his theoretical orientation and the goals of therapy.

To put this together, let us assume that Joseph ben Jacob comes to see Counselor Shmooze for family problems. According to Joseph, his family is a mess. He and his father are quite close, but his brothers all hate him. He cannot understand why. "After all, I did tell them that I'll be their leader one day even though I'm the youngest, but that's what my dream said, so I know it must be true." Together they created the genogram shown in Figure 11.2 (at the end of this chapter).

Several relational patterns leapt off the page at Counselor Shmooze. First, the bitter sibling rivalry reported by Joseph was actually part of a multigenerational pattern of emotional cutoffs between siblings. What happened between Great-Grandfather Abraham and his brothers was a bit of a family secret; after he left home, he appears to have never contacted them again, but no one knew why. The battle between Grandfather Isaac and his older brother Ishmael was better documented. That conflict escalated to the point that Ishmael and his mother were driven into exile and seldom if ever heard from again. Joseph's own father, Jacob, literally had to run for his life from his brother Esau, and the reconciliation they later effected produced an uneasy truce at best. This was not just a problem for the males, either. Joseph's mother, Rachel, had serious conflicts with Leah, her sister and Jacob's other wife (having two or more wives was common in the culture Joseph came from, especially for a wealthy man such as his father was). By participating in the conflict with his brothers, Joseph was simply (and unconsciously) keeping the family "rule" of sibling battles. What he missed was the clear pattern that these rivalries could and often did escalate to the point of exile or death for someone.

Another family pattern was the prominence of toxic secrets. One of the favorite family stories was how Grandmother Rebecca secretly conspired with Jacob to trick Grandfather Isaac and cheat brother Esau out of his birthright. Among his own brothers, Ruben's having sex with Bilhah, his father's concubine, while Jacob was away burying Joseph's mother Rachel was a very poorly kept secret. Everyone knew it happened, but no one talked about it. Counselor Shmooze could not help but wonder what other secrets lay hidden in Joseph's family that either he did not know about or had not revealed.

A third pattern that appeared very obvious to Counselor Shmooze was the tendency of a parent to select one child to be the favorite. Grandfather Isaac and Grandmother Rebecca had been very close at one time, but later in their relationship each parent chose one of the boys as the favorite. Counselor Shmooze recognized it as a classic pattern of triangulation.

Joseph's own parents were very close, and he was without a doubt his father's favorite. As Counselor Shmooze questioned Joseph, he began to be convinced that this triangle, while very close and emotionally satisfying as long as Rachel was alive, actually served to further destabilize the rest of the family. Clearly, Joseph's family lived out a pattern of dysfunctional relationships which had existed for generations. Counselor Shmooze's work with Joseph would be challenging at best. Because he had already been emotionally cut off by his brothers, keeping Joseph from being killed or exiled long enough for therapy to do any good would have to be Counselor Shmooze's first priority.

This "case" example illustrates that genograms can be very useful for organizing data, conceptualizing a case, and treatment planning. They can also be very helpful to the client in creating some appropriate goals for therapy. For example, Counselor Shmooze might say to Joseph, "Looking at your genogram, who has at least some of the strengths you'd like to have when our work together is a success?" Joseph might reply, "Well, I'd like to have Uncle Esau's ability to forgive. He's too much of a brute, so I wouldn't want to be just like him, but I would like his ability to forgive." Then Counselor Shmooze could help Joseph review the stories he knew about his uncle and make plans to develop the desired characteristics in himself. Counselor Shmooze would likely keep the genogram readily available for every session to help make sense of whatever bit of reality Joseph was sharing at the time by putting that reality into context.

Structure Grams

There are at least two primary means of drawing structures of a family. Both are grounded in the work of Salvador Minuchin's Structural Theory, and, in contrast to genograms, both focus primarily on the here-and-now rather than development across time.

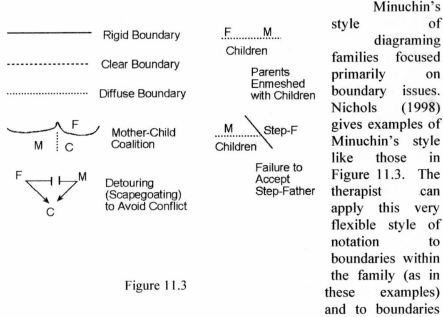

Minuchin's style of diagraming families focused primarily on boundary issues. Nichols (1998) gives examples of Minuchin's style like those in Figure 11.3. The therapist can apply this very flexible style of notation to boundaries within the family (as in these examples) and to boundaries

Figure 11.3

between the family and other systems (such as school, church, "outside interests", etc.).

Looking only at the parental subsystem of Joseph's family, Counselor Shmooze could diagram the boundaries like this:

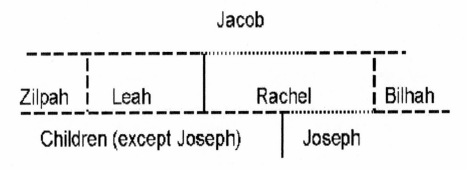

Figure 11.4

This makes it easy to see that Jacob had clear and appropriate boundaries with Leah (his first wife) and with the two concubines Zilpah and Bilhah, but he was enmeshed with Rachel and with Joseph. It also easily shows the rigid boundaries between Joseph and his siblings, and between Rachel and Leah, the two wives and sisters. Leah's and Rachel's boundaries with their maids, Zilpah and Bilhah, respectively, were clear and appropriate.

For Counselor Shmooze, this diagram revealed one more dynamic of Joseph's family. There really was no parental subsystem. In reality, there were two parental subsystems. The first was occupied by Jacob alone. While he was very fused with Rachel, he ruled the family fairly much the way he had ruled all his life - alone and by his own wits. The other parental subsystem consisted of the women of the household. This subsystem was where much of the conflict took place, often in disguised fashion. Counselor Shmooze began to create two hypotheses about his work with Joseph. First, since Joseph was fused with his father, he likely would have learned the same style of "go it alone and live by your wits." Father Jacob was also a very religious man, so religion would likely be highly important to Joseph as well. Second, since Joseph was fused with his biological mother Rachel as well, he likely would have learned a covert style of conflict from her. Counselor Shmooze decided that if anyone were to be killed in this family, Joseph would not be the one to do the killing. He would be more likely to set up his opponent to make them look stupid or make them cause their own down fall. Based on this evidence, Counselor Shmooze decided that one goal of therapy would be to help Joseph deal more openly and appropriately with conflict. A related goal would be to help him structure clear, appropriate boundaries, instead of the diffused or rigid ones with which he was more familiar.

A different method of diagraming structure focuses on power and closeness issues instead of the boundaries. In this method, a circle represents the emotional "space" of a family (or other) system. The "twelve o'clock" position of the circle represents the power position - the one who is actually exerts the most power and influence in the system. The physical space in the circle represents the emotional space in the system. The further apart family members are on the circle, the more emotionally distant they are. The lower they are (i.e., the closer to the "six o'clock" position), the less power they actually have.

Counselor Shmooze constructed this type of structure gram with Joseph (Figure 11.5). Two facts are worth noting. Sometimes people are outside the circle of power. In this case, Counselor Shmooze drew Jacob as outside and above the circle because he was so aloof from everything happening in the family.

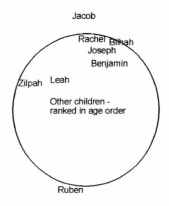

Figure 11.5

This drawing clearly shows that Rachel and her two children enjoyed more power and status with Jacob than Leah or any of the other children. Even Bilhah, Rachel's maid, enjoyed more influence than Leah, Jacob's first wife, because of her connection with Rachel. The ranking of children in order of age is consistent with Jacob's culture, as Counselor Shmooze knew. However, Ruben's position outside and below the circle was especially interesting. Ruben was the first born son and therefore, according to normal cultural rules, to be the one who was in charge of the sibling subsystem and who maintained the father's good name. Jacob's choosing to replace him with Joseph, the youngest (until Benjamin was born), while very consistent with the family "rules", was nevertheless an insult in larger cultural terms. After looking at this diagram, Joseph was able to understand why Ruben had acted out the way he had. He and Counselor Shmooze were also able to predict that Ruben would be very likely to try to do something to get back in favor with his father and thus regain his "rightful" position near the top.

Ecomaps

Ecological maps, or ecomaps as they are usually called, are a means of depicting the ecological system that encompasses a family or an individual. Like structure grams, ecomaps focus on here-and-now existential functioning. That fact makes both structure grams and ecomaps very compatible with present-oriented theories such as solution-focused therapy (Hodge, 2000). Ecomaps' inclusion of larger system issues also makes them very compatible with holistic approaches such as the Metasystems Paradigm.

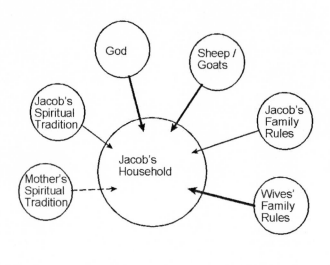

Figure 11.6

Believing in a thorough assessment, Counselor Shmooze helped Joseph create an ecomap of his family. The greatly simplified result is found in Figure 11.6. The heavier the line from a sphere of influence, the greater the leverage that sphere of influence has to create change in the family. (In a more complete ecomap, a one generation family genogram would be included in the center circle, with the lines of influence pointing toward the person or person in the family who is most affected by that part of the environment. A more complete ecomap would likely include many more influences, such as the culture of the Canaanite people living around Joseph and his family.)

When Joseph looked at the completed ecomap with Counselor Shmooze, there were few surprises. He was well aware of the very strong influence of sheep and goats on the family. After all, most of the family's considerable wealth came from and was tied up in the flocks of sheep and goats they owned. Anything that affected the size and health of the flocks directly affected the family. God's great influence was similarly no surprise. Jacob often told about his dreams, which he believed were from God, and he even claimed that his limp was the result of a face-to-face encounter he had with God. Joseph, too, believed his dreams were from God.

Naturally, Jacob's religious traditions were a strong influence on the family. The family worshiped his God. They told stories of this God meeting Great-Grandfather Abraham, and of this God's promise being fulfilled by Grandfather Isaac. By contrast, Leah and Rachel's gods had not been openly worshiped or even talked about since the family left the maternal grandparents' home many years ago. The influence of their religious traditions on the family was weak at best.

Joseph was not surprised to see maternal and paternal grandparents missing as spheres of influence. His paternal grandparents had been dead for years. He did not remember them at all. His maternal grandparents were cut off from the family and had been for years. This insight only reinforced his belief of the importance of his present family as his sole source of spiritual and emotional support.

What caught Joseph by surprise was the exceptionally strong influence of Leah and Rachel's family rules on the family. Jacob was a trickster and prided himself as such, but Joseph's maternal grandfather, Leban, was a master at the back-stab and the double deal. Even Jacob enjoyed telling stories at family gatherings about the covert conflicts between Leban and him. These family stories served to create rules for Jacob's family which said, in essence, that conflict must always be covert, and that the best man is not necessarily the strongest but the one with the sharpest wits. Joseph could immediately see how some of his rather naive and straight-forward statements to his brothers had unwittingly violated the family rules, and had only aggravated an already explosive situation between him and his brothers. Counselor Shmooze then helped Joseph create a personal goal which would help him more closely fit the family rules, while at the same time remaining true to his religious and personal beliefs.

One major advantage of using ecomaps is being able to conceptualize the entire relational ecology of a family (or other) system on a single sheet of paper. Clients who are strongly prone to linear thinking can see that, as Salvador Minuchin likes to say, "Life is more complex than that." For example, if the therapist is working with the parents of an only child who is alleged to have attention-deficit disorder, the parents may only frame this as a parent-child issue. By using an ecomap, the therapist can show that other influences play a role, too, such as the child's school teacher, the school system itself, the church, neighborhood playmates, the extended family, and community support (or lack of support) for the concept of attention-deficit disorder. Social organizations such as scouts are also influential building blocks in a child's life. The client can then decide which parts of the relational ecology can be a part of the solution, and which parts help define and maintain the problem that brought the client to therapy in the first place.

Ecomaps can be used for organizations as easily as they can with families. This author frequently serves as a process consultant to church groups and (less often) to businesses. Creating a complete ecomap for the organization helps the organizational leaders identify the forces that are acting on the organization. Once those forces are identified, the leaders are in a better position to decide where they have the most leverage to produce the change they desire for the organization.

Conclusion

Diagrams called blueprints help architects make sense of a client's ideas about a building. Diagrams called genograms, structure grams, or ecomaps help counselors and therapists make sense of a client's ideas about reality. The greatest advantage of any sort of diagram is that it brings together a mass of data and impressions into a coherent, intelligible whole.

Genograms are favored by therapists who place an emphasis on multigenerational influences in their work with clients. Genograms are superior for tracing the development of a belief or behavior pattern across generations. They reveal family themes or mottos by revealing repeating patterns.

Structure grams and ecomaps are more here-and-now focused. They are snapshots in time, and like a photograph, show nothing of what went on before and only a hint of what might go on in the future. These diagrams are ideally suited to therapists and counselors whose orientation is similarly limited to the here-and-now. They can, however, also be effectively used by therapists or counselors who, like Counselor Shmooze, operate from a more holistic or developmental approach to therapy.

Whatever style or type of diagraming a therapist or counselor may choose to use, these tools provide tremendous flexibility. Like language, there is a certain required grammar and syntax to using diagrams, but the possible arrangements is almost limitless. The diagram is most effective when the client can look at it and say, "Yes, you have revealed the truth."

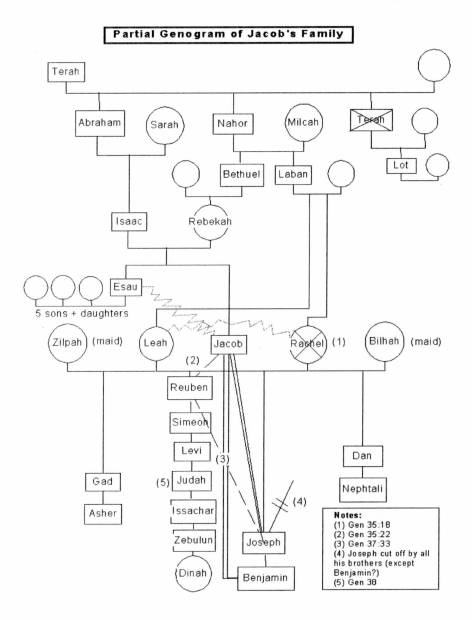

Partial Genogram of Jacob's Family

Figure 11.2

171

Living Into the Lesson

1.   One type of diagram not discussed in this chapter is a time line. A time line is simply a horizontal line with a specified beginning date and (usually) a specified ending date. It includes vertical tick marks for significant events between those dates. Construct a time line for your school career, beginning with your first entrance into school and ending with your anticipated graduation. Mark every school change and graduation. Mark other significant school events (e.g., "elected homecoming queen"). What parts of your school life does the time line help put in perspective for you? Discuss with another student.

2.   The author states that diagrams can be useful for clients who do not seem to be able to grasp "obvious" connections and for clients who are primarily visual learners.   Can you think of any other appropriate uses of the diagrams discussed in this chapter?   Are there any situations where you clearly would not use them?

3.   Refer to the genogram of Joseph's family (Figure 11.2). What is the place of the youngest in this family (Benjamin)? Could you have discovered this pattern as easily without the use of a genogram? If so, what other method could you use?

4.   Imagine you are Counselor Shmooze and you are working with Joseph. What would you guess Joseph's goal for therapy would be? Which of the therapy techniques presented in this text would you use for your work with him?

5.   What evidence for conflict between Jacob and his wives do you see in Figure 11.2? If they had not been as conflicted, do you think the boys would have had as severe a rivalry? Justify your answer.

6.   When parents choose a child as a favorite and allow the relationship with the spouse and with other children to suffer (a repeated occurrence in Joseph's family), what could the function of that choice be? I.e., What does this choice make possible for the parent that treating everyone alike does not make possible?

7.   Refer to the boundary diagram of Joseph's family (Figure 11.4). If you were Counselor Shmooze working with Joseph, what coalitions would you expect? Consider both within and across generational

lines. If you had only this diagram, not the genogram (Figure 11.2), what information would you lose? Would that be a problem for therapy?

8. Refer to the closeness and power diagram of Joseph's family (Figure 11.5). Rachel died giving birth to Benjamin. If Joseph had not been exiled by his brothers shortly after Rachel's death, what might have happened to the family dynamics as Benjamin grew up? What effect on the power dynamics of the entire family might Joseph have had if he learned from Counselor Shmooze how to set and maintain appropriate boundaries?

9. Create an ecomap of your current family. Be sure to include as many spheres of influence as you can, and draw lines to indicate who in the family these affect and how strong the effect is. Talk about your map with at least one other student. Help each other to make sure you include all the important influences in your family's relational ecology.

10. Of the five types of diagrams discussed in this chapter (including time lines in Question 1), which do you think you will use most often? Which will you use least often? Why?

Chapter 12 - Drug/Alcohol Interventions

Experience isn't what happens to a man. It is what a man does with what happens to him. - Aldous Huxley

Some Native American tribal nations have used hallucinogenic substances as part of their religious rites for more than 1000 years. Archeological evidence indicates similar practices in Central and South America dating back some 3500 years. Sumarians in Mesopotamia used opium poppies, which contain the narcotics morphine and codeine, 7000 years ago. Viking warriors ate the mushroom *Amanita muscaria* before going into battle. Since the Vikings called themselves "Berserkers," their mushroom-stimulated wild, fearless behavior gave rise to our word "berserk." Ancient Egyptians made a rather potent beer as a staple of their diet. There is hardly any culture that has not made at least some use of mind-altering substances (Grilly, 1998).

Even animals sometimes seek out intoxicating substances. In this author's back yard once stood a wild cherry tree. Birds would flock to the tree every year as the wild cherries became over ripe - naturally fermented. They would eat the fermented fruit until they became so drunk they would literally fall out of the tree. According to Grilly (1998), llamas chew coca leaves just like their Indian masters; perhaps this is where the native peoples learned how to do it. Even ants herd some beetles to collect their intoxicating secretions.

Of course, use does not necessarily imply abuse. No one would argue that using a mind-altering substance to relieve pain is illegitimate. Many people alter their minds every day with some form of caffeine, a perfectly legal psychostimulant found in coffee, tea, cola drinks, and chocolate, among other foods. Millions of people drink alcoholic beverages without ever developing problems that could be called "abuse" or "dependence."

According to the American Psychiatric Association's *Diagnostic and statistical manual of mental disorders* (2000) [usually abbreviated DSM-IV], substance abuse is demonstrated by a "maladaptive pattern of substance use leading to clinically significant impairment or distress....." Some examples of "clinically significant impairment" include failure to fulfill major role obligations at work, home, or school, or using the substance in situations in which it is physically hazardous. There are, of course, other examples. What is in common is that the person abusing the substance does not necessarily have to see it as a problem for the diagnosis to be given. For example, in some parts of the United States, repeated arrests for drunken brawling is accepted as just "boys will be boys," yet this behavior clearly meets the standards for substance abuse.

Substance dependence (addiction) is more severe and more serious. It, too, includes a maladaptive pattern of substance use which leads to "clinically significant impairment or distress." However, for a dependence diagnosis to be given, at least three of the following criteria must be present during the same 12 month period:

- tolerance (either marked increased need for the substance or marked diminished effect after continued use)
- withdrawal (usually withdrawal symptoms are the exact opposite of the effect of the drug; for example, cocaine produces a "high", so one of the withdrawal symptoms is a "crash," a very deep depression. Withdrawal symptoms are drug specific.)
- substance use is taken in larger amounts or over a longer period than intended (i.e., use is not under the user's voluntary control)
- a persistent desire (and perhaps attempts) to cut down or control substance use
- a great deal of time is spent in activities necessary to obtain the substance
- important social, occupational, or recreational activities are given up or reduced because of the substance use
- use continues despite knowledge of having persistent physical or psychological problems that are caused by or made worse by the substance use (e.g., drinking despite knowledge that it makes an ulcer worse)

Abuse and dependence are two separate problems, and these are different from intoxication or use. The therapist confronted with substance use, intoxication, abuse, or dependence in a client system will need to study both the pharmacology of the substance itself and specific techniques applicable to the presenting problem. The balance of this chapter will focus on the general principles which apply both to abuse and dependence to give the beginning counselor a good foundation from which to build this more specific and essential knowledge.

Substance abuse is a major problem in the United States. According to the DSM-IV, 60% of males and 30% of females in America have had at least one alcohol-related incident in their lives (e.g., driving while intoxicated, missing work or school due to a hangover, etc.). That same source estimates that approximately five-percent of the U.S. population meets the criteria for alcohol dependence in any given year.

Alcohol is by no means the only abused drug, of course. The DSM-IV (2000) estimates that about one-percent of U.S. adults abused stimulants in any given year, and almost one in eleven adults abused cannabis. Twice as many adults abused cocaine as abused amphetamines. These patterns may change as drug availability and fashion dictate, and they do not begin to touch the many who abuse prescription drugs. What is very clear is that sooner or later, almost every therapist or counselor will face someone who is either a current or former drug abuser.

Systemic Interventions for an "Individual" Problem

At one level, substance abuse is obviously an individual problem. That is, abuse and dependence cannot occur unless an individual voluntarily practices a maladaptive pattern of substance use despite recurrent, significant adverse consequences (abuse), or despite the presence of tolerance, withdrawal, and compulsive use (dependence) (DSM-IV, 2000). Indeed, this is one class of mental disorders which cannot develop without the active complicity of the person with the disorder. Since two people can, theoretically, use identical amounts of a given substance, and yet one may never develop problems related to substance use while the other person may develop significant problems with abuse or dependence, it seems reasonable to assume that the difference is related to individual, intrapsychic variables.

The recovery movement, as personified in groups such as Alcoholics Anonymous (AA) and Narcotics Anonymous (NA), supports this individual focus. Indeed, the first of AA's Twelve Steps begins, "We admitted we were powerless...." Each AA (and NA) member is responsible for working out his or her own sobriety, with the support and encouragement of other members. From a research perspective, the emphasis on individual variables has yielded a rich understanding of physiological and genetic factors which may contribute to vulnerability, as well as the power of environmental and conditioning components of the problem. We also know now that drugs can be very powerful in their own right. For example, there are many stories of persons becoming addicted to crack cocaine after a single use. Yet other people claim to be able to use crack for long periods of time without falling into compulsive, non-voluntary use. As important as these intrapsychic and physiological variables are, there must be something more.

The "something more" is family relationships. Clearly, the presence of an addiction in a family affects every family member. Depending on the level of maladaptation, abuse which falls short of dependence may very well negatively affect the entire family, also. A classic example of this is the wife of an alcohol-abusing husband who compensates for her husband's weekend-long drinking binges by keeping the children quiet and out of harm's way. She learns to organize her life around his drinking in order to prevent at least some of the negative consequences of her husband's alcohol abuse. This author has a client who has an unmarried adult son living at home because the son habitually abuses marijuana to the point that he has been fired from almost every job he has ever held. The client has rescued his son from financial trouble for more than 30 years, which certainly has negatively affected the client's own emotional and financial resources.

Research on addict families has shown that family of origin is a crucial factor in understanding the development and function of an addiction. For example, addicts contact members of their family of origin much more frequently than comparable "normals" or even other psychiatric patient groups (Stanton and Todd, 1982). This does not appear to be simply related to the addict's "fear of separation" or some similar attachment disorder. Indeed, families tend to put very real pressure on the addict not to leave, and they willingly endure (even covertly encourage) the addict's lying, stealing, and other indignities to make sure he (or she) stays firmly attached to the family.

Families of addicts often show family traditions of addiction and abuse which become obvious on a genogram. The substance abuse may skip a generation, only to pick up again. Even in the skipped generation, other addiction-like behaviors such as compulsive gambling and television-watching or being a "workaholic" may well be present. A form of "pseudo-individuation" is often present. Like my client's son, who "yo-yos" in and out of the family home, many substance abusers protest that they are "free" and autonomous. As proof, they often display aggressive behaviors toward family members. However, they only do so under the influence of the drug. This allows the family members to discount the aggressive attacks (i.e., "You don't really hate us. You won't really leave us. You're just high."), and the addict to unconsciously concur ("Yes, I don't really hate you, and I won't leave you. I just can't help myself when I'm high") (Stanton and Todd, 1982). The payoff for both the abuser and the abuser's family is that they get to pay homage to the cultural value of the child leaving home and becoming an "individual" without really risking the loss that implies. This same pattern of interactions is frequently present even in the non-abusing generation (the "dry drunk," as AA often calls it).

Of course, there are other systemic pay-offs to substance abuse other than pseudo-individuation. These may occur singly or in any combination. One of the more common (at least in this author's experience) is using the drug or alcohol as a form of self-medication for anxiety. That use is obvious for the one who abuses a central nervous system depressant, like alcohol, or a tranquilizer, like marijuana. However, the other family members also reap a pay-off. They get to focus on the user's problem, which keeps them from having to look at their own issues. For example, mom and dad can fret and worry endlessly over Sue's frequent attendance at Ecstasy parties (a very legitimate worry, considering how dangerous Ecstacy is), but the unspoken payoff is that this worry diverts their attention from their own unsatisfactory relationship. Users frequently "know" this in their Back Stage, so they continue to use despite the best attempts at rehabilitation. If they were to become sober, mom and dad might fall apart. So the user frequently plays out a Martyr script.

The exact opposite may also be true. Sometimes it is not the abuser who volunteers as the "family spear catcher." Sometimes that role is thrust (pun intended) on them. Family members may be operating from a Back Stage life script which says, I am no good, so to feel good about me, I must have someone who is lower than I am. The substance abuser gets recruited for that role - to be the family "black sheep," the one who everyone is better than. In this case, the substance abuser typically plays out a Victim role, but it is a role grounded in reality. This person truly is the family's Victim. The easiest way for the counselor to distinguish which of these dynamics is operating is to watch for who sabotages the therapy. If the abuser/addict is a volunteer to "save" the family, she or he will sabotage the therapy. If the family recruited the abuser/addict, the family will undercut the therapy, all while protesting they are doing what they are doing for this family member's good.

Other systemic functions of drug or alcohol abuse can include escape from boredom, a compensation for a lack of assertiveness, and a means of modulating intimacy. The point of a systemic orientation to therapy is not trying to discover "why" someone does something, but rather discovering what the function of the symptom is. The truly wise therapist treating substance abuse will always look to the family members (both family of origin and family of procreation) as well as the individual in trying to elicit the symptom's function, no matter how strongly the addict/abuser protests he or she has nothing to do with family (Stanton and Todd, 1982). After all, whatever the "cause" of the substance abuse, it grew and was nurtured in the family environment. Unless the family changes its emotional and relational environment, the same ingredients which made the abuse a reasonable "solution" will be waiting to set back the newly recovered abuser.

In doing this family work, many of the systemic interventions already presented in this text are readily applicable. In this author's more than 20 years' experience in working with alcohol and other drug abusers, a genogram is almost a requirement. Very heavy use of circular questioning is an absolute must. An individually focused therapist might ask the daughter, "How do you feel when your parents argue?" By contrast, a systemic therapist, like Counselor Shmooze, would ask the wife, "When you argue, how does your daughter react?" It is a truism in working with families where substance abuse is present that all family members are exceptionally skilled at "ignoring the elephant in the living room." Circular questioning forces family members to become aware of their impact on others.

One technique not mentioned so far in this text is emotional mapping. As already indicated, one of the more common payoffs for both the substance abuser and the family members is an avoidance of pain and anxiety of all sorts - physical pain, perhaps, and also the pain of shame, inadequacy, sadness, fear, etc. By not passing through these emotions and instead going directly to the bottle, the "line", the pill, or the syringe, the addict/abuser avoids the sense of emptiness, powerlessness and hopelessness that he or she expects to be intolerable (Perlmutter, 1996). The addict/abuser may express feelings of self-pity, suffering, resignation, or disgust, but these secondary emotions serve only to mask the real terror lurking hidden Back Stage.

An emotional map begins with the standard genogram symbols and adds color to indicate who expresses what emotions to whom. Each counselor can develop his or her preferred color scheme. This author uses the following codes:

- red - anger/rage (rage indicated by zig-zag line; anger by straight line)
- purple - sexual feelings (appropriate by straight line; incest/abusive by zig-zag line)
- light blue - positive emotional closeness
- black - depression, emptiness
- green - hope
- brown - shame/despair
- orange - fear
- yellow - compassion/pity

While this list is by no means exhaustive, it does open up some of the emotional tone of the family, vividly displaying which emotions are allowed in a given family and which are not. As a practical matter, because several colored lines likely will be running to each family member, the emotional map should be drawn much larger than a conventional genogram. In this author's experience, it is best to keep each page of the emotional map to a single family unit at most. For example, one page may reference the abuser's family of origin, while another page may show cross generational emotional connections.

A key concern in any family intervention is when to bring the family members in. Generally speaking, the earlier family members can be recruited to come to therapy with the addict/abuser, the more likely they are to stay connected and the more beneficial the outcome is likely to be (Edwards, 1990). The therapist should be willing to use any available leverage to get the family in (legal, Department of Human Services, etc.). More importantly, the therapist should do the recruiting, not the addict/abuser. However, there are times when families should be recruited much later in the process. When it is obvious from the case history given by the substance abuser that family members selected him or her for the Victim Role, the therapist should begin family therapy with the family separate from the substance abuser. Only when they have begun to work on their own issues should they be brought in to work with the substance abuser on those issues.

Cognitive/Behavioral Interventions

Any of the cognitive/behavioral interventions described in Chapters 6 and 7 of this text can be applied to working with substance abusers. Because of their power and utility, they ought to be part of the tool kit of every therapist who works with substance abusers. One helpful way to apply those cognitive/behavioral skills is by providing both the abuser and the family information about the conditioning process of addiction. The basis of the following information came from the "Matrix" model developed by therapists at the University of California at Los Angeles and presented to the AAMFT National Conference in 1998.

Introductory Phase

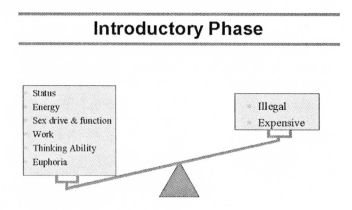

The introductory phase of the addiction process beings with the drug bringing far more benefits than costs. The user likely feels increased social status and energy. Most drugs of abuse claim to enhance sexual performance and drive; whether that is actually the case is beside the point -

the user typically believes it is true. Often the relief that the drug gives actually enhances work performance and produces at least occasional euphoria. The only down side is that many drugs of abuse are illegal, and a drug habit can quickly get expensive. Typically at this point, the strength of the conditioned response is relatively weak. Events such as parties or "special" occasions do stimulate pleasant thoughts of drug use, but because the use is infrequent, use remains totally under the user's control.

Maintenance Phase

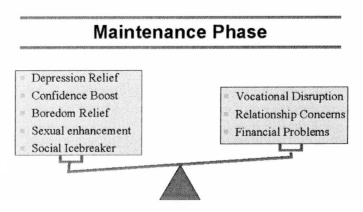

If the user progresses on to abuse, she or he enters the maintenance phase. The drug use still produces depression and boredom relief, and still boosts confidence in both sexual and work performance. Being part of the drug scene makes for an instant icebreaker, an important benefit for one who fears he or she is socially inept. On the down side, the emotional and financial costs of the drug use are beginning to take their toll. By now there are occasional vocational disruptions (including school, if the user is an adolescent), the cost of the habit is becoming harder to manage, and those with whom the user has ongoing relationships often express concerns about the effects of the drug on the relationship (even if they do not know the user is in fact using). Though the positives still outweigh the negatives, it is the strength of the conditioned response which keeps the drug use going at this point. The "triggers" (conditioned stimuli) for drug use now include parties, Friday nights, the presence of friends, concerts, sexual situations, and any "good times." These triggers elicit pleasant thoughts of eager anticipation for drug use. There is a mild physiological arousal, as the body physiologically prepares for the on-coming "high." This physiological response only makes the cravings grow stronger as the time for use actually approaches. At this point, the use is still under voluntary control, but only barely.

Disenchantment Phase

Social Currency	Nosebleeds-infections
Occasional Euphoria	Financial Jeopardy
Relief from Lethargy	Relationship Disruption
	Family Distress
	Impending Job Losss

The disenchantment phase marks a transition from abuse to dependence. By now, the abuser is losing control. The costs, such as nosebleeds or infections (depending on the route of administration), financial jeopardy, relationship disruptions, family distress, and impending job loss outweigh the still-present benefits of the drug's being a social currency, and giving occasional euphoria and relief from lethargy and boredom. The user knows all the costs. What keeps the using going is the very strong conditioned response operating on the Back Stage. Now weekends, friends, and any "unpleasant" emotions can trigger strong cravings and physiological arousal. The conditioned response is so strong that the user continually thinks of drug use, even in the absence of the conditioned stimuli. Of course, what the user thinks about is the pleasure that the drug formerly produced. However, on the Back Stage the user tells himself , It was great once, and it can be again if only I do the drug "right" (translated, take more, or more often).

From the disenchantment phase it is only a short slide down the slope to the disaster phase. The drug still likely produces relief from fatigue and depression (not all do by this point), but even so, the costs far outweigh these minimal benefits. The user's body is beginning to show failure by weight loss, and a host of physical problems (exactly which ones depending on the drug of abuse and route and duration of administration). In addition, there is often severe depression when the drug is not "on board." Bankruptcy, unemployment and family dissolution are common. Any sane person would have quit long before now, and the addict is certainly sane enough to recognize the costs. However, Back Stage, the strength of the conditioned response is by now overwhelming. Any and every situation or emotion can be a trigger for drug use. With the presentation of the trigger, the body responds with a powerful anticipatory response, which guarantees automatic use of the drug. Often the user has obsessive thoughts of drug use, though usually the Back Stage is filled with the fears of the pain of not using rather than the joys of using.

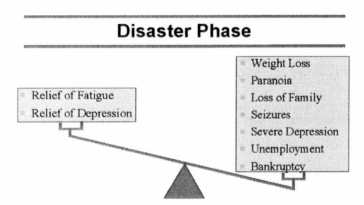

Disaster Phase

| Relief of Fatigue |
| Relief of Depression |

| Weight Loss |
| Paranoia |
| Loss of Family |
| Seizures |
| Severe Depression |
| Unemployment |
| Bankruptcy |

The skillful counselor will help abusing/addicted individuals and their families recognize their own triggers and the responses those triggers provide. Family members will have to recognize how they enabled or cooperated with the user's getting the drug, especially in the early stages of use. Once these patterns are clearly stated (moved from Back Stage to Front Stage, in the Metasystems language), the counselor and the clients can begin to plan alternative responses. That is, they can begin to plan ways to avoid the triggers (the conditioned stimuli) that are possible to avoid, and alternative responses to give instead of the drug use (the conditioned response) to all the various triggers. Building on this is a relapse prevention plan, which involves all the members of the family working together to face the inevitable temptations to relapse (especially during the "Wall" period, which typically occurs between six and 20 weeks post-discharge from inpatient treatment).

"Spiritual" Interventions

Alcoholics Anonymous (www.aa.org) is well known for its insistence that belief in a Higher Power is necessary for deliverance from addiction. This is indeed the Second Step of the famous Twelve Steps, and most Twelve Step programs include a similar statement. AA, in keeping with its Twelve Traditions, is very insistent that each person in recovery must define what the Higher Power is for him or her self. Other groups are not so reticent. In doing research for this text, this author was able to discover Twelve Step groups which explicitly identified themselves with a variety of religious traditions from Buddhist to evangelical Christian to Muslim. What all of these groups have in common is a core belief that substance abuse has, at a minimum, a spiritual component and therefore requires some sort of spiritual intervention. Muslims might be encouraged to practice the Five Pillars of Islam. Christians might be counseled to attend public and private worship. Buddhists might be encouraged to pray and practice self-denial to forever break the cycle of desire.

The thesis of this author's doctoral dissertation (Perry, 1980) was even more radical. My thesis was that substance abuse not only has a spiritual component, but is at its core a spiritual disorder. That is, the abuser is trying to satisfy a legitimate spiritual need, such as forgiveness, acceptance, or fellowship, via a chemical means. This spiritual core only adds to the strength of the conditioned responses already discussed, because the chemical does satisfy those desires - after a fashion. The alcohol abuser, for example, can find the acceptance she is missing at home by joining other alcohol abusers in their ritual of getting drunk together. The cocaine abuse can find forgiveness of all sorts of "sins" in the euphoria of the chemical skyrocket. Of course, the need is never really satisfied by the drug, and sooner or later the drug wears off, leaving only emptiness where the illusion of fullness formerly existed. So the user tries more and more of the same, trying to keep the illusion from ending, because the emptiness is so devastating.

I tested this thesis in my dissertation research and found that it was significantly (at .01) true. My clinical work with substance abusers since that date continues to confirm that impression, so I have confidence my research was not skewed by the relatively small (n = approximately 50), homogeneous (exclusively military member) sample.

All the major therapy professions' codes of ethics would prohibit a therapist's imposing his or her religious beliefs on a client. However, there is a growing awareness that spiritual issues are an important part of any therapy. My experience strongly suggests that this is especially true in working with substance abusers. In constructing an ecomap (see Chapter 11), for example, the counselor will want to inquire carefully about spiritual influences in the relational ecology. While the abuser may not have been active in organized religion (commonly the case), my experience is that there are still spiritual influences - perhaps a very religious grandmother, or a family story about the ancestor who was a preacher or priest. These influences set Back Stage expectations and hopes for which the substance appears a "solution." That fact strongly suggests that spiritual resources should be a part of the solution to the abuse that the therapist and client co-create.

Of course, groups like AA or NA are invaluable in working with any substance abuser. These groups exist solely to help others find the sobriety the members fought for and found. Members know all the lies and rationalizations from having used them themselves. The mantra "90 meetings in 90 days" sets an expectation that the substance abuser will continue recovery by establishing new patterns of relationships as soon as he or she leaves inpatient treatment. The recovering abuser will find her or his sponsor more willing and able to listen at all hours of the day or night than any therapist could be. Family members often (though not as often as the person in recovery) find invaluable support in groups like Al-Anon or Al-ATeen.

The real trick from the counselor's perspective is finding the right group for the individual client and his or her family. Some clients will want one of the explicitly faith-group oriented groups. Others will be more comfortable with the deliberately ambiguous "Higher Power." Even those who gravitate to AA or NA will find that not all groups are created equal. By the Twelve Traditions of AA, each group is autonomous, so there can be great variation in what happens from group to group. If a client tries a particular group and does not feel comfortable there, encourage him or her to try another. The odds are high that the next group will be different.

Spiritual resources alone will not resolve a substance abuse problem. If they could, the many prayers that abusers prayed on the way down to disaster would have turned them around. Nevertheless, spiritual resources need to be considered a vital part of an overall treatment program. The specifics will vary with the need of the client and the ability of the therapist. Counselors who feel the need for more training in working with spiritual issues can find a variety of books and workshops readily available to extend their skills in this essential area.

Conclusion

Substance abuse has been a problem from the earliest recorded human history. Over the years mental health professionals have discovered that the problem is exceedingly complex and therefore an integrated treatment approach works best. This chapter suggests just a few of the interventions which will be necessary. Pharmacological interventions (such as prescribing an anti-anxiety medication for people coming off of alcohol abuse) are often necessary, but are, of course, the province of medical doctors. They are beyond the scope of this text's target audience. The gender and sociocultural variables which are very important to accurate treatment planning are likewise beyond this text's scope. The truly proficient substance abuse counselor should have detailed, specific knowledge of the abused drugs (including, of course, alcohol and abused prescription medications) when working with substance abusers.

Even the suggestions for therapy in this chapter are only that - suggestions. Probably more than any other area of therapy, those who work with substance abusers will need special supervision in the field. The best place to learn is in the crucible of therapy.

Living Into the Lesson

1. The author cites a source which claims that drug abuse can be traced back at least 7000 years and in almost every human culture. The negative consequences have been known at least that long, too. What makes drug abuse such a persistent human problem despite the well-known consequences of that abuse?

2. Take a position pro or con on this statement: marijuana should be legalized for medical purposes only. Support your position with research of your own.

3. Create a 3-generation genogram of someone who abuses drugs or alcohol (your subject, your subject's parents, and your subject's parents' parents). If you don't know anyone who will admit to substance abuse, check with the local AA or NA chapter. They likely have someone who will be glad to help. What evidence do you see to support the family dynamics mentioned in this chapter?

4. You are working with a family concerned about the 16 year old son's marijuana use. In the room are mom, dad, and sister, age 15. Work with a group of other students - one for each role, one to play therapist, and one to be the observer - and use circular questioning to unpack how each family member is affected by the boy's daily use of an illegal drug .

5. You are working with a single mother of a 13 year old daughter. In the course of working with mom on parenting issues, you discover she is abusing her Xanax prescription. Role play the case with two other students and practice using circular questioning.

6. Map the emotions of your family when you were a teen. Who talked with whom? With what types of emotions? What emotions were allowed? Which were not accepted?

7. The author makes a strong point that the therapist, not the chemically dependent person, should recruit family members for therapy. Why? What are the risks of allowing the substance abuser to do the recruiting? What are the risks of having the therapist do it?

8.   The author presents a four-phase model of the conditioning process for drug addiction. What makes some people progress all the way to the disaster phase, while other people stop short at one of the other phases? What, besides conditioning and family dynamics, might account for this variation?

9.   Take a habit of your own (it could be a "good" habit or a "bad" habit) and apply the four-phase model to your own situation. What are the benefits of the habit? The costs? Who helps/helped reinforce the conditioned response (the habit)? What automatic thoughts can you identify in your own habit-history? Is the habit totally automatic, or do you still have some conscious control over it? What has made the difference in your being in the stage where you currently are? What change in the habit do you see coming, if any?

10.   Do you buy the author's thesis that substance abuse issues are at their core spiritual issues? Why or why not? What evidence do you have for your position?

11.   Check with the local AA and NA organizations. Obtain a list of local meetings to which you could refer a potential client. What do you learn from looking over these lists?

12.   Obtain a copy of the Twelve Steps. What spiritual components can you identify in addition to the Higher Power reference (Step Two)?

13.   Suppose you are an evangelical Christian, and you have a client recovering from prescriptions drug use who tells you she a member of Wicca. What would you need to be able to work with this client on her spiritual issues in recovery? How would you ensure your own beliefs did not hinder the progress of therapy? What would be different if you considered yourself non-religious and you were working with a devout Muslim?

14.   Construct a three-generation spiritual genogram of your own family. The symbols are the same as a regular genogram, but the notations refer to the transmission of religious traditions and strength of religious practice. How could you use a spiritual genogram in working with your substance-abusing client? Where might some "solutions" to the substance abuse be found?

15. Assume you have a client who is the spouse of a substance abuser. The client tells you the substance abuser refuses to acknowledge there is a problem and asks you what to do. What do you tell the client?

Chapter 13 - "Disarming the Bomb"

Nearly all men can stand adversity, but if you want to test a man's character, give him power. - Abraham Lincoln

If you were to survey 100 people to discover which emotion was the most troublesome, in all probability you would find that anger would, by far, rank number one. In fact, Carrere and Gottman (1999) found that it is possible to predict eventual divorce in premarital couples from simply observing the first three minutes of a problem-soaked conversation. Those who eventually divorced expressed negative emotions significantly more frequently than those who remained married. Divorce is by no means the only negative "fall out" from anger in a relationship. Approximately 2000 children are killed in their homes each year, and 1100 of these were killed by their mothers (Miller, 1989). Being a child in a family where parents abuse each other makes the child 15 times more likely to be abused or killed than children who live in non-abusive families (Stacy and Shupe, 1983). U.S. Bureau of Justice statistics confirm that both women and men are more likely to be assaulted or killed by someone they know than by a stranger (Bachman, 1994). This is not just a family matter, as some would claim. Every year the medical costs from domestic violence total between $3 and $5 billion. Businesses lose another $100 million per year in lost wages, sick leave, absenteeism, and non-productivity (Domestic Violence for Health Care Providers (3rd Ed.), Colorado Domestic Violence Coalition, 1991.). While it is possible that all this pain and chaos stems from emotions other than anger, it does seem reasonable to assume that anger and rage play a very significant role.

Yet common experience shows that anger is a near-universal experience. People differ in their outward expressions, but there is probably no one (with the possible exception of some saints) who does not experience anger. Still, not everyone who gets angry commits assault or murder. Clearly, not every incidence of anger is an appropriate focus for therapy. So the first task of this chapter will be to differentiate between pathological and normal anger. Following that introduction, our attention will turn to treating both pathological and non-pathological anger.

The Meaning and Function of Anger

Many authors treat anger and rage as though they were simply different points on the same continuum, with emotions like irritation and frustration being at the low end of that scale. I do not believe this is the most helpful way to look at these emotions. My clinical experience indicates that anger and rage are qualitatively different.

Jacobson and Gottman (1998) came to a similar (though admittedly not identical) conclusion in their research on abusers. They found that some batterers (the "Pit Bulls") fit the stereotypes. These men became visibly and physiologically aroused as the battering approached. There was a clear build up of the anger until it exploded. Other batterers (the "Cobras") actually became physiologically calmer (as measured by decreased heart rate) as the battering approached. Cobras are not out of control when they batter. Their dramatic lashing out is coldly calculated to produce just the response they desire. Jacobson and Gottman's conclusion is that the risk to the woman trying to leave an abusive relationship and the type of therapy appropriate for the batterer depends on whether the batterer is a Pit Bull or a Cobra.

In my understanding, Pit Bulls are angry when they batter. Anger is an emotion which can be modulated. It is possible to be "a little angry" and it is possible to be "so angry I can't see straight." It is even possible to talk someone down from their anger. For example, a quick, sincere apology can often turn around a rapidly building anger, as can giving a reasonable alternative explanation that the angry person had not previously considered. Furthermore, the one who is angry can exert some conscious control over the anger. For example, it is very common for a couple having a heated verbal argument, when the telephone rings, to have one of them answer the phone and even joke with the person on the other end, and once the phone call ends go right back to the heated verbal argument. The final crucial distinguishing mark of anger is that anger seeks to "fix" the problem and reconnect with the other person. Anger serves to protest some real or perceived threat and to motivate the angry person to remove that threat by the classic "fight or flight" response. Even the Pit Bulls are trying to "fix" their spouse so they can have a "happy relationship" (as defined by the Pit Bull). One of the major tasks of therapy for abused women is to help them feel their anger at being abused so they can be motivated to "fix" the problem rather than to continue helplessly submitting to the abuse.

By contrast, Cobras represent rage. Rage may indeed look like out-of-control anger, but it may, as Jacobson and Gottman's research showed, look very different. Rage cannot be modulated. Rage tends to be global, not specifically targeted like anger, and trying to talk someone out of their rage is guaranteed to only increase the rage. If a phone call interrupts someone in a rage, for example, the rage-full person likely will speak to the person on the telephone with the same degree of venom as they are using on the original target of their rage. While anger seeks ultimately to "fix" the problem, rage seeks only to destroy. Rage-ful people   tend to be unremorseful about the damage they inflicted because they have a low opinion of and need for other people. In their view, the other person deserves whatever they get. While it is certainly possible to move from anger to rage (indeed, it is a sadly common outcome when anger is simply "stuffed" and not allowed to perform its intended function of "fixing" the problem), the move is still a qualitative jump and not simply a slide along a continuum.

Even with non-pathological (i.e., non-abusive) anger, the outward manifestation can vary greatly. Some people, for example, display anger by shouting. Their heightened physiological arousal shows in their red faces and bulging neck muscles and (likely) clenched fists. Other people display anger by becoming very emotionally cold and distant (e.g., the "passive-aggressive" person). Their heightened physiological arousal is often more difficult to spot, but can be seen in rapid, shallow breathing, increased pupil size, and very rapid reaction to any "hostile" or "threatening" (as subjectively assessed) move. Of course, there are many possible variations on these basic themes. Counselors need to remember that regardless of its intensity or pathology, relational anger is at its core a protest against a real or imagined threat to the relationship, and that anger has as its goal the removal of the threat and the restoration of the relationship as it "ought" to be. This is one of the fundamental tenants of attachment theory (Sperling and Berman, 1994).

Confronting Anger in Intimate Relationships

The counselor's first task when working with angry relationships is to assess whether this is indeed an angry relationship or a rage-full one. If it is rage-full, as determined by the goal of the behavior and the actions when the emotion is present, the only safe course is to separate the clients and work with them individually. Client safety is always a primary concern for every helping professional. Remembering that rage tends to be global rather than selective, the counselor will proceed with extreme caution when dealing with the rage-full person. To use Jacobson and Gottman's image, this work is indeed like being in a pit full of cobras. They can and will bite without warning, and without anger before or remorse after the event. Because this work is so exceptionally dangerous for everyone, the beginning therapist should immediately refer a Cobra to a more experienced clinician, or proceed only with very careful, direct supervision. This work is beyond the scope of this introductory text.

If the primary emotion is anger rather than rage, as determined by the goal of the behavior and the actions when the emotion is present, the therapist next has to assess whether this is pathological (i.e., emotionally, verbally, or physically abusive) or non-pathological anger. If it is pathological, the therapist will need to take immediate steps to de-escalate or defuse the anger and provide for the safety of both clients.

As an aside, each therapist should know the legal requirements for mandated reporting of abuse in her or his state, and should have, before allowing clients to reveal any possible abuse, already warned the client about the mandated reporting requirements in their state. At a very minimum, this warning should be included in the written Informed Consent document the client receives in the first few minutes of the first session of therapy (see Chapter 1), and ideally should be verbally stated as well as written.

As previously stated in this chapter, attachment theory holds that anger and anxiety are normal reactions to any perceived or actual threat to the relationship. Since most people do have Secure attachment styles (approximately 56% - Sperling and Berman, 1994), the odds are that the individuals in the couples or families coming to therapy for non-pathological anger problems will have Secure attachment styles. That assumption is predictive of successful resolution to the problem. Once the threat is resolved, the attachment drive, as manifested by the anger and/or anxiety, should subside and the relationship should return to its normal, secure base. Depending on the exact nature of the presenting problem, any of a number of therapeutic techniques can be useful in achieving this goal. For example, psychoeducational approaches which teach communication and conflict resolution skills could be sufficient. Other clients might respond better to cognitive/ behavioral therapy, which provides them alternative explanations and specific strategies to increase the number of positive interactions in the relationship.

As the table "Attachment Styles for Adults" at the end of this chapter suggests, clients with a Preoccupied attachment style will often be the identified patient where non-pathological anger is a presenting problem. Persons with this attachment style not only want but actually need relationships, because self-worth is totally, or almost totally, dependent on being attached to the other person. Not surprisingly, then, any perceived threat to that relationship will be felt by the person with a Preoccupied attachment style as seriously as a threat to survival itself. Invariably, the goal of the angry expression is to communicate, "You are unavailable to me right now and I cannot accept that level of pain, so you must change and become available to me again."

Counselor Samuel Shmooze knew that maintaining a systemic focus is essential in helping these couples. He was meeting with Alice and Chad, who came to him complaining of Alice's "irrational" anger. This was a first marriage for both of them, and they had been married 3 years.

A   I can't help it. He's just so thoughtless. He never pays any attention to me. I mean, he's home, but he might as well be gone. All he does is sit there on that damn computer.

C   That's not true. I spend lots of nights with you. We watch tv together. We talk during supper. I even call you sometimes during the day.

T   Umm, let me see if I understand. Chad, when you sit and talk with Alice at supper, how does she act?

C   Fine. I mean, we talk and all. It's very nice.

T   Okay. And Alice, when Chad is on his computer....

C   (interrupting) I'm hardly ever on that damn thing! Besides, I have work to do!

T   I understand. As I was saying, Alice, on those times when Chad is on his computer, how does he act?

A   Like I'm not even there. I feel like a piece of furniture, not his wife.

T   Chad, on those times when you are on the computer, how does Alice let you know she's not happy?

C   Oh, you couldn't miss it. Sometimes she'll come to the study door and say something really biting, like, "If you love that thing so much you can just make love to it to night." Sometimes she just stays in the kitchen, but the way she slams the pots and pans around, you can't miss that she's ticked. It's amazing we still have those pots and pans.

T   So this happens often enough that you wonder about the future of the cookware?

C   Yeah, I guess it does.

A   See! I told you he ignores me all the time!

T   Alice, when you say or do those things, what is it you hope Chad will do in return?

A   I want him to pay attention to me! I want him to come over to me and hug me and let me know that he loves me. That's what I want.

Counselor Shmooze's use of circular questioning helped him to understand that Alice's feelings of abandonment were not totally irrational - Chad did at times ignore her. Just as importantly, at other times he focused appropriately on her. This was his clue that Alice's attachment style was Preoccupied and that it was Chad's very inconsistency that prompted her frantic efforts to keep him consistently "loving" (i.e., attached). Had Counselor Shmooze started using "why did you..." or other types of linear questions, he could easily have further polarized an already polarized situation.

Counselor Shmooze developed a treatment plan with Alice and Chad which included primarily solution-focused therapy, with heavy emphasis on the behavioral component. The goal of therapy was to give Alice enough secure attachment experiences that she could begin to relax and not feel the former level of panic during times when Chad was unavailable. To compliment these behavioral changes, Alice would be assisted to creating some positive self-talk to help her overcome her low self-worth.

Couples with a Fearful attachment style will often present as very similar to those with a Preoccupied style. Often, though not always, a distinguishing difference will be that the anger will be reciprocal in the Fearful attachment style. The person with the Fearful style may well have unconsciously selected someone who would indeed prove untrustworthy and undependable as a mate. Even if the spouse does not enter the relationship as undependable and untrustworthy, he or she cannot help eventually responding to the spouse's expectation that he or she is. The more undependable the spouse is, the more angry the Fearful spouse may become. Completing the circle, the more angry the Fearful spouse becomes, the more absent (and perhaps angry) the undependable spouse becomes.

These couples, too, require serious therapy. Both may have a Fearful attachment style. This makes creating the trust necessary to form a Secure attachment all the more difficult. Even if one partner does not have a Fearful style, living with constant suspicion and distrust is wearing at best. The partner may well be very discouraged by the Fearful person's constant demands for contact and yet inability to accept the contact that is given. Since Bowlby's initial theoretical work in the late 1940s, attachment theory has held that attachment style is fixed, at least in large measure, by age two (Sperling and Berman, 1994). Given that fact, a psychodynamic therapy like object relations therapy or Adlerian therapy may be useful. However, it is by no means the only option. Attachment theory also holds that it is the continued validation of the person's early working models in the form of continued success or lack of success in forming secure bonds that accounts for the persistence of this early learning experience. Therefore, any therapy that disrupts the behavior sequence of self-fulfilling prophecies and which also builds healthy trust experiences will make a significant difference. Obviously, doing this work in couple or family sessions is more effective than doing it with individuals. The therapy session can and should be a training ground for ways the couple will treat each other outside of the therapy room.

People with a Dismissing attachment style represent a particular challenge. To use the language of Transactional Analysis, they operate from a "I'm okay-You're Not Okay" position. This means that they frequently feel justified in their becoming angry and in fact blame the partner for the anger. Although not every person with a Dismissing attachment style will become abusive, this style is remarkably similar to the "typical" abuser. "Abusive husbands most frequently explain that they wouldn't hit their wives if (a) 'She'd only listen to [obey] me'; (b) 'she'd take better care of the kids and the house'; (c) 'she'd stop nagging or yelling at me'; and (d) 'she'd stop talking back to me' " (Rosenbaum and O'Leary, 1986, p. 393). It is well known that abused children tend to grow up to become abusers. If being abused happens to be in the background of the Dismissing person (which fits the theoretical model), it certainly makes the Dismissing person's compulsive self-reliance and refusal to depend on others understandable.

If abuse is present in the current relationship, the counselor's first task is to ensure the physical and emotional safety of the one being abused. Often abusers will bring weapons into therapy (such as a pocket knife doubling as a key chain) and "play" with them during the session. Whether intentional or not, such actions can be intimidating and should be explicitly prohibited. If the abuser has a history of very rapidly escalating out of control, the therapist should take further precautions to ensure that nothing that could be used as a weapon (such as a letter opener or a paper weight) is readily accessible on the desk top. Establishing and signing a firm escape plan as a contingency should anger get out of control between sessions becomes the next order of business. This should be completed before the end of the first session.

The work of therapy begins in earnest when the Dismissing person begins to recognize his or her triggers and physiological cues that anger is building towards an explosion. Counselor Shmooze was doing this work with Adam and Mary.

T	Mary, how do you know Adam is getting mad?
M	He gets unusually quiet. He won't even answer when I ask him if he wants a beer.
T	Adam, do you know what Mary is talking about?
A	Yeah, I guess so. I never thought about it before.
T	And what is your first clue that you're getting mad?
A	That's easy. It's when she does something bubble-headed like she usually does.
T	You're describing your view of Mary. Tell me how you feel. Tell me where you first feel the anger in your body.

A   I don't know. I never thought about it.

T   That's okay. There's always a first time. Where in your body do you usually first feel your anger?

A   I guess my shoulders get tight. Yeah, I get tight in my shoulders, and then the back of my neck gets tight.

T   You're doing great. Is this tightness before you get quiet?

A   Uh, I don't know. About the same time, I guess.

The conversation continues with Counselor Shmooze getting Mary to describe what she sees, what cues she observes in Adam that he may not be aware of. Adam also helps Mary identify the behaviors she shows which are not helpful once the escalation has started.

Once cues and triggers are identified, therapy moves to adjusting the attitude of both the abuser (or person with Dismissing attachment style) and the spouse. Both parties will, for their respective reasons, need to check out their irrational beliefs which lead to the angry interactions, and create alternative explanations for the data which lead to more satisfying results. Similarly, both need to learn to use proper self-talk at the first sign of cues and triggers so that both stay more calm than before (Rosenbaum and O'Leary, 1986). Other therapeutic interventions might include teaching about the "cycle of violence" and teaching various relaxation techniques. Communication skill training, to include non-toxic ways of expressing dissatisfaction, can also be a component of the deeper work with attitudes and feelings.

Using Private Fictions and Teleology With Couples/Families

One primary sign of any system's health, from the internal system inside a single individual to the global system of a league of nations, is that system's ability to successfully negotiate conflict. That point is significant. It is not the presence of anger or conflict which is a problem. It is the way the conflict is handled which is predictive of the system's ability to meet its member's needs and thus the system's ability to survive. Further, people tend to use the same conflict management patterns for both intrapsychic and interpersonal conflict. Some of these patterns, such as always being defensively angry, are clearly dysfunctional, while other patterns may well be functional in one setting and dysfunctional in another (Heitler, 1990).

Regardless of its source, there are five basic responses to a conflict situation (Heitler, 1990). One is to fight. People who fight tend to use projection and blame or criticize the other person in lieu of seeing those qualities in themselves. The goal of the anger is to impose the angry person's goal on the other person and thus "fix" the problem. Alternatively, people can "fight" internally by becoming self-critical, attacking their own thoughts and feelings. Self-critical people tend to escalate feelings in order to gain control in a frustrating situation. People who use anger as a primary conflict resolution style frequently operate from a Getter lifestyle - "I must get power and control in relationships or I do not have any worth."

The second basic response is submission. People who habitually submit tend to become depressed. This depression can and often does grow to clinical levels (though, of course, not all clinical depression results from submission). Where submission is a primary conflict resolution strategy, one person becomes very dominant and the submissive partner sinks further into resentment or depression. The submissive person may well operate from a Martyr lifestyle - "I'm more virtuous than you because I don't fight back and I give in to you."

A third basic response is fleeing. People can certainly physically flee a conflict situation by leaving the scene of the conflict, but people can also flee by ceasing to talk or by changing the subject. They can also "flee" internally by suppressing or repressing from conscious awareness their own uncomfortable thoughts or feelings. Behavioral cues to a "flee" strategy include compulsive behaviors, obsessional thinking, addictions, or schizoid isolation. Naturally, these symptoms often produce relationships which are as distant or disengaged as relationships where members physically flee the conflict.

The fourth primary response to conflict is to freeze. In other words, the person simply waits in hopes that the situation will spontaneously improve. People who choose this strategy tend to be anxious, passive people. Likely, their experience has proven to them that whatever they do will only make the situation worse, so they wait, shivering, not knowing what will happen next. The chronic anxiety and tension present in these families is a major clue to what is going on. Another major clue will be the client's staying solidly "stuck" despite the therapist's best efforts to move them. The Back Stage rule is: Anything I do will make matters worse, so it is better to live in this pain than it is to even attempt to solve anything.

The fifth, and obviously most beneficial, response to conflict is problem solving. Problem solving requires healthy ego functioning on the part of all parties in order to listen to one's own thoughts and feelings, and to listen just as closely to the other's thoughts and feelings. The goal of any therapy attempting to "disarm the bomb" is to increase the client's skill at and likelihood of using problem solving skills.

Since anger, by its very nature, seeks to resolve the conflict, one effective way to move from unresolved anger to a solution is to make the conflicted parties' private logic overt. In other words, the trick is to move the private logic from the Back Stage to the Front Stage, where it can be examined and changed as necessary.

Counselor Shmooze continued working with Adam and Mary to uncover their private logic and their Back Stage goals in their conflict resolution styles. They already understood that their typical response to conflict was for Adam to fight and Mary to freeze. While Mary interpreted her freezing as her attempt to keep matters from growing worse, Adam interpreted it as a passive-aggressive attempt to wrest control from him. This interpretation only reinforced Adam's already-present view of others as dangerous and not to be trusted.

T   So, Adam, help me understand. Complete this sentence for me, please. "I must not be controlled by others because ..."

A   (Pause) ... because I'll get hurt if others get a chance.

T   Good. And "Others will hurt me if they get a chance because ...."

A   ... people are basically mean.

T   And "People are basically mean because ... "

A   ...because they only think of themselves.

T   So, when you ask Mary to do something and she doesn't respond, for you she is being mean and self-centered.

A   I guess so. That seems right. But Mary is so good, so thoughtful, I never would have called her self-centered.

T   Right. Part of you knows that she is the loving, thoughtful woman you married. But another part of you feels that any time she disagrees or doesn't do what you want, she is being mean and self- centered.

A   Ouch. I hate to admit it, but you're right.

T   So, Adam, I want you to visualize a time in your past, before you met Mary, when you felt like this. It doesn't matter when it was. Just pick a time and get it clearly in your mind.

A   (Long pause) Okay.

T   Now, describe what was going on.

Adam vividly described several incidents where people had been rejecting of him. He described his hurt at these rejections, and his decision that he would never allow himself to be hurt again. Mary listened intently. She saw a vulnerable side of her husband she had never seen before. This made him seem less frightening, and freed her, with Counselor Shmooze's help, from her frozen defensiveness to be able to actively cooperate with the problem solving strategies to follow. Adam began to be able to use Mary's thoughtfulness as a resource to help him distinguish interpersonal cues when his normally self-protective response was appropriate from times when a more open, cooperative stance was appropriate. This mutually supportive style of interaction increased the number of positive interactions in their relationship and reinforced the work already accomplished.

The key for the therapist is to pay close attention to the presenting symptoms as a way of entering the client's Back Stage and uncovering both the private logic maintaining the current pattern of interaction and the goal or purpose of that pattern. Emotions, because of their ability to signal internal states, are crucial sources of data in this discovery process. Working purely from a cognitive or rational basis will likely prove futile. The habit patterns are too ingrained in emotional logic to respond to "oughts" and "shoulds." The patterns are also too entrenched in habit to respond easily to careless or unfocused therapy. Once this careful behavioral and emotional assessment is performed, the specific therapeutic techniques which will carry out the resulting treatment plan can be selected according to the client's needs.

Conclusion

Most of the case examples in this chapter focused on couples' interactions. However, the same principles apply to other interactions, including those between parents and children, co-workers, and members of the extended family. For example, a securely-attached teen may still respond angrily to her parents' "unfair" restrictions on her dating. A fearfully-attached volunteer in a service club may drive other members crazy with his long-winded bragging about his accomplishments and minimizing of others' accomplishments. The variations are endless, but the same principles still apply.

Once a person interprets an event or an action as a threat, the amygdala (in the limbic system of the brain) automatically triggers the previously learned response. That is why simply knowing "I should not act like that" is not helpful. The amygdala will have triggered the protective response long before that conscious thought can ever arise out of the neocortex. To change the response, the person must do the Back Stage work of changing the perception of the threat so that either the amygdala is not triggered or the conditioned response is more appropriate to the actual threat level.

Attachment Styles for Adults

Belief About Others	Internal View of Self	
	Positive (Low Dependence on others)	Negative (High Dependence on others)
Positive (Low need to avoid them)	***Secure*** It is relatively easy for me to become emotionally close to others. I am comfortable depending on others and having others depend on me. I don't worry about being alone or having others not accept me. Generally, others are trustworthy and loveable, and I am loveable and worthy. My relationships are a source of support and comfort. <u>Results</u>: self-esteem; comfort with closeness; trust; healthy dependence	***Preoccupied*** I want to be completely emotionally intimate with others, but I often find that others are reluctant to get as close as I would like. I am uncomfortable being without close relationships, but I sometimes worry that others don't value me as much as I value them. My only self-worth comes from gaining close relationships with others, but I find others sometimes available and sometimes not, and I find it difficult to understand others. <u>Results</u>: Over dependence; aloneness; interpersonal anxiety; desire for approval; lack of confidence; preoccupation with relationships
Negative (High need to avoid them)	***Dismissing*** I am comfortable without close emotional relationships. It is very important to me to feel independent and self-sufficient, and I prefer not to depend on others or have others depend on me. This is because I find others as untrustworthy and undependable. I [defensively] see myself as too good for others and relationships are not worth the effort. <u>Results</u>: Avoidance of intimacy; lack of trust; value on independence; compulsive self-reliance; emphasis on achievement	***Fearful*** I am somewhat uncomfortable getting close to others. I want emotionally close relationships but I find it difficult to trust others completely or to depend on them. I sometimes worry that I will be hurt if I allow myself to become too close to others. I find others as untrustworthy and undependable. I worry that I am unlovable and therefore that others will threaten what control I do have over my life. <u>Results</u>: Low self-esteem; lack of trust; interpersonal anxiety; desire for contact and intimacy; need for approval; aloneness; anger/hostility

- adapted from Sperling, M.B., and Berman, W.H. (Eds) (1994). *Attachment in adults: Clinical and developmental perspectives.* New York: The Guilford Press.

Living Into the Lesson

1. This chapter began with some depressing statistics about domestic violence. Discuss with your class mates why you believe this plague is so common in our culture. Do you believe domestic violence is more common now, or simply more openly discussed?

2. Discuss an incident in which you or someone you know well was angry. What were the outward manifestations of the anger? What was the (perhaps Back Stage) goal? What happened or could have happened to lessen the intensity of the anger? To what extent does this incident illustrate the criteria for anger given in this chapter?

3. Take an incident of "road rage" you know of or learned of through the news media. What happened? Given the facts of the case, what was the (perhaps Back Stage) goal? What happened or could have happened to lessen the intensity of the incident? To what extent does this "road rage" illustrate the criteria for rage given in this chapter?

4. Take an informal survey of ten people (even strangers will do). When you are angry, how do you show it? Do others know you are angry? On a 1 to 10 scale, with 10 being totally out of control, what is the most angry you have ever been? On that same scale, how angry do you typically allow yourself to get? Share your results with your classmates.

5. What are the laws regarding the mandated reporting of abuse in your state? What types of abuse must be reported? To whom? Are there any exemptions from the requirement?

6. Take a position pro or con and debate this proposition with your classmates: Mandated reporting of abuse makes abusers less likely to report abuse in its early stages because of their fear of the legal consequences.

7. The author indicates that people with a Secure attachment style sometimes can be helped with a psychoeducational intervention, while people with a Preoccupied attachment style will need more extensive therapy. What makes the difference? In the case with Alice and Chad, what evidence did you see of a Preoccupied style?

8. What would attract someone to a person who has a Fearful attachment style? How well would this attraction "wear" as the relationship progressed? Roleplay the interview between Counselor Shmooze and Alice and Chad, but this time with Alice having a Fearful attachment style. What attachment style does Chad have? How does this fit?

9. Watch the classic movie "Gaslight" (It was first released in 1944). Which attachment style would you give the husband? How does the wife respond? If this couple came to you for therapy, how would you treat them?

10. What were the rules regarding conflict in your family of origin? What where the dominant conflict resolution styles? What is your primary conflict resolution style now? If it is different from your family of origin, how did it change?

11. In working with Adam and Mary, Counselor Shmooze used some Gestalt therapy tools. Go back to the case material with Chad and Alice and roleplay these tools using that case. "Chad," "Alice," and "Shmooze" should pay attention to their own feelings as the role play progresses. What does this experience teach you about these techniques?

12. The 1946 classic movie "It's a Wonderful Life" shows a man driven to near suicide by life events. Watch the movie and look for his conflict resolution style. If he had been your client before the suicide attempt, how would you have helped him?

Chapter 14 - Exorcizing "Ghosts"

If you hate a person, you hate something in him that is part of yourself. What isn't part of ourselves doesn't disturb us. - Herman Hesse

Counselor Shmooze was meeting with Bubba, a soon-to-be divorced 45 year old man. Bubba had been married twice before. This now made his third divorce, and, as he expressed it, "three strikes is out in anybody's ball game." He knew that the odds both of re-marrying and of having yet another divorce were both good unless he made some major changes. That was the presenting issue that brought him to Counselor Shmooze's office - to find what changes he needed to make and then how to make those changes.

On the surface, Bubba had his life together relatively well. He had a master's degree and a good job. In Counselor Shmooze's office he displayed good contact with his emotions and very good insight. Still, there was something missing, one key ingredient that kept the whole picture from making sense. Counselor Shmooze and Bubba returned to the genogram they had constructed during their second session together and dug deeper.

T   Bubba, who taught you about sex? I don't mean the "where babies come from" stuff. I mean, who taught you, "guys do this," "gals do that"?

C   I don't know. My parents, I guess.

T   According to what you put on the genogram, your parents had a good relationship. What did you learn from you mother about what it takes to keep a woman happy?

C   (Pause, with a blank stare at Counselor Shmooze) We never talked about that.

T   Okay, your father then. What did your dad teach you about what it takes to keep a woman happy?

C   We didn't talk about that, either. I guess I just learned by watching. They never fought. They just went into the bedroom, closed the door, and when they came out, everything was settled.

T   How about other members of your family? Did anyone teach you what it takes to please a woman?

C   No, that's silly. You just know these things.

Over the course of the hour, Bubba came to realize he was being "haunted" by a ghost - the ghost of his father (who was still very much alive). Bubba's father demanded perfection, and Bubba had largely internalized that same demand. That was one reason Bubba was so successful in most areas of his life. However, in the area of relationships, he had never been a success, even in high school. Every time he embarked on a new relationship, the "ghost" of his father said, "Do it right, son, just like I do it right with your mother." Yet Bubba didn't know how to "do it right." The harder he tried, the more he failed. He masked his insecurity very well behind a facade of self-confidence and physical strength. He was excellent at starting relationships, but by his own Back Stage assessment, a miserable failure in maintaining them.

As the Introduction pointed out, all behavior is ultimately relational. Sometimes the behavior is for the benefit of or is stimulated by people who are physically present. Other times, the behavior is produced by a relationship with people who are physically absent but very emotionally present. These are "ghosts," in the often-metaphorical language of Metasystems. The ghost may be someone living, as in the case of Bubba's father, or it may be someone dead or even someone who is purely fictitious.

Since Bubba and his father had a close relationship all of Bubba's life, he very easily saw from the genogram the Front Stage influences his father had on him. His father taught him to hunt and fish, and his father gave him his love of music and his love of working with his hands. Of course, the Back Stage influences were hidden in plain sight. Once Bubba understood that he had been keeping up a Back Stage relationship with the ghost of his "perfect" father, he was in a position to begin to change his life story to one that allowed him to be less than perfect and still not feel like a disappointment to his father. Not at all surprisingly, he also began to have more success in relationships with the women in his life.

When is "exorcism" appropriate?

Exorcism is a rite for getting rid of a ghost or apparition that is troubling a person or a location. The use of this metaphorical term points to a key truth in dealing with ghosts in our clients - not all ghosts need to be exorcized.

In Bubba's case, the ghost of his father had brought him success in his work life. In that area, he and his father had talked openly, so he did not allow his perfectionism to be carried to extremes. Bubba readily acknowledged that hearing the voice of his father inside his own head had kept him from dropping out of his master's program when his second divorce hit, and at other times as well. In this case, playing to an audience comprised primarily of his father enabled Bubba to reach for personal superiority that he might otherwise not have attempted. This was, in short, a "good" ghost, not a troublesome one, a "ghost" Bubba definitely wanted to keep around.

The ghost of his father haunting his relationships, however, was definitely troubling. Adding to it were the ghosts of his many failed relationships, each haunting Bubba with their message, "See, you couldn't please us. You're a failure. You're just a sham." As the number of ghosts crowding his relationships increased, the likelihood of his failure increased. In this area, he needed an exorcism.

The metaphor is appropriate for another reason. A literal exorcism is not a purely rational process. The same applies to metaphorical exorcisms. Ghosts which operate on the Front Stage rarely bring people to therapy. By definition, these ghosts are known and recognized by the client. Clients can freely talk about them. They may even be embraced by the client. Those Front Stage ghosts that clients want to get rid of can be dealt with by logic, education, or a variety of other Front Stage interventions. Similarly, not all ghosts that inhabit the Back Stage are troublesome. In "The Wizard of Oz" Dorothy found her Back Stage filled with helpful ghosts of people from Kansas who, in disguised form (as Back Stage ghosts often are), helped her survive in "Oz" the aftermath of the tornado. These are ghosts she was glad she had. However, troublesome ghosts that haunt the Back Stage need exorcism, i.e., the trans-rational process of depth therapy.

In summary, when the counselor notices that the client appears to be driven in some way which does not appear to make sense, that is a clue to start looking for a Back Stage audience to whom the client is unconsciously playing. The rest of this chapter will give a few examples of when and how this might occur.

Divorce and post-divorce therapy

Divorced or divorcing couples are prime candidates to be haunted by ghosts, and there are plenty of them to be haunted. According to the U.S. Census Bureau, 40 percent of all marriages in 1991 were remarriages for one or both parties. That same report, which focused on women of various ethnic backgrounds, indicates that among first marriages that ended in divorce, the median length of marriage for those women in their 20s at the time of divorce was 3.4 years, the median length of marriage for the women in their 30s was 4.9 years, and the median length of marriage for women in their 40s was 7.6 years. Taking all ages into consideration, 38 percent of marriage that end in divorce do so before the fifth anniversary, and 65 percent do not make the tenth anniversary (Norton and Miller, 1992).

Healthy marriages are able to flexibly, perhaps even synergistically, promote growth for each spouse as well as for the relationship. Almost by definition, divorcing couples have failed in one or more of these crucial tasks. In addition, marriage is often a major source of identity for both men and women. Loss of the marriage can therefore mean a lost of identity, with concomitant feelings of failure and lowered self-esteem.

Counselor Shmooze was working with Carmen, a 32 year old mother of two children ages 3 and 2 years, during her separation and divorce. Her husband had announced that he was having an affair and he was leaving her for the other woman. Shortly after that announcement, he moved out of the house. Although Counselor Shmooze prefers to work with couples even through the divorce process, in this case, that was not a possibility. He had helped Carmen and Pedro, her husband, negotiate the logistics of their separation - the temporary child care and living arrangements, visitation, dividing the bills, etc. Even though Pedro refused to come in, Counselor Shmooze was careful to ensure, to the best of his ability, that all the agreements were fair to all parties. Counselor Shmooze had enough experience with divorcing couples to know that if either person perceived an agreement as unfair, the likely end result would be more battles elsewhere - usually over the children and visitation issues.

In his exit speech before moving out, Pedro had blamed the affair on Carmen, specifically on her lack of interest in sex during their entire marriage. Naturally, Carmen felt responsible for the breakup of the marriage and wanted to deal with her feelings of guilt. She admitted to Counselor Shmooze that she and Pedro had an active sex life prior to marriage, but after marriage sex just seemed less important to her. When the kids came, sex became even less important to her. "Sex was okay, I guess, but I would have been just as happy if I never had to fool with it again," she said. "It's just too much bother."

There was no obvious reason for Carmen's enjoyment of sex prior to marriage and her lack of sexual interest after marriage. She had no history of rape or other forms of sexual abuse. There was no other trauma in her history. Although the lack of desire began prior to her first pregnancy, Shmooze confirmed that both pregnancies and deliveries were uncomplicated. Carmen remembered enjoying being pregnant, and she spoke with a tone of wonder and tenderness as she spoke about holding her newly delivered child in her arms. She did not suffer post-partum depression in either case. There appeared no reason at all for Carmen's change, and yet it was a fact she admitted that could not be ignored. Counselor Shmooze's intuition told him it was time to start "ghost-busting."

T So, Carmen, tell me. Has anything like this ever happened before?

C (Long pause) Well, yeah, I guess so. I mean, I've never

T   Never?

C   Not since high school. (Pause). Wow, that was something.

T   Tell me about it.

C   He was about the cutest boy in the whole world. I had this major crush on him. He was like, he'd call me and my heart would just flip flop. We were always together. When we couldn't get classes together, it was, like, torture until we could see each other again. [Shmooze noted that Carmen was starting to talk like a teenager again, which meant she was reliving the experience - a good sign for therapy and a good clue that a ghost was in fact haunting her, probably the ghost of this boy.]

T   Sounds wonderful.

C   Oh, that's not the half of it. [Carmen continued to talk about her relationship with this boy in glowing terms for five minutes.]

T   Were you sexually active with him?

C   Oh, yeah. I gave him my virginity. Some people would say he took it, but he didn't take it. I gave it. I really loved him.

T   I feel that. But he's not Pedro?

C   (Laughs). No, he's not Pedro. Not by a long shot.

T   So what happened? Seems like it was such a perfect relationship.

C   It was until I found out he was screwing my best friend. I could have scratched her eyes out! I've never spoken to either of them again. [Carmen's voice trailed off, and Shmooze noted she appeared to be on the verge of tears.]

T   (Softly) You must have been devastated.

C   I was. (Long pause)

T   Let me try something here. Tell me if this fits your experience. "I loved this boy so deeply and he hurt me so badly, I can never risk really loving anyone again."

C   (Head snapping up and looking straight at Shmooze with a surprised expression) Huh? (Pause) Ooo, yeah. You're right. I never thought about that before, but you're right. I'd never let anyone get that close to me again.

By listening carefully to Carmen, especially to her emotions, Counselor Shmooze was able to uncover her private logic that dominated the Back Stage of all her relationships with men. As they continued to work together, Carmen discovered that her private logic only applied to relationships with men. She maintained several long term relationships with women she had grown up with, and she was close to her family of origin. It was only male peers who had proven "too dangerous" and therefore who must be kept at arms length.

As they continued working together, Carmen came to see that she had unconsciously chosen Pedro precisely because he would do to her what she already expected. Pedro had a reputation as a "ladies' man" who "proved" his manhood by multiple female conquests. She had told herself and her friends that the problem is that the other women just hadn't been "woman enough" to keep a man like him satisfied, and during their dating she acted on that self-image by being actively sexually involved, in every sense of that term. Once they married, however, the ghost of her first love came back. While her Font Stage appeared as confident as ever, her Back Stage realized that marriage is for keeps, and she could really get hurt. So she unconsciously started pulling back from Pedro in self-protection, just as she had every other close relationship in her past. Of course, the inevitable result of her choice of partner and her changed behavior was that she proved once more that her private logic was valid and accurate.

Carmen is like many people in our culture. She was not afraid of intimacy, although that was her conclusion when she first saw her private logic under the "klieg lights" of the Front Stage. In fact, she craved intimacy. What she feared was the devastating pain that always seemed to accompany the intimacy. As Counselor Shmooze explained it to her, "It's like being given your very favorite food in the whole world, and then, just when you've eaten just about half of it, you're given a painful electric shock. It wouldn't take very long to conclude that the gain ain't worth the pain." Carmen's strong desire for true intimacy propelled her into relationships, and yet her fear of the "inevitable" hurt kept her from giving herself deeply enough to ever find what she wanted so badly.

Multigenerational legacies

Will came to see Counselor Shmooze after he was fired from the job he had held for the past 10 years. Will was devastated. He had worked hard at his job and he knew it. He believed he was at least as good at his work as the other "jerks" (his term) he worked with. The boss had told him, "You're just not a team player." "I don't understand it," Will fumed. "I job-out at my desk all day long instead of standing around the coffee pot wasting time like those jerks I work with, and I'm 'not a team player'."

Donna, Will's wife, had tried to be supportive of her husband, but in recent weeks he had become increasingly depressed as his job searches proved repeatedly fruitless. Both agreed his interest in sex had decreased to near zero, despite Donna's frequent attempts to initiate sexual intimacy. His energy and drive had similarly bottomed out. In short, when Will first came to Counselor Shmooze's office, he met all the criteria for a moderate clinical depression.

Their work began with some of the solution-focused techniques Counselor Shmooze frequently employs. Will was able to specify concrete behavioral goals he wanted to work for, and by the second session he had forced himself to actually begin to put some of them into action. With progress toward a goal becoming evident, Will's depression began to lessen and by the third session he was beginning to feel the first glimmers of hope.

Even so, Counselor Shmooze's intuition told him there was more to the story than simply getting Will a new job. After all, he had a good job previously, but he had lost it for not being a "team player" even though all evidence supported his contention that he did in fact work hard. Counselor Shmooze decided that a ghost must be haunting Will's Back Stage and that this ghost must be named and exorcized if his next job was not to end the way the last one had.

The fourth session began with the search for the ghost.

T   Will, you're a hard worker. So tell me, who taught you to work so hard?

C   That's easy. My parents. They always made a big deal any time I did anything. Didn't take me long to realize that if I wanted their approval, I had to achieve. Guess I kinda became a classic overachiever - working so high above my head my nose ought to bleed.

T   Well, I can understand that, and that's also part of what puzzles me. Who told you that you were an overachiever? I mean, can't you simply be an achiever?

C   I don't know. I was just trying to make a joke.

T   Yeah, you're right. I get too serious sometimes. (Pause) Still, something felt right to me when you said it.

C   Well, I did work hard and I did do well.

T   I bet you did. So what didn't you do so well in?

C   Oh, that's easy. I was what you'd call a nerd. Never had many friends. Stayed pretty much to myself.

Didn't even date much, until I met Donna. She's been my life saver.

T   "Donna's been my life saver because...."

C   ... Because she knows the ins and outs of social things, like how to get along at church and stuff. I'm lost in stuff like that.

T   Okay, and who are you most like in your family?

C   Grrrrr, I wish you hadn't asked that. As much as I hate to admit it, I'm like my mother in that regard. Wish I weren't, but when it came to relationships, she didn't have a clue, and neither do I.

The conversation quickly centered on Will's mother, whose mother had died in childbirth whose father had run off almost immediately after she was born. As a result, she had been raised by a succession of family members. When Will's parents married, they settled down into a very closed family. As Will talked, he realized that his father had friends, but his mother did not, and they never went anywhere as a couple.

T   Will, I want you to talk with your mother right here, right now, in your imagination. You can talk out loud or you can talk inside your head, which ever is easier for you. I want you to ask her what was her goal in staying away from people who could be her friends.

C   How should I know? I've never talked to her like this, and I don't particularly want to start now.

T   That's okay. You don't have to do it for real. Just use your imagination and see what happens.

Will closed his eyes and began to talk. As the conversation developed, Will connected emotionally with some facts he had known for years but never really appreciated. His mother had learned through bitter experience that people can and will leave you. The best way to avoid getting dumped is to not depend on anyone. His mother had compensated for her social inferiority, that is, her discomfort with and unwillingness to form social relationships, by being a hard-working mother. She did everything she could for Will and his sister.

C   Whoa, now I see! I've become just like her! I'm not comfortable with people either, so I work hard to get the attention I need.

T   (Smiling) Yeah. Seems like part of you knows better, but part of you believes "I cannot handle relationships so I must work hard and that way people will only notice my hard work, not how scared I am of people."

Will came to realize he had been haunted by the ghost of a man he had never met - the ghost of his maternal grandfather, the same ghost who had haunted his mother's life. He had lived his life as though others were going to do to him what his maternal grandfather had done to his mother; she had nonverbally (and unconsciously) taught him to believe this is the way life is. With this insight, Will was able to decide for himself how much involvement was the "right" amount. He decided that he would likely always be an introvert, but he could use Donna as a coach to help him gain the social skills he lacked and previously believed were unattainable for him. Writing this new direction for his private fiction gave him increased confidence, and soon Will landed a great new job.

Trauma

Brian had been a successful paramedic for five years. One night, however, he and his crew responded to a fiery car crash that changed his life. Even though he did not know the victims, and even though he had seen badly burned people before, Brian became so sick that he could not continue working. His crew had to complete their work without him, and the watch captain had to take him directly home in the captain's car. The next day the captain called Counselor Shmooze's office and made an appointment for Brian.

For the first 30 minutes of the first session, Counselor Shmooze simply encouraged Brian to tell his story, to tell what happened to him that night. Following the Critical Incident Stress Debriefing protocol, Counselor Shmooze first asked Brian to simply describe the events, and then he asked him to go back and tell what he thought during those events, and finally he asked Brian to express what he felt during those minutes on that dark, sad road.

T   Brian, I really appreciate your sharing your story. You've been very open, I believe, and that certainly makes my job easier. But I'm puzzled. Help me understand. What makes this incident different? What about this one bothered you so much?

C   I haven't got a clue. I've seen lots worse. I'm a professional. I don't know. They warned us about critical incidents in school, so I guess this one just got me.

T   Well, who ever warned you in school was right. You ought to thank them. And maybe you're right - maybe this is just one of those things for you. [Shmooze was consciously trying to normalize some of Brian's feelings and to remind him of some of his cognitive resources from his paramedic training.] (Pause) Still, I'm curious. Has anything like this ever happened to you before?

C   No, I told you, I've never had any problems on the job before.

T   No, I mean to you personally. Ever been in a car wreck or in a fire or anything like that?

C   [Long pause. Then with voice lowered] Well, there was that one wreck when I was 16 years old. But it wasn't my fault!

In the remaining minutes of the first session, Brian related the details of the fatal auto accident he was a part of shortly after he got his driver's license. He was driving his best friend when a drunk driver ran a red light and rammed their car broadside. Brian was thrown from the wreck and badly injured. His best friend, however, was trapped in the wreckage and burned to death. As the story unfolded, Counselor Shmooze carefully assessed Brian to make sure he was going to be able to function. Brian adamantly insisted he had gotten over that incident years ago and that he was safe to return to work. Realizing that returning to normal activities is often healing for persons following a trauma, Counselor Shmooze encouraged him to do so and scheduled a follow up appointment.

The next appointment began with Counselor Shmooze's asking again about the fatal accident. Brian was resistant at first, stating that he had dealt with that years ago and it did not have anything to do with his problems a few weeks ago.

T   I'm sure it probably doesn't have anything to do with anything. I'm just curious. What was your best friend's name?

C   Bobby.

T   I'd like you to do something for me. I want you to talk to Bobby and tell him you're sorry he's dead. You can do this out loud or you can do it inside your head, whichever is most helpful for you.

C   This is crazy. I haven't thought about him for years.

T   That's okay. I'm a little crazy. Just humor me and tell him you're sorry he's dead.

C   (Sighs) Bobby, I'm sorry you're dead.

T   And what does he say to you?

C   Huh?

T   He's your best friend. He wouldn't simply ignore you when you said something sincere to him. What does he say to you?

C   He says, That's okay. I know it wasn't your fault. It was that drunk.

T   Good, good. Now tell him you're sorry you couldn't get him out of that car.

C   (Long pause, then softly) Bobby, I'm sorry you got burned in that car. That's a hell of a way to die. I really feel awful that I couldn't get you out. (Eyes begin to mist up) God, Bobby, I could hear you screaming as I was lying there in the street. I wanted to help you, but I couldn't even move. I couldn't even move!

T   (Pause) And what does Bobby say to you?

C   "Yeah, it was awful. I thought you were dead, too. I knew you would get me if you could." (Sobbing) I would have, Bobby, I would have. I wanted to get you and help you but I couldn't.

T   That feeling of helplessness must have been really awful for you. Try this out and see if it feels real. Say, "I feel awful about not being able to help Bobby, and when I saw those people burned in the car I felt helpless again. I should have been able to help Bobby and I should have been able to help them."

C   I really feel awful about Bobby, and I should have been able to help him and I should have been able to help those people the other night. But I couldn't! I couldn't help Bobby and I couldn't help them!

T   Good, good. And because I couldn't help them....

C   I don't deserve to live. It should have been me who died, not Bobby! He didn't do anything. I was driving. I talked him in to going out that night. It should have been me (sobbing).

Counselor Shmooze continued listening to Brian's story. Brian had known the facts of the case all the time. The facts were Front Stage. But the emotional meaning - his guilt over surviving a crash that killed his friend

214

- was hidden on the Back Stage. The similarities, vague as they were, between the current crash and the one that killed his best friend were enough to set off the "haunting" by Bobby's ghost.

By the end of the session, Brian had received Bobby's total forgiveness for his having survived. Six months after the original critical incident, Brian again had to respond to a fatal fire scene. Although some of the old feelings came flooding back, he was able to "talk" with Bobby quickly and quietly in his head at the scene and get Bobby's help getting on with his work.

Conclusion

These case studies are merely illustrative of some of the types of material that may contain ghosts. Remembering that all behavior is relational, if a client appears to be stuck and unable to move despite the client's stated desire and the therapist's best efforts, or if the client appears to be acting out of all proportion to the precipitating situation, the counselor should suspect that the client is in reality responding to a ghost. The key is to always ask What is the function of this behavior? In what context does it make prefect sense to act this way? Working with ghosts requires both the therapist and the client to be willing to experience some strong emotions. This type of therapy is not for the faint of heart, but it can be a way of healing.

Living Into the Lesson

1.   Take the case material at the beginning of this chapter. Work with two other students - one student to play Counselor Shmooze, one to play Bubba, and one to be observer. Start your role play as given in the transcript, then follow it on to uncover Bubba's ghost. The observer should give feedback after the role play to the two characters on how believable their reactions were and on alternative ways they could have played their roles.

2.   Keep a journal for one week (if you do not already regularly do so). What ghosts affect your Front Stage? What clues do you see from the journal about any Back Stage ghosts?

3.   If you were working with a divorcing couple in their 30s with two small children, what items would you include in their negotiated separation agreement? What would be different, if anything, in a separation agreement between a couple in their 50s? Share your answers with other class members. Did you overlook any important areas?

4.   The author makes the point that most people do not fear intimacy, they fear the pain they experienced in previous intimate relationships. Do you agree? Why or why not?

5.   Think about people you have known who have divorced. What kinds of ghosts might have been responsible for these break ups? What difference might it have made if the ghosts could have been brought onto the Front Stage early in the relationship?

6.   Take a position pro or con and stage a debate: No fault divorce should be abolished and divorce should be more difficult to obtain. Support your position.

7.   Refer to the case material with Counselor Shmooze and Will in this chapter. Given the situation, what solution-focused techniques would you use with this client? Role play the interaction (note: the one playing Will should be depressed and hopeless; if this is easy, you are not doing it right!).

8.   One of the key concepts of Bowenian therapy is multigenerational transmission of emotional processes. How does Counselor

Shmooze's work with Will illustrate that concept? In what ways is it different?

9.   What clues are evident in Will's case history that tipped Counselor Shmooze to the presence of a "ghost"? If this were not included in a chapter about ghosts, how soon would you have caught those clues?

10.   Bring in material on critical incident stress debriefing. What is a "critical incident"? Who is vulnerable? Can anyone do the debriefing?

11.   Dr. Charles Figley, internationally known expert in trauma, warns about "secondary trauma" - the trauma that happens to mental health professional who must repeatedly listen to stories of trauma to others. Make a concrete plan for your own dealing with listening to stories of trauma and abuse. Share it with at least one class mate.

12.   Some theories of therapy believe in "resistance" on the part of clients and teach counselors how to overcome that resistance. Given this case material in this chapter, does Counselor Shmooze, as a personification of the Metasystems model, believe in resistance? What evidence do you have for your conclusion?

13.   Counselor Shmooze uses a particular Gestalt therapy technique with Brian - having him visualize and re-experience his friend Bobby's death. Why was this technique appropriate with Brian? Wouldn't simply telling him the connection be as effective and faster?

14.   Another technique Counsel Shmooze uses with Brian is having Brian repeat a statement of private logic suggested by Counselor Shmooze. What is the point of having Brian repeat the sentence?

Chapter 15 - Next Steps

To the man who only has a hammer in the toolkit, every problem looks like a nail. -
Abraham Maslow

This text has presented basic techniques of counseling and therapy which are compatible with the Metasystems Model of doing therapy. I never intended it to be a comprehensive walk through all possible styles of therapy. To stay with Maslow's woodworking image, this text has given the beginning student a few basic tools - a basic "hammer," "saw," and "screwdriver." In keeping with the Metasystems model, this text assumes there is no such thing as "one size fits all" therapy. Not every problem is a nail and not every therapeutic model is the right hammer.

As our understanding of human behavior expands, all mental health professionals must work to keep up with the latest information. Our clients and our society deserve our best. So one "next" step for the reader of this text is to realize that this is just the first tentative, "baby step" in the direction of competence to heal. The readers of this text as much as the author must be life-long learners. As Jimi Hendricks, the great guitarist of the 1960s, said in his song "Purple Haze," "Them not busy bein' born is busy dyin'." Make a plan to constantly be born anew in your knowledge and your excitement about your chosen profession.

A part of that plan will be supervision. All mental health professions require some supervision as a prerequisite to licensure to practice. Make the most of that experience. Learn all you can from your supervisors. Risk being open and share your failures and your uncertainties. You learn and grow far more from your failures than from your successes. Even after you complete all the requirements for licensure, make a plan for continued supervision. Most often, that will be sharing cases with a peer. This text includes exercises which require students to work together to give you a taste of what that will be like. Practice with other students now so you will know how to work with peer colleagues in the future.

In our current era, the *Diagnostic and Statistical Manual of Mental Disorders* of the American Psychiatric Association (DSM) has become the "lingua franca" of the mental health world. You will need to learn how to use these diagnostic criteria. Many managed care companies require a diagnosis under these standards for reimbursement, so even if the counselor objects to the DSM's medical world view, it often becomes a requirement. Some, including this author, believe that it can be helpful by giving the counselor a convenient fiction to describe the behavioral symptoms. It's a "fiction" in Adlerian terms because it does not matter if , for example, "panic disorder with agoraphobia" actually exists or not. The term becomes a convenient short-hand for a cluster of behavioral symptoms that the client and therapist want to jointly address. Regardless of the motivation, students will need to learn how to effectively use the DSM.

Once the symptoms are described, the counselor needs to put together a treatment plan to help the client move from the problems that brought them to therapy to the goals they specify. The treatment plan becomes a map to guide the counselor and the client on their work together. It helps the counselor decide which of the many issues the client brings are important enough to warrant attention, and which to simply ignore. Learning how to construct and use treatment plans is an important next step. To return to our woodworking analogy, the treatment plan helps the counselor decide whether to use a pair of pliers or a saw, and if a saw, what kind of saw - a circular saw, a scroll saw, or a chain saw. The goal will help dictate the specific tool.

The difference between the casual woodworker and the master craftsman is the master's ability to use data that are not available to the average person. The master has a "feel" of the wood and the tool that can almost be spiritual. So in therapy, the master therapist is the one who learns how to use all available data - the data available to the physical senses (the data which will form the basis of a DSM diagnosis), and the more "spiritual" data available only to the intuition. Learn to use your emotions and your intuition. In the formal language of psychotherapy, pay attention to transference and countertransference. This is hard to do, because our society teaches most of us, especially males in our culture, to ignore or run from so-called negative emotions like anger or pain. When we are working with an individual of the opposite gender, sexual feelings or reflexes may prove very frightening. Learn when and how to use this emotional and intuitive data. That will come only from supervision and/or personal therapy. As this book has tried to make clear, emotional data must be experienced and not merely thought about. If you cannot deal with your own emotional data, it is certain that your client will never be able to do so, either. At least, they will not be able to do so as long as they stay with you.

These are only some of the next steps. What keeps this profession as exciting to me now, twenty-five years after that first frightening day on a locked ward at St. Elizabeth's Psychiatric Center, is that there is so much to learn. My clients teach me so much. They shape me as much as I, hopefully, shape them. I pray you will know the same joy and fulfillment in your work.

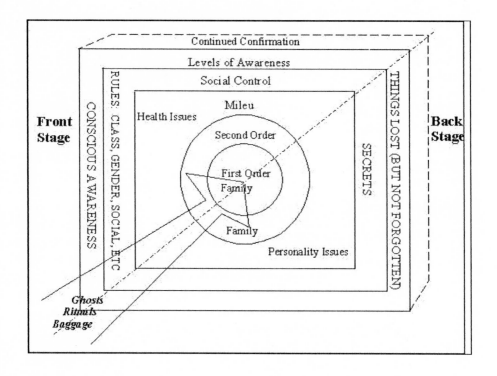

References

Alford, B.A., and Beck, A.T. (1997). *The integrative power of cognitive therapy.* New York: Guilford Press.

American's Children 2000 (2000). [On-line]. Available: http://childstats.gov/ac2000/ac00.asp.

American Association for Marriage and Family Therapy (2001). AAMFT code of ethics. Washington, D.C.: Author.

American Psychiatric Association (2000). *Diagnostic and statistical manual of mental disorders* (4th Edition, Text Revision). Washington, D.C.: Author.

American Psychological Association (1992). Ethical principles of psychologists and code of conduct. Washington, D.C.: Author.

American Psychological Association (Sept. 1994). [On-line]. Available: http://www.apa.org/practice/peff.html.

Bandura, A. (1978). The self-system in reciprocal determinism. *American Psychologist, 33,* 344-358.

Beck, A.T., Rush, A.J., Shaw, B.F., and Emery, G. (1979). Cognitive therapy of depression. New York: Guilford Press.

Beck Institute (2000). Meta-analysis shows the effectiveness of cognitive therapy. [On-line]. Available: http://www.beckinstitute.org/beck.html.

Boszormenyi-Nagy, I. (1962). The concept of schizophrenia from the perspective of family treatment. [CD-ROM]. *Family Process, 1:*1.

Broderick, C.B., and Schrader, S.S. (1991). The history of professional marriage and family therapy. In Gurman & Kniskern, pp. 3-40.

Carrere, S., and Gottman, J.M. (1999). Predicting Divorce among Newlyweds from the First Three Minutes of a Marital Conflict Discussion. [CD-ROM]. *Family Process, 38:*293-301.

Chubb, H. (1990). Looking at systems as process. [CD-ROM] *Family Process, 29:*2.

Dattilio, F.M. and Bevilacqua, L.J., eds. (2000). Comparative treatments for relationship dysfunction. New York: Springer Publishing Co.

Derrington, A. (1999). "Why you should never, ever feel guilty or blue." *Financial Times, Weekend* (Sept 25/25, 1999). [On-line]. Available: http://www.rebt.org/derrington.html .

de Shazer, S. (1988). *Clues: Investigating solutions in brief therapy.* New York: Norton.

Edwards, J.T. (1990). *Treating chemically dependent families.* Minneapolis, MN: The Johnson Institute.

Ellis, A. (1997). Experiential Therapy vs. Rational-Emotive Therapy. [On-line]. Available: http://www.rebt.org/essays/june97essay.html.

Ellis, A. (2001). Questions and Answers about Rational Emotive Behavior Therapy. [On-line]. Available: http://www.rebt.org/faq.html

Figley, C.R., and Nelson, T.S. (1989). Basic family therapy skills, I: Conceptualization and initial findings. *Journal of marital and family therapy*, *15*:4, 349-365.

Figley, C.R. and Nelson, T.S. (1990). Basic family therapy skills, II: Structural family therapy. *Journal of marital and family therapy*, *16*:3, 225-239.

Goffman, E. (1956). *The presentation of self in everyday life.* Garden City, NY: Doubleday.

Griffin, W.A., and Greene, S.M. (1999). *Models of family therapy.* Philadelphia: Brunner/Mazel.

Grilly, D.M. (1998). *Drugs and human behavior* (3rd ed.). Boston: Allyn and Bacon.

Gurman, A.S., and Kniskern, D.P. (Eds.) (1991). *Handbook of family therapy* (Vol 2.). New York: Brunner/Mazel.

Gutheil, T.G. (February 1993). Documentation: Burden or blessing? *The Harvard Mental Health Letter*, 8.

Harvard Medical School (March 2000). Personality Disorders - Part I. *The Harvard Mental Health Letter*, 1-5.

Heitler, S. (1990). *From conflict to resolution: Strategies for diagnosis and treatment of distressed individuals, couples, and families.* New York: W.W. Norton & Company.

Hodge, D.R. (2000). Spiritual ecomaps: A new diagrammatic tool for assessing marital and family spirituality. *Journal of marital and family therapy, 26*:2, 217-228.

Huber, C.H. (1999). Ethical, legal, and professional issues in the practice of marriage and family therapy (2nd ed.). Upper Saddle River, NJ: Prentiss-Hall.

Imber-Black, E. (1998). *The secret life of families: Truth-telling, privacy and reconciliation in a tell-all society.* New York: Bantam Books.

Ivey, A.E. (1986). *Developmental therapy: Theory into practice.* San Francisco: Jossey-Bass.

L'Abate, L., Ganahl, G., and Hansen, J.C. (1986). *Methods of family therapy.* Englewood Cliffs, N.J.: Prentice-Hall.
Jacobson, N.S., and Gottman, J.M. (1999). *When men batter women: New insights into ending abusive relationships.* New York: Simon & Schuster.

Jacobson, N.S., and Margolin, G. (1979). *Marital therapy: Strategies based on social learning and behavior exchange principles.* New York: Brunner/Mazel.

Keefe, J. W. (1987). *Learning styles theory and practice.* Reston, VA: National Association of Secondary School Principals.

Levenson, E.A. (2000). A Monopedal Presentation of Interpersonal Psychoanalysis. [On-Line]. William Alanson White Institute. Available: http://www.wawhite.org/whatisi.html.

Levy, S.Y., Wamboldt, F.S., and Fiese, B.H. (1997). Family-of-Origin Experiences and Conflict Resolution Behaviors of Young Adult Dating Couples. Family Process, 36:297-310.

Living Systems: The Brain/Mind Learning Principles (2001). [On-line]. Available: http://www.esc13.net/socialstudies/livingsystems.htm .

Lundin, R.W. (1989). *Alfred Adler's basic concepts and implications.* Muncie, IN: Accelerated Development, Inc.

McGoldrick, M., Gerson, R., and Shellenberger, S. (1999). *Genograms : Assessment and intervention* (2nd ed.). New York: W.W. Norton & Co.

Minuchin, S. and Fishman, H. C. (1981). *Family therapy techniques.* Cambridge: Harvard University Press.

Nichols, M..P. (1987). *The self in the system: Expanding the limits of family therapy.* New York: Brunner/Mazel.

Nichols, M.P. and Schwartz, R.C. (1998). *Family therapy: Concepts and methods.* Boston: Allyn and Bacon.

Norton, A. J., and Miller, L.F. (1992). Marriage, Divorce and Remarriage in the 1990's. U.S. Department of Commerce, Economics and Statistics Administration, Bureau of the Census, Current Population Reports, Special Studies #P23-180.

Olson, D.H. (1999). *PREPARE/ENRICH Counselor's manual.* Minneapolis: Life Innovations.

Paul, N.L., and Grosser, G.H. (1964). Family resistance to change in schizophrenic patients. [CD-ROM]. *Family Process, 3*:2.

Perlmutter, R.A. (1996). *A family approach to psychiatric disorders.* Washington, D.C.: American Psychiatric Press.

Perry, C.W. (1980). *Education for responsibility: A chaplain's role in alcohol rehabilitation.* Unpublished doctoral dissertation, Emory University.
Pipes, R.B., and Davenport, D.S. (1994). *Introduction to psychotherapy: Common clinical wisdom* (2nd Ed.). Boston: Allyn and Bacon.

Potter, P.A., and Perry, A.G. (1997). Fundamentals of nursing: Concepts, process, and practice (4th ed.). St. Louis: Mosby.

Rigazio-DiGillio, S.A. (2000, May). *Building on the client's story line: Practice tools to guide assessment and treatment.* Presentation to Alabama Association for Marriage and Family Therapy Conference, Guntersville AL.

Rosenbaum, A., and O'Leary, K.D. (1986). The treatment of marital violence. In Jacobson, N.S., and Gurman, A.S. (Eds.) *Clinical handbook of marital therapy* (pp. 385-405). New York: The Guilford Press.

Schiraldi, G.R. (2000). *The post-traumatic stress disorder sourcebook: A guide to healing, recovery and growth.* Los Angeles: Lowell House.

Sperling, M.B., and Berman, W.H. (Eds.) (1994). *Attachment in adults: Clinical and developmental perspectives.* New York: The Guilford Press.

Stanton, M.D., and Todd, T.C. (1982). *The family therapy of drug abuse and addiction.* New York: The Guilford Press.

Sweeney, T.J. (1989). *Adlerian counseling: A practical approach for a new decade* (3rd Ed.). Mincie, IN: Accelerated Development, Inc.

Sullivan, H.S. (1964). *The fusion of psychiatry and social science.* New York: W.W. Norton.

Thomas, C.L. (Ed.) (1997). *Taber's cyclopedic medical dictionary* (18th ed.). Philadelphia: F.A. Davis Company.

Tomm, W. (1993). *Family constellation: Its effects on personality and social behavior* (4th ed.). New York: Springer Publishing Co.

Tuckman, B. W. (1965). Developmental sequences in small groups. Psychological Bulletin, 63, 384-399.

U.S. Department of Justice, Bureau of Justice Statistics (2000). "Homicide trends in the US: Intimate homicide." [On-line]. Available: http://www.ojp.usdoj.gov/bjs/homicide/intimates.htm.

Warner V., Weissman, M.M., Mufson, L., & Wickramaratne, P.J. (1999). Grandparents, parents, and grandchildren at high risk for depression: A three-generation study. *Journal of the American Academy of Child and Adolescent Psychiatry, 38*, 289-296.

Walter, J.L., and Peller, J.E. (1992). *Becoming solution-focused in brief therapy.* New York: Brunner/Mazel.

Yingling, L.C.; Miller, W.E., Jr.; McDonald, A.L., and Galewaler, S.T. (1998). GARF assessment sourcebook: Using the DSM-IV global assessment of relational functioning. Bristol, PA: Brunner/Mazel.

Printed in the United States
1530200006B/139